D0891875

Understanding
HERMANN HESSE

Understanding Modern
European and Latin American
Literature

James Hardin, *Series Editor*

volumes on

Ingeborg Bachmann
Samuel Beckett
Thomas Bernhard
Johannes Bobrowski
Heinrich Böll
Italo Calvino
Albert Camus
Elias Canetti
Camilo José Cela
Céline
José Donoso
Friedrich Dürrenmatt
Rainer Werner Fassbinder
Max Frisch
Federico García Lorca
Gabriel García Márquez
Juan Goytisolo

Günter Grass
Gerhart Hauptmann
Christoph Hein
Hermann Hesse
Eugène Ionesco
Milan Kundera
Primo Levi
Boris Pasternak
Luigi Pirandello
Graciliano Ramos
Erich Maria Remarque
Jean-Paul Sartre
Claude Simon
Mario Vargas Llosa
Peter Weiss
Franz Werfel
Christa Wolf

UNDERSTANDING

HERMANN
HESSE

The Man, His Myth, His Metaphor

LEWIS W. TUSKEN

UNIVERSITY OF SOUTH CAROLINA

Published in Columbia, South Carolina, by the
University of South Carolina Press

Manufactured in the United States of America

02 01 00 99 98   5 4 3 2 1

Library of Congress Cataloging-in-Publication Data

  Tusken, Lewis W., 1931–
    Understanding Hermann Hesse : the man, his myth, his metaphor /
  Lewis W. Tusken.
      p.   cm. — (Understanding modern European and Latin American
  literature)
    Includes bibliographical references and index.
    ISBN 1-57003-211-4
    1. Hesse, Hermann, 1877–1962—Criticism and interpretation.
  I. Title. II. Series.
  PT2617.E85Z952 1998
  833'.912—dc21   97-45364

Our task as human beings is this:
Within our own unique personal lives
To move one step further along the path
From animal to human being.

Hermann Hesse,
in "Thou Shalt Not Kill"

Contents

Illustrations

following page 132

Hermann Hesse's birthplace in the Black Forest city of Calw.

Hesse's beloved Nagold River in Calw.

Hermann Hesse Platz in Calw.

The Demian Pub in Calw.

Hesse at age 4.

The Heckenhaurer Bookstore (center building) in Tübingen, where Hesse worked from October 1895 to August 1899.

The "Petite Cénacle," the group comprised of Hesse (front) and his student friends in Tübingen, 1899.

"The connoisseur"—Hesse, circa 1907.

Hesse in 1955, age 78.

Bronze bust of Hesse by Otto Bänninger.

Items from the desk of Hesse on display in the Hermann Hesse Museum in Calw. The inscription reads, "What one writes lasts forever."

Editor's Preface

Understanding Modern European and Latin American Literature has been planned as a series of guides for undergraduate and graduate students and non-academic readers. Like the volumes in its companion series, *Understanding Contemporary American Literature,* these books provide introductions to the lives and writings of prominent modern authors and explicate their most important works.

Modern literature makes special demands, and this is particularly true of foreign literature, in which the reader must contend not only with unfamiliar, often arcane, artistic conventions and philosophical concepts but also with the handicap of reading the literature in translation. It is a truism that the nuances of one language can be rendered in another only imperfectly (and this problem is especially acute in fiction), but the fact that the works of European and Latin American writers are situated in a historical and cultural setting quite different from our own can be as great a hindrance to the understanding of these works as the linguistic barrier. For this reason the UMELL series emphasizes the sociological and historical background of the writers treated. The philosophical and cultural traditions peculiar to a given culture may be particularly important in gaining an understanding of certain authors, and these are taken up in the introductory chapter and also in the discussion of those works to which this information is relevant. Beyond this, the books treat the specifically literary aspects of the author under discussion and attempt to explain lucidly the complexities of contemporary literature. The books are conceived as introductions to the authors covered, not as comprehensive analyses. They do not provide detailed summaries of plot because they are meant to be used in conjunction with the books they treat, not as a substitute for study of the original works. The purpose of these books is to provide information and judicious literary assessment of the major works in a compact, readable form. It is our hope that the UMELL series will help increase knowledge and understanding of European and Latin American cultures and will serve to make the literature of those cultures more accessible.

J.H.

Acknowledgments

Many thanks are due the Faculty Development Board of the University of Wisconsin–Oshkosh for approving two summer grants that enabled me to complete a first draft of this book. I am extremely grateful to my former colleague Professor Emerita Carol Bedwell for her careful reading of that draft and her many thoughtful suggestions, most of which I followed. A friend and colleague, Dr. Harold Round, was especially helpful in pointing out the nuances of meaning of the Latin verb *ludo,* which aided in no small way my interpretation of *The Glass Bead Game.* For a thorough editorial reading of the final draft, I am indebted to Sheri Bodoh, a literature major and an excellent student in my Hermann Hesse honors course. I am grateful, too, to the many other Hesse honors students whose interest and lively discussions over the years prompted my decision to attempt a book-length study of this fascinating author.

Thanks to Volker Michels of Suhrkamp for information and for permission to quote from Hesse's works and letters; to Paul Rathgeber, director of the Hesse Museum in Calw, for permission to reproduce several photographs; to the editors of *Monatshefte,* the *Modern Language Review,* and *Modern Fiction Studies* for permission to adapt material from my Hesse articles previously published in their respective journals; and to the editors of Francke Verlag for permission to adapt material from my chapter in *Theorie und Kritik. Festschrift für Gerhard Loose.* I wish also to thank editors James Hardin, Joyce Harrison, and Bill Adams of the University of South Carolina Press and copy editor Kimberly F. Johnson for their advice and direction in preparing the manuscript.

I owe more than a small debt of gratitude to Pat Wagner, secretary of the foreign language department, and to Mary Anne De Zur, secretary of the philosophy department, both of whom I interrupted countless times for help over computer hurdles.

Last, but not least, I am indebted to my wife, Sally, for doing without me on numerous Saturdays, and to my sons, Michael and Eric, for their constant, long-distance encouragement.

Chronology

1877	Hermann Hesse is born on July 2, in Calw, a small Black Forest city near Stuttgart. Father is Johannes Hesse, an Estonian German and former Pietist missionary in India. Mother is Marie Gundert Isenberg Hesse, daughter of Indian missionary, Hermann Gundert, and widow of Charles Isenberg.
1881–86	Family moves to Basel, Switzerland, where father edits Pietist mission magazine. Hesse acquires Swiss citizenship.
1886	Returns to Calw.
1890–91	Attends Latin school in Göppingen to prepare for state examination, required for acceptance into Maulbronn Seminary. Confirmation into Pietist Church. German citizenship reinstated.
1891–92	Suffers nervous collapse after seven months at Maulbronn. Sent to sanatorium in Bad Boll. Threatened suicide forces removal to second institution in Stetten. Has brief respite at home but must return to Stetten. Following release, begins Gymnasium in Cannstatt on November 7, 1892.
1893	Makes second suicide threat but manages to complete school year. Begins second term, but acute depressions continue, and Hesse begs to drop out, returning to Calw on October 18. End of his formal schooling.
1894–95	At home in Calw. Reads "half the world's literature." Works as apprentice in Perrot's machine shop from June 5, 1894, to September 19, 1895. Formulates vague plans to emigrate from Germany to Brazil.
1895–98	Apprenticeship in Heckenhauer's bookstore in Tübingen. Continues systematic study of literature, philosophy, history, and art history. Meets regularly with small circle of friends, the *petite cénacle*.
1899	First publications: romantic poems and prose vignettes, *An Hour beyond Midnight*. The latter causes further alienation from family when mother finds "some sentences so indecent that no girl should read them."

1899–1903 Employment at bookstore in Basel, Switzerland. Beginning of independent life. Trips to Italy in 1901 and 1903. Studies art history and writings of historian Jakob Burkhardt. Mother dies in April 1902. Hesse does not attend funeral. Becomes engaged to Maria Bernoulli in spring 1903. Signs contract with Fischer Publishing House and resigns bookstore position.

1904 First major work, novel *Peter Camenzind,* a three-edition success, enables him to marry. Monographs on Boccaccio and St. Francis of Assisi. The latter will remain a major influence on Hesse's life and thought. Begins married life in isolated, primitive farmhouse in village of Gaienhofen.

1905 First son, Bruno, born.

1906 Publishes second novel, *Beneath the Wheel;* co-editor of liberal journal *März.*

1907 Has home built in Gaienhofen, where he and Maria are "settling for life."

1909 Second son, Heiner, born.

1910 Publishes artist novel, *Gertrud.* First work to receive negative reviews.

1911 Third son, Martin, born. Takes trip to India with friend Hans Sturzenegger. Marital problems beginning to surface.

1912 Moves from Gaienhofen to outskirts of Bern into old patrician house of deceased friend Albert Welti.

1914–19 Novel *Roßhalde* (1914) depicts problematic life of artist, reflecting own marital difficulties. World War I begins. Hesse's pleas for peace and his Swiss residency are cause for charges of draft-dodging and cowardice. Attempts to enlist, but age and ill-health prevent acceptance. Operates office in Bern in cooperation with German embassy, editing and publishing books for German prisoners of war. Overwork, financial difficulties, and continued criticism cause breakdown of self and wife. Following father's death in 1916, Hesse commits himself to a sanatorium, where he is treated by Dr. Joseph Lang, a disciple of Jung, whose theories remain in evidence in Hesse's work. Publication of novel *Demian* (1919) under pseudonym Emil Sinclair marks a new and maturer stage of his writing, bringing wider recognition. Moves alone to Montagnola in southern Switzerland.

	Sons stay with relatives. Takes up painting as relaxation.
1922	Publishes novel *Siddhartha.*
1924	Second marriage, to Ruth Wenger, twenty-four-year-old voice student. Ruth takes up separate quarters after short period; divorce follows in 1927.
1927	Publication of *Der Steppenwolf,* an "experimental" novel. Hesse's fiftieth birthday. First Hesse biography published, by close friend Hugo Ball.
1930	Publishes novel *Narcissus and Goldmund.*
1931	Marries third wife, Ninon Dolbin, an art historian living in Vienna. As fourteen-year-old, Ninon had written letter of admiration to the budding author, and they had remained in contact. Friend and patron Hans Bodmer finances a house of their own design in Montagnola, where they will spend the rest of their lives. This marriage proves successful.
1932	Publication of *Journey to the East,* Hesse's "personal fairy tale." Begins work on his magnum opus, futuristic novel *The Glass Bead Game.*
1933–45	Hitler era. Hesses shelter and aid numerous artist-refugees fleeing the Third Reich. Many family members and friends of Jewish wife disappear. Hesse's works declared "undesirable" in Germany, though not banned. *The Glass Bead Game* published in 1943. Hesse continues to answer personally the countless letters received from readers.
1946	Publishes collected essays "War and Peace," a commentary on war and politics since 1914. Receives Goethe Prize and Nobel Prize for Literature.
1952	Hesse's seventy-fifth birthday. Collected works published in six volumes.
1955	Receives Peace Prize.
1957	Collected works published, in seven volumes.
1962	Dies on August 9 in Montagnola, aged eighty-five. Later years had been plagued by sciatica, painful eyes, poor vision, and arthritis. Burial in cemetery of San Abbondio near Montagnola.

Abbreviations and Editions

Quotations from or references to Hesse's primary writings and correspondence and references to several works of critical literature will be cited parenthetically in the text and abbreviated as indicated below.

GS I-VII   *Hermann Hesse. Gesammelte Schriften,* 7 vols. Frankfurt am Main: Suhrkamp, 1968.

KuJ I-II   *Hermann Hesse. Kindheit und Jugend vor 1900,* vol. 1, 1877–95. Selected and edited by Ninon Hesse. Frankfurt am Main: Suhrkamp, 1966.

                Hermann Hesse. Kindheit und Jugend vor 1900, II 1895–1900. Ed. Ninon Hesse, continued and expanded Gerhard Kirchhoff. Frankfurt am Main: Suhrkamp, 1978.

GB I-IV   *Hermann Hesse. Gesammelte Briefe,* 4 vols. Frankfurt am Main: Suhrkamp, 1973, 1979, 1982, 1986.

HHudP   *Hermann Hesse und die Politik.* Proceedings of the Seventh International Hermann Hesse Colloquium, 1992. Edited by Martin Pfeifer. Bad Liebenzell: Verlag B. Gengenbach, 1992.

HHudR   *Hermann Hesse und die Religion.* Proceedings of the Sixth International Hermann Hesse Colloquium, 1992. Edited by Friedrich Bran and Martin Pfeifer. Bad Liebenzel: Verlag B. Gengenbach, 1990.

PC   *Peter Camenzind* (Hermann Hesse)

NG   *Narcissus and Goldmund* (Hermann Hesse)

BG   *The Glass Bead Game* (Hermann Hesse)

Understanding
HERMANN HESSE

Introduction

The Nobel laureate Hermann Hesse has always occupied a slightly precarious position on his world-literature pedestal. Ralph Freedman has noted that he "is not always acknowledged as a literary master."[1] George Field has observed that "his partial success in portraying the higher ideal or synthesis may raise him above the stature of the problematic transitional writer."[2] Most interesting is that Joseph Mileck compares him to Thomas Mann, saying "Hesse possesses none of Mann's Olympic equanimity, his works are not as wide in range, as deep in meaning, as clear in outline . . . and he is beset by the timeless tragedy of man's existence."[3] When critics of this stature note shortcomings, there is obviously basis for their judgments, but there is also a need for a closer look at Hermann Hesse. If stylistic mysteries have complicated interpretation, there is, nonetheless, an Olympic equanimity behind them which gives his final vision of humankind a depth of meaning that begs better understanding than criticism has afforded it. And if he was "beset by the tragedy of existence," he gradually came to realize that life was much bigger than the tragedy—that only ego, insecurity, self-pity, and limited perception perpetuated the tragic view.

After reading *The Glass Bead Game,* Thomas Mann spoke of the "dangerously advanced intellectuality" and the "revolutionary level" of Hesse's thinking.[4] This level of Hesse's vision develops and reveals itself in his life and major prose works, culminating only in the final paragraph of his final novel. His "ultimate wisdom," which he has intentionally obscured and which has been only partially understood, badly needs to be more clearly traced and explained. Hugo Ball, Hesse's close friend and early biographer, recognized the intentional obscurity: "To have talent means to him to hide the talent."[5]

And what Boulby noted years ago—that "there is in Hesse's works a more complex and more coherent set of structural patterns than has yet been shown"[6]—is very true. The intention of this study is to clarify this web of structural patterns, which, in turn, will reveal a more profound level of Hesse's thinking. He is indeed standing on Olympic heights when his last protagonist, Joseph Knecht, performs his final act. The narrative content of Hesse's novels is most important, for it is in easily overlooked details—especially duality motifs, image-metaphor variations, and other parallels—that the intricacies of a progressive, thematic continuum become evident.[7]

The introductory biographical chapter traces Hesse's life to 1904 and is followed by a discussion of his first two novels, *Peter Camenzind* and *Beneath the Wheel.* The third chapter follows his life into 1919, when his wartime activities and his first marriage ended. The period of the World War I conflict, 1914–1918, is a turning point in Hesse's life and a part of his story that could receive more critical attention. The prisoner welfare work he carried out, the human insights he gained, and the emotional and spiritual crises he endured molded his character and made him more determined than ever to follow his own star, regardless of the folly around him. In fact, the series of essays and meager creative efforts (aside from *Demian*) are preludes to virtually every theme he would deal with in his subsequent novels. These early works witness his agonized struggles to discover a positive core in human existence and to believe that humanity has a purpose—both objectives that he accomplished, paradoxically, during the war, the most tragic period in his own life, when there was every reason to give up hope for his own and the world's future.

The remainder of the book consists of individual studies of the seven major novels that followed *Beneath the Wheel: Roßhalde, Demian, Siddhartha, Steppenwolf, Narcissus and Goldmund, Journey to the East,* and *The Glass Bead Game.* The last, his magnum opus, is discussed chapter by chapter. Further biographical data, when relevant, are included in the respective analyses of the novels, as are occasional commentaries on other minor works. The biographical approach to understanding Hesse is especially helpful, not only because it details the circumstances under which his works were written but also because it helps to determine his *Erzählhaltung*—his stance toward his subject matter—and, thus, to reveal his message in relation to his own ability to "live it" at a given time. All critics agree that Hesse's novels are part and parcel of his own inner conflict. Freedman calls his writings "a single creative autobiography" (4); Mileck points out the "intimate relationship between his life and his art";[8] Eugene Stelzig entitled his study *Hermann Hesse's Fictions of the Self;* [9] and Hesse himself wrote to Helene Welti, "The writer doesn't exist to play pretty things to the readers on a flute, but only to show and explain his own being and experience through the magic of the word, be it beautiful or ugly, good or evil. . . ." (*GB II* 167). And Hesse would always insist that, not only the writer, but every human being must seek his own direction. Readers might well ask, then: What good is Hesse interpretation if his "truth" was his alone? He, himself, had few kind words to say for critical efforts. Joseph Mileck, in fact, begins the preface of his *Hermann Hesse: Life and Art* by quoting from a 1956 response that Hesse sent to a young reader who had asked him for an explanation of Kafka. In his reply Hesse unceremoniously calls the act of interpreting an "intellectual sport . . . one that is good for clever people . . . who never get to the heart of a work of art because they stand at the gate fumbling with their hundred keys, blind to the fact that the gate is really not locked" (ix).

Mileck felt obliged to respond somewhat defensively by agreeing, at least partially, with Hesse that a "work of art is essentially its own explanation" (ix). This how-to-approach-literature battle has long raged among literary critics and will undoubtedly continue. It focuses, in part, on the question of relating an author's life to his works, but it seems a question that should be answered simply: to each his own. Whatever methodology critics may otherwise espouse, in Hesse's case his message is what should be sought, and it can be fully understood only by knowing the man and the mind behind it. Nonetheless, Mileck's defensive comment is, itself, worthy of reaction. One need not fear to offer a mild rebuke to the then-seventy-seven-year-old Hesse, who perhaps no longer clearly recalled the role that interpretation had played in the myriad book reviews that he had written, or how the Jungian keys presented to him by Dr. Lang had permitted him to refocus his own life, or what he had said about Dostoevsky's *Brothers Karamazov*—that there was a "deep need to interpret this miracle" (*GS VII* 172)—or the roles that he had assigned to his fictional characters Demian, Hermine, and Narcissus and to the guide Leo in *Journey to the East.* Even Hesse's "immortals" did not begin their journeys alone.

It has seemed Hesse's fate to appeal primarily to those who want "freedom from," as was illustrated with his "discovery" in the United States during the Vietnam era. But his real message is "freedom to," with its incumbent responsibilities. He was deeply concerned with humanity's future and with the question, "What does it mean to be a human being?" Such a search, by its very nature, has heavy religious implications. After his parents failed to bring him into the Pietist fold, he concluded early on that God can only be a "voice within" and is not to be fettered by doctrines and dogma. He would express his religious faith in *Siddhartha,* but as Hesse himself noted, little attention has been paid to it by Christian theologians,[10] though he is as important to contemporary religious thought as were Lessing and Goethe in their time. His writings are, in large part, an attempt to give religion back to life. His stories are the stories of all who journey to the East, for all whose lives must have meaning that may not be found in familiar religions or isms. Hesse's "new mythology" reaches out to the common core behind all religions, beyond the unique myths that he felt separates them, leaving them unable to move beyond their particular metaphors. The approach of the Christian millennium is naturally connected with a renewed interest in spirituality, at least in the West, and it was primarily for the West that Hesse wrote. Hans Küng, an exception to the disinterested theologians, sees the present age, in fact, as a "transition period" that "encompasses a new relationship to religion" and goes so far as to say that "none of the great writers of the twentieth century seem to me more suited than Hermann Hesse to

3

draw this paradigm change of religion."[11] If this noted scholar-theologian offers such a daring opinion of Hesse's vision, perhaps there is more curiosity warranted than has occurred.

Last, but not least, Hesse's irony is worthy of an introductory comment. There are touches to be found in *Demian* and *Siddhartha,* but his first real attempt to stand back and look at himself is found in the person of Harry Haller in *Der Steppenwolf.* The fact that irony is rarely mentioned in the Hesse-Haller relationship, however, is evidence that most critics do not see Hesse, at this point, standing above his creation; the book appears to be far too serious. He even found it necessary to explain his stance in a prologue to a new edition fifteen years after the initial publication. It is not until *Journey to the East* that ironic distance becomes an overt feature in Leo-Hesse's chastisement of the wayward journeyer H.H.-Hesse. And in *The Glass Bead Game,* his symbolic tale of the game of life, his final vision and its incumbent message are carefully, playfully, and enigmatically presented. It was, in fact, the irony of ironies that Hesse's God within, who permitted him to listen to no other voices his life long, finally made it clear to him that his all-important self was important only because it was a component part of universal being.

CHAPTER ONE

Biography

Beginnings and Forebodings

Everyone has a life of dreams, despair, fears, and faith, but few put this private world on public display as did Hermann Hesse, both in letters and in his writings, although much of the latter is mixed with fiction. Like Goethe before him, he readily admits to the confessional nature of his work. Hesse's earliest goal was to become a "poet or nothing,"[1] a decision he trumpeted loudly to his parents when he was barely into his teens, but his self-centered and rebellious nature nearly led to the "nothing" side of the coin. Twice he was to acquire a pistol and threaten suicide, but eventually a long, slow, inner struggle for recovery and self-expression took shape and produced an impassioned seeker after the meaning of life. This interior journey is what provides Hesse's stories with spirit; they are not chronologies of exciting external events. His life and fictional lives, although depressing affairs during his early and middle years, gradually become quietly inspiring because of his sheer doggedness of will to make life meaningful and positive.

Hermann Hesse was born in the small city of Calw, Baden-Württemberg, a short distance from Stuttgart in southwestern Germany. It is a picturesque city nestled in a valley of the Black Forest with the Nagold River flowing through its center. Not every resident is able to point out the birthplace of its most famous son, even though the house, marked by a modest plaque, is located directly on the old central marketplace across from the city hall.

The German word *Heimat* has various nuances of meaning. It can mean homeland or hometown, but it also expresses the strong emotional ties and roots associated with the place that a German thinks of as home. Even though Tessin in southern Switzerland would eventually become Hesse's permanent residence, he would never forget the small Black Forest town, calling it "the most beautiful city I have known."[2] He would pay tribute to it in his early prose as *Gerbersau* and describe its streets, the river, the houses, and outlying fields and forest with deep nostalgia. Hesse's letters, too, are full of descriptive passages, not only of the city itself but of the closeness he felt with his family during early childhood. It is fortunate, indeed, that saving correspondence was a practice on both sides of Hesse's family. Numerous family events were chronicled and personal feelings laid bare, and the collected letters from, to, and about Hermann Hesse give a picture of his life which is intimate and quite complete. Bernard Zeller says of the Hesse letters, "The collection is larger and their content more substantial than is the case with any comparable German author."[3]

Hesse was born in Calw because of his parents' association, both professional and spiritual, with the Pietist Church. His father, Johannes Hesse, was a native not of Germany but of Weissenstein, Estonia—a Baltic German who had decided at the age of eighteen to devote his life to God and to missionary work. His own father, Carl, Hermann's paternal grandfather, was a medical doctor, locally respected, well liked, and community minded; founder of an orphanage; leader of Bible studies; and a man with a rather peculiar mixture of joviality and religious fervor. His wife, Hermann's paternal grandmother, was always "inclined to melancholy" and began to have extreme headaches shortly after they were married, which may expose a still deeper shade of her husband's personality. When this wife lay dying in childbirth, she asked her husband to pray to God that she be spared, but, with tears in his eyes, he told her not to fight it but to "let go and join Jesus" (*KuJ I* 523–7).[4] A new twenty-one-year-old bride soon took over as the mother of the family, but she too died giving birth, and a third wife took her place two years later. Johannes Hesse was the product of the first wife and appeared to have inherited her melancholy and bad nerves, traits which were also to plague Hermann Hesse all of his life. Johannes Hesse's decision to enter into the missionary field prompted him to write a letter of inquiry to the Pietist Mission Church in Basel, Switzerland. He was given a position as assistant to a missionary in India, where he spent four years before recurring dysentery and general ill health required him to return to Europe.

Hesse's mother, Marie Gundert Hesse, with a family background in Baden-Württemberg, also came from missionary stock and was born in India. Her father, Hermann Gundert, had attended the same Maulbronn Cloister where his grandson Hermann Hesse would suffer his first breakdown. The grandfather was still a relatively free spirit and not sure of his commitment when he left Maulbronn to enter the theological seminary in Tübingen. A rash of suicides among the students broke out in the summer of 1833, however, and Hermann Gundert promptly decided to become a missionary in India without ever explaining why he struck this particular bargain with God (*KuJ I* 537). He fulfilled his promise and went on to be a man of great Christian devotion, preaching the Pietist gospel at various mission houses in India for many years. Volker Michels points out that "this grandfather . . . still today is one of the Europeans most frequently mentioned on the west coast of India because he didn't take anything from the Indians, but brought them something" (*HHudR* 153–4). He was a philologist and talented linguist, as well: he could preach in a number of Indian dialects and speak fluent English and French. Years of his life were devoted to compiling a German-Malaysian dictionary. While in India he married Julie Dubois—not out of love but because he required a wife for his position. They spent their honeymoon traveling by oxcart to his mission house assignment, Dr. Gundert giving sermons along the way. According to her husband, Julie Dubois "wasn't pretty, didn't sing, didn't play an instrument, didn't draw, but was open and natural" (*KuJ I* 540). She was also five years older than her husband and produced three living children; the last, Marie Gundert, the future mother of Hermann Hesse, was born on October 18, 1842. Four years later the family went on home leave to Europe, and when the parents returned to India, Marie was left behind at the mission headquarters in Basel, a customary fate for the children of missionaries. As a twelve-year-old she was sent to a girls' school in Baden-Württemberg, but she was far too full of fantasy and energy and had considerable difficulties. She read "forbidden poems," and when she stood by a friend who had gotten into trouble, she, too, was punished, the incident was reported to her parents, and she was withdrawn (*KuJ I* 554–5). The parallel behavior patterns between Marie Gundert as a young girl and her son Hermann years later are very interesting. Judging by the letters in which Marie begs her son to give up his errant behavior, one can see that she recognized in him the inclinations of her own youth, after which she had submitted to the Pietist denial-of-self doctrine. This, however, would not be the case for her son, for his spirit was not to be broken. It is perhaps this battle of wills more than any other factor that set a would-be writer and future Nobel laureate on his path.

In 1857 Marie Gundert returned to India to help her parents, having learned English and French after her withdrawal from the girls' school. On board ship, she fell in love with a young Englishman, but after arriving in India she waited in vain for his promised letter. Her mother eventually told her that John Barns, her erstwhile lover, had written to her father asking for her hand but that Hermann Gundert found the young Barns, apparently on the basis of the marriage proposal alone, "too impulsive and a man of the world" (*KuJ I* 555). Marie was heartbroken, but several months later, following counseling with another missionary, she reconciled with her father, sacrificed her worldly love, and pledged her life to the missionary efforts of her parents (*KuJ I* 555–6).

In 1859 Hermann Gundert became extremely ill and returned to Basel, expecting to rejoin his wife and daughter after his recovery, but he was not to see India again. Mother and daughter then returned to Europe in May 1860, and the family made its home in Calw, where Hermann Gundert had been assigned to the Pietist Publishing House. Two years later he would take charge of the work and remain in Calw until his death.

Marie's early romantic inclinations seemed destined to have a British flavor, for she now met an English missionary student, Charles Isenberg, in Cannstatt. They were soon in love, but a long wait was required while he finished his training. After their engagement in 1864, he set out for India, where she was to join him and they would marry. The wedding took place, apparently with her father's blessings this time, on November 10, 1865, in Talatscheri, the very city where Marie had been born twenty-three years earlier. Her brother, whose mission was there, performed the ceremony. Several months later she learned from friends that John Barns, her first love, had been waiting and hoping all of these years and had again written to her father when he learned of Marie's engagement (*KuJ I* 556). There is no record of Marie's reaction to this news, but even the silence bespeaks her Pietist resolve.

The marriage of Charles Isenberg and Marie Gundert produced two living sons, Theodor and Karl. One month after Karl's birth, his father suffered a severe hemorrhage and had to return to Germany, where he died in February 1870. There was no option for Marie and her two sons but to join her parents in the living quarters of the Calw Publishing House. Its original purpose had been to print Christian literature to counter the worldly literature that had been a product of the Enlightenment. The strong Pietist movement in the area had enabled the publishing house to flourish, and Dr. Gundert was a busy man. He was supposed to have one-third of his time free to continue his own linguistic work, including completion of the Malaysian-German dictionary, so Marie was a welcome helpmeet. The Basel Mission House administration likewise showed sympathy for the dedicated and devoted Dr. Gundert by sending a new assistant, another missionary recovering from the rigors of life in India. Johannes Hesse had had to compromise his missionary zeal because of the Indian climate and his fragile health, but he welcomed any assignment from the Basel Mission as God's calling and arrived at his new post on December 10, 1873.

Less than a year later, Johannes Hesse and the widow Marie Isenberg, four years his senior, were married. External circumstances would appear to make the match a marriage of convenience, but abundant epistolary evidence shows that they devoted their lives to each other. Marie's sons by her first marriage were soon joined by their half-siblings, Adele Hesse, born in 1875; Hermann, born on July 2, 1877; Marulla, born in 1880; and Hans, born in 1882. Two other children died in their early years. Unhappiness and misfortune seemed to follow the last born, Hans. As a child he was often beaten by a sadistic teacher, and as an adult he ended up working in a lackluster job as a technical correspondent after several false starts in other career directions. In 1935 he committed suicide. Hans is mentioned less often in letters, and there are fewer letters to him from his older brother than to his sisters. He seemed always to stand in the background of the family, which is perhaps natural for the youngest sibling, but whether his lack of meaningful accomplishment, in contrast with that of his famous brother, played a role in his unhappy life and death is difficult to assess.

What did it mean to be born into a devoted Pietist family and community in late-nineteenth-century Germany? This Protestant religious sect, itself a protest against a Lutheran or Evangelical church that had seemed too worldly and too impersonal, was an attempt to return to an intimate personal relationship with God and Christ. The sect was a cousin and offshoot of the equally devout *Herrenhüter* group, from which would evolve the Moravian church, still in existence in the United States with most of its adherents in Pennsylvania. The Pietists gained their major sectarian recognition as a result of the Pietist philosopher Johann Albrecht Bengel, who wrote and preached in seventeenth-century Stuttgart. The movement gathered momentum in the eighteenth century and expanded into Basel, Switzerland, which became one of its European centers of strength. In England the Pietists were related to the early Methodists. Pietism is a religion of love, both for God and for fellow humans. Consequently, it is a paradox, visible in numerous Hesse family letters, that these pious and devoted Christians, for all their humility and goodwill, could not help but be puritanical and self-righteous because they believed so passionately that theirs was the only path to God. They would willingly sacrifice their health, even their lives, to bring their beliefs to others, as is evident in their missionary zeal. If one of their number should stray or have doubts, they would demonstrate endless patience in their attempt to return the lost sheep to the fold. It is paradoxical, too, that someone leaving the Pietist community—Hermann Hesse, for example—could not help but continue to recognize and admire the genuineness and devoutness of his former brethren's faith.

His Pietist upbringing long remained a major factor in Hesse's inner struggle. For years he would feel a sense of guilt—not always openly expressed, but obviously present—for his desertion. He especially felt a sense of guilt toward those who loved him and wanted to save him from himself. These feelings reached crisis proportions in his middle teen years, manifesting themselves in physical symptoms as well as in rebellion and mental breakdown. He continued to harbor guilt feelings toward his parents, especially his father, which would haunt him long after Johannes Hesse's death in 1916. Only gradually would the mixture of bitterness and guilt subside. Other traits of character that undoubtedly resulted from Hesse's Pietist background were a strong need to differentiate between and to deal with the polarities of right and wrong, the sense of mission and duty which permeated the Pietist belief, and the idea of a personal relationship with God. When all of these collided with a gifted intellect, a rebellious will, and a poetic nature, such an upbringing had to leave its mark. Hugo Ball writes, "In this [Hesse's] home, the Psalms were sung and the Bible read, comparable only to the way Catholic priests perform their daily prayer readings" (18), adding that "Hesse's childhood was filled with the smell of flowers from the beyond, with angels of death, with stroking hands [a reference to Hesse's gentle mother], tears and anxieties, all of which go far beyond the usual measure" (27).

Marie Hesse described the birth of her son in her diary: "On Monday, July 2, 1877, after a difficult day, God in his mercy, presents us at 6:30 in the evening, the deeply longed for child, our Hermann, a very large, heavy, beautiful child, who is immediately hungry, who turns his light blue eyes toward the light and turns his head toward the lamp by himself, a splendid example of a healthy, strong boy" (*KuJ I* 8). The latter part of the comment seems nothing short of prophetic, for "striving toward the light" would be a constant and recurring metaphor in Hesse's prose. His "journey to the east," it seems, began at birth. Two years later there is both pride and a touch of anxiety in the mother's diary comment: "Little Hermann is developing very quickly, he recognizes all of the pictures immediately, whether they are of China, Africa, or India, and he is very bright and entertaining, but his stubbornness and defiance are on a grand scale" (*KuJ I* 8).

Such a child added greatly to the tension in the cramped living quarters, where the high-strung father also had his workplace, and all felt a sense of relief when Johannes Hesse was called back to Basel in 1881 to become editor of the mission magazine. Here they were able to live comfortably in a larger house, and a field nearby gave the children an outdoor play area, which had been lacking in Calw.

In today's vernacular Hermann would be characterized as a "hyper child" or, possibly, as having an attention deficit disorder. Johannes Hesse readily confessed to his own nervous condition and often hovered on the verge of breakdown. There is even a sense of guilt, evident at times in letters, that he is responsible for passing the bad nerves on to his son. In addition to nervous tension, the young Hermann seemed to be possessed of a rebellious nature and sense of self-righteousness that easily got out of control. At his fifth birthday party, he argued with a playmate called Arnold and told his mother that it was "stupid to give such a bad boy as Arnold a beautiful name like Arnold, a Biblical name at that." When his mother explained that Arnold was not a biblical name, Hermann insisted that it was—he knew better and they had forgotten. He went on to say that his own name was not nice, it was not biblical, and they should have named him Seth. Adam and Eve had named their *good* little boy Seth (*KuJ I* 10–11). The episode shows not only child's temper and strong self-will but also a self-righteousness that does not bode well for his early life. Later on, however, when he was able to control and evaluate it, this self-will (*Eigensinn*) became his guiding principle. It is also the focus of Stelzig's study, in which he calls Hesse's self-will his "favorite virtue" and a "transcendental or theologically based version of individualism" (45), thus also a result of his Pietist upbringing. The birthday argument also reveals the heavy emphasis given to scripture in Pietist education. Hesse knew the Bible well, and allusions to it would play a major role in many of his works.

Even though he became a model boy in Sunday school for a while, his parents considered sending him to an institution or to another family to be cared for. Johannes Hesse wrote in November 1883, when Hermann was in his seventh year, that the other family members were far too nervous and weak for him, the whole household not disciplined enough. The elder Hesse noted Hermann's gifts, as well, saying that the child watched the moon and the clouds, played the harmonium, drew amazing sketches, and made rhymes incessantly (*KuJ I* 13). Hermann's natural curiosity about the world around him, and his consequent inability to focus sufficient energy on his "spiritual development" according to the Pietist formula, while not an insurmountable problem at this point, would eventually become a serious parent-child obstacle.

In February 1890, Hermann's first real separation from the family took place when he was sent off to the Latin School at Göppingen. At the time the school enjoyed an enviable reputation as the best preparatory institution for the dreaded, but highly esteemed, state examination.[5] Those who passed were given a tuition-free education at the Theological Seminary in Maulbronn and, thus, were guaranteed a future as teacher or clergyman. That he should have such a future was the expectation of Hermann's parents. In later reminiscences he recalled his departure from the train station, where his mother had brought him, when he suddenly realized that he was going to be alone in the world for the first time and that he would be expected to adjust and survive—life strategies that he was not sure he had learned properly (*GS IV* 602). He arrived at Göppingen with his harmonica, violin, and trumpet, which again suggests the difficulty that he had in focusing his energies and activities. His first reaction to Göppingen was very positive, and it set a precedent for him of having faith in new beginnings. This, in turn, can be interpreted to show that the young Hesse usually expected more out of his experiences than he received. Once he had settled into a daily routine, Hermann would often suffer growing depression. It is ironic, however, that once Hesse had established his own life as a writer, he compelled himself to be even more disciplined than he was required to be in his early years. Not all of his Pietist indoctrination was lost.

Shortly after classes had begun, he wrote home to tell his little brother Hans to study hard, so that he, too, could come to Göppingen (*KuJ I* 32). He wrote proudly to his parents to say that he had been called into the principal's office to be praised and told that he would surely pass the state examination and that the principal wanted to make a "sound man" out of him. The young scholar left the office beaming with pride, determined to do his part and make the principal's job an easy one (*KuJ I* 45); a similar scene, with some variation, would appear as a prelude to tragedy a number of years later in *Beneath the Wheel*. His mother found, perhaps for the first time, great cause to rejoice over her son's enthusiasm, writing to Hermann's sister Adele to say "our dear God has lifted so many of our concerns for Hermann" (*KuJ I* 48).

An incident that perhaps triggered more difficulties than were immediately apparent took place in September 1890, just before Hermann was scheduled to return to Göppingen. He and a friend had built a fire while out hiking, were discovered by a forest ranger, and were dragged by their collars back into the city. When Hermann resisted the treatment, he was given a roughing up by the ranger and spent most of the night "howling" in bed. (*KuJ I* 61–2). Despite his rebellious reaction to authority within family surroundings, Hesse was still very sensitive to what others thought of him and how they treated him. But it did not seem to occur to him that what he was doing was wrong if *he* did not find it wrong. There was shame involved when rules were broken in the Pietist community, and for Hermann, this would carry over to breaking laws in the larger community.

Hermann had only a few days to recover from the affair before returning to school. In his first letter he complained of headaches—a constant refrain from then on—but, nonetheless, he could report stoically that the heavy assignments were not getting him down (*KuJ I* 65). He even found time to write a Christmas play, but the plot leaves little doubt that he was not well psychologically. The action, described in a letter, takes place on Christmas Eve within a family setting where the mother has died. A begging, hungry child comes to the door, tells of her own mother who has died, and says that she is looking for her. The girl, brought in and warmed in front of the fireplace, continues to hallucinate about her mother and then collapses and dies herself. Hermann even assigned roles for the family members to play (*KuJ I* 74). This is the first of several instances in Hesse's life when letters indicate that he is not dealing well with reality, that an escape mechanism has been triggered. The incidents are associated with periods of heavy stress, and at times he would lose full control.

Shortly after returning to school in mid-January, the promising scholar felt himself slipping—things were not going well anymore, his feet and chest had been hurting for three days, and he was having trouble breathing. The state examination date had been set for July 15, and if he were to fail, he did not "know what he should do" (*KuJ I* 80). When a practice exam was scheduled for the students on February 24, he reported having been sick for twelve days. However, he claimed to have found a "great method" to cope with it: he tells himself firmly that he is not sick (*KuJ I* 85). Nevertheless, in a confirmation class, he was suddenly unable to breathe and had to stand up to recover; breathing problems became a daily occurrence (*KuJ I* 89).

One major event during the spring of 1891 helped to take Hermann's mind off the overpowering specter of the state examination—his confirmation on April 13. This most important step within the devotional life of the Pietist was celebrated with the traditional ceremony, although there was a note of sadness for the family, as well, because Marie's two sons by her first marriage had left the church. Even without their presence, however, the confirmation seemed a successful milestone for Hermann. Somehow, the aspiring student then managed to survive the months between April and July, when he was to take his examination. When the appointed day arrived, Hermann's mother accompanied him to Stuttgart for moral support and could actually report that he was in good spirits (*KuJ I* 101). When the examination results came in, Hermann was ranked twenty-eighth out of seventy-nine, and his next goal was the seminary at Maulbronn.

In an essay written later in his life, entitled "From My Schooldays" (*GS IV* 596–609), Hesse pays tribute to two Göppingen teachers who left positive impressions on him. The first, a Herr Schmid, was a teacher of Greek, and his meager handful of pupils—only five in Hesse's class—were called "the Greeks" and "the Humanists." The boys thought of themselves as an intellectual aristocracy. The rank-and-file teachers were hated and feared and had powers that they often abused by pulling hair and ears and slapping faces—sometimes hard enough to draw blood—but Herr Schmid stood out for Hesse. Strangely enough he was a bitter, sarcastic man whom the other students did not like but whom the young Hesse gradually learned to respect by getting to know him more closely. After Hesse's twelve-day absence for sickness, Schmid tutored him in his dingy household, where his sickly wife was a constant burden. Schmid took Hesse on a walk or two and showed interest in his ideas and dreams for the future, and the boy was won over.

The second Göppingen teacher was Rector Bauer, who became an idol for Hesse. In the rector's younger days, he had had the reputation of being a spare-the-rod-spoil-the-child disciplinarian (to which one of Hesse's older relatives testified), but by the time Hermann enrolled, Bauer had mellowed, although he remained fully capable of instilling fear. From Hesse's physical description of the rector, Bauer must have been an Einstein look-alike and was seldom without his long, hooked pipe that reached nearly to the floor and blackened the ceiling of his room with its smoke. Hesse remembered the pipe as a "scepter and symbol of power." Bauer was his "leader, his model, his judge," and a revered "half-god" (604). He was able to demand the young Hesse's best efforts and to inspire the highest ideals. Hermann could be happy for days if Bauer told him, "You did that very well, Hesse," and would suffer despair if Bauer said, "I'm not satisfied with you, you can do better" (605).

In his essay "From My Schooldays," which was an attempt to portray himself psychologically during the Göppingen years, Hesse recalled that he responded positively when he felt a sense of respect for his teacher. He could "thrive and flourish when he could feel reverence and adoration and strive toward noble goals," and this happened in the classrooms of Schmid and Bauer (*GS IV* 606). It seems apparent that Hesse was sensitive and eager to please, and that he needed to be considered a good boy. A short time later, when called upon to obey the demands of his own conscience in spite of an absence of approval from parents and teachers, he would begin his long, despairing journey as an outsider. It would be years before he could learn to live as his own judge and tolerate the criticism of others with relative equanimity.

In any event, Hesse looked back at his Göppingen studies as the "only short period of my school years when I was a good student," and when he recalls his Latin and Greek classes, they "always smelled a bit like the Garden of Youth and the tobacco smoke of Rector Bauer" (*GS IV* 609).

From Seminarian to Author

The proud and tired scholar spent August and early September of 1891 hiking through the countryside around Calw, reading in the library where it was cool and quiet, and constantly bothering his younger sister, Marulla, much to his mother's consternation.

It is interesting to read the letters of Hesse's maternal grandfather, Hermann Gundert, who often mentions his namesake and who, himself, had attended the Maulbronn Seminary in 1827. The grandfather had definite suspicions regarding his grandson's character and expressed his thoughts with no little irony in letters to his own son, yet another Hermann. In his opinion, his young grandson would enter the seminary by the "will of God"; Grandfather Gundert seemed to be saying that Hermann would require an additional portion of grace in order to focus on his studies. A month or so after Hermann began at the seminary, the grandfather wrote to a friend, "I'd like to say something nice about them [Hesse and a Gundert relative], but their age prevents me from saying more than that they have attacks of the Christian spirit now and then, but otherwise are quite willing to leave themselves open to all the spirits" (*KuJ I* 119). When Hesse let himself be hypnotized and went to bed in his socks, collar, and tie, causing a minor scandal in the school, his father wrote with strong words of chastisement and warning: "The business with the hypnosis has shocked us terribly. All of these unseen things are anathema to me. Our body is a temple of the Holy Spirit, our soul a tool of His will. Intoxication or narcosis, be it alcohol, morphium or hypnosis, dirties and debases that which God has created to serve Him, which He has saved and made holy" (*KuJ I* 132). The father's solemn, God-fearing nature and his son's adventurous spirit, in strong contrast here, would continue to clash. Such a thing as hypnosis had never taken place in the seminary before and was immediately forbidden by the authorities. Grandfather Gundert continued to complain, however, that his grandson was now carrying on with yet other stupidities in his spare time.

However, time was spare, indeed, at Maulbronn. The boys had forty-one hours of class per week, including Saturdays. Sunday was little different, except that tightly scheduled "quiet activities" replaced the classes (*KuJ I* 111). Despite the regimentation and restrictions, though, Hesse's letters home were positive, enthusiastic, and even ironic: In their study of the Book of Luke, Hermann said they had "reached the gratifying conclusion that they know with certainty that Luke really was the author"; in their history class, they were "far enough along to know enough about Lycurgis to know that nothing is known about him"; after overcoming one hundred difficulties, they had "advanced far enough to believe, nay, even *know* that Homer probably even lived" (*KuJ I* 127).

That the young scholar had not given up his "free-time stupidities," as his grandfather called them, in favor of disciplined devotion to his assigned studies is evident from the content of a poem that, at least, was inspired by those same studies:

> Oh, if only I could climb to heaven in winged flight with Apollo
> In his golden chariot, joined by merry Bacchus;
> Drink the glowing nectar out of Elysian gold.
> Glowing with intoxication, I would pour out upon the slumbering earth,

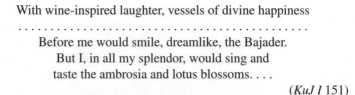

With wine-inspired laughter, vessels of divine happiness
. . . .
Before me would smile, dreamlike, the Bajader.
But I, in all my splendor, would sing and
taste the ambrosia and lotus blossoms. . . .

(KuJ I 151)

Such is not the stuff of which Pietist pastors are made, but, nonetheless, Hesse seemed to be in control of his life. He enjoyed a Christmas vacation at home, and his first letters after returning to Maulbronn were light-hearted and enthusiastic. The kibitzing grandfather, however, who was apparently given all of Hermann's letters to read, observed: "He finds time for everything possible. Now he's even taken a liking for drama, they're assigning roles and reading Schiller. . . . Proper guidance is lacking" *(KuJ I* 157).

In January of 1891, a scandal of major proportions echoed through the Pietist Church in the Baden-Württemberg area. A certain Pastor Christoph Schrempf, following a crisis of faith, had declared from his pulpit that he could no longer allow himself to conduct baptisms and hold catechism classes. Hesse reflected on this incident in a later essay, "In Memory of Christoph Schrempf," written in 1944 upon the occasion of Schrempf's death. The pastor had left the church at the time of the scandal, and Hesse noted that he was discussed with "hate and scorn." Hesse also recalled that the incident was discussed by his parents at home and among the boys at the seminary, where it created a sense of foreboding. In the essay, he reflects that Schrempf had given up his position and his source of daily bread because of his beliefs and had placed himself among the cursed, which was no small thing. Schrempf remained a figure that Hesse did not forget, one who "smelled of hellfire but also of courage and pride" *(GS IV* 768ff.) and who could well have become a rebel-protagonist in a later Hesse novel. In *Demian,* for instance, Hesse expresses a similar respect for the biblical Cain and the thief who died on the cross next to Christ, the one who would not convert at the last minute to save his soul. In a letter to his sister Adele in 1946, during the very difficult postwar period, Hesse again recalled Schrempf as "one of those who couldn't be bought, who preferred to leave life rather than humanity" *(GS VII* 444). The Schrempf condemnation also reflects upon the Pietist community. Normally, if one of their own fell into disbelief, Pietists were patient and understanding, but this time one of their leaders had embarrassed and betrayed them. Under these circumstances, they became intolerant and defensive. Such reactionary behavior may reveal their insecurities and the safe-haven nature of the corporate church. The Schrempf case also helps to explain the abyss that would shortly open between Hesse and his parents and why the ranks would close behind him at the seminary.

On January 31, 1892, Hermann wrote: "I can only tell you that things are really going well, that I'm glad for the warmer weather and that we can again take walks in the corridors" (*KuJ I* 165). February 14 brought an even more exultant letter: "I am happy, content, and satisfied. There is an atmosphere in the seminary that agrees with me. Most of all, it is the close, open relationships between student and teacher, but then, too, the good relationships among the students" (*KuJ I* 170). The new year could hardly have appeared more promising. But in her diary, Hesse's mother would later write that 1892 was one of the most difficult years of her life (*KuJ I* 162). At the root of the tragic circumstances was her son Hermann.

The initial event leading to the catastrophe that would force him to leave Maulbronn and slowly and painfully embark on an altogether new path may have been a rift of some kind with his violin instructor. In a letter written on March 4, he reported to his parents that things were going well as far as his health and school were concerned, but he requested that they send him his violin so that someone else could use the seminary instrument. On March 7 in the late afternoon, his father received a telegram saying that Hermann had been missing since two o'clock in the afternoon. By ten o'clock he still had not been found, and one of his professors wrote a long letter to Hesse's father. According to reports of his friends, Hermann had been in a state of great agitation since before Christmas and had been writing "rapturous" and "extravagant" poems, but these periods alternated with others when he was "calm and happy." He had spoken of his intention to run away, but no one had taken him seriously (*KuJ I* 178ff.).

At 11:55 the next morning, a telegram arrived at the Hesse household saying that Hermann had been returned. His mother's diary account tells at least the outer story. At first she was afraid that he had done something "sinful and disgraceful," but after reading a letter from Professor Paulus, a member of the Maulbronn faculty, she came to the conclusion that *Weltschmerz* and mental confusion had caused him to run away; it was not a planned evil deed. When found by a hunter, Hesse was trying to make his way back to Maulbronn, shivering with cold after having spent the night in a haystack. The professors took the misadventure very seriously and feared a partial mental breakdown. The problem with the violin teacher several days earlier seemed to have played some role, but Hesse offered no clearer explanation (*KuJ I* 181ff.). He would write a fictionalized account of his failure at Maulbronn some fourteen years later—*Beneath the Wheel*—but whereas he builds toward and motivates the dismissal of Hans Giebenrath (his fictional counterpart), he remained silent on the circumstances surrounding his own situation. In his *Life Story Briefly Told* (written sometime during the immediate postwar years and published in 1925), he would reflect that "storms broke over me, which led to my flight from the cloister school, to punishment with a difficult incarceration and to my leaving the seminary" (*GS IV* 473). And in the only other direct reference he made to the incident, he wrote to his sister Adele in 1946, "I had committed a great misdeed; I had run away from my school, from the Maulbronn Cloister" (*GB III* 320).

His father's reaction was predictable. He did love his son, but life, to him, had to follow the path that was prescribed by his Pietist Christianity. Two days after the event, he wrote to his son expressing the family's concern and love, but the letter was also a stern statement saying that Hermann had "overstepped certain bounds . . . there is no time for such adventures." The main questions were: "how will things now continue for him in Maulbronn; will something like this ever happen again; can he survive with any honor; will God be able to give him his blessing?" When such things happen, "one comes before a court. There are investigations and inquiries. Everything—even hidden details—are brought to light. But this is a blessing. As soon as one takes it seriously and accepts his failings in all humility, takes himself to court more severely than do others . . . then the event is a blessing" (*KuJ I* 184–5).

Here the elder Hesse is repeating the words of Hermann's mother, mentioned earlier—that the spirit must be broken and that to live decently means surrender to God's will, implying that this will had been divined by the Pietist Church. According to the letter, if Hermann had doubts about the Christian faith, he should set them aside until he is able to understand. He should hold to the ten commandments; he should ask himself concerning the first: "What are my gods, i.e. my ideals?" Perhaps he is "worshipping idols." He should ask himself, concerning the second commandment, if he has ever "spoken ill of God or sacred things"; as concerns the third commandment, has he ever "abused or profaned [his] time that is dedicated to God? Man does not live by bread alone. He must also have divine nourishment. He must pray. And then comes the fourth commandment." Here his father can only beg God to protect his son from "everything that threatens those who transgress this commandment." How happy he, Johannes Hesse, would be if he could "begin again and correct [his] failings." Hermann, his father claimed, stood now at the "wonderful juncture in life that can be compared to planting time." He should "sow good seeds of this spirit." Then he shall "reap a harvest of eternal life, the fulfillment of all good things, peace and bliss—here on earth. With the Savior all is well" (*KuJ I* 185–6).

The son's answer is short and his reaction almost as if he were an outside observer of the whole affair: "So you don't despise the frivolous dreamer who brought you so many worries?" But he also asked permission to stop the violin lessons; otherwise there would be no "good side" to life in the seminary (*KuJ I* 186–7). Permission was granted, but the puzzling problem with his music teacher had to remain a mystery. If there was something more involved than a personality clash or a humiliating dressing down, it was not mentioned in letters. It is tempting to conjecture that the violin teacher made a homosexual approach to the fourteen-year-old, which would explain his flight, his silence, and the strange behavior. There is, however, no evidence to make such a charge, and it is unlikely that Hesse would have remained silent about it for his entire life, but neither did he give the incident any frame of reference, which is suspicious. There is a strong hint of an untold story, whatever its nature. In the analysis of *Demian,* we will pursue the possibilities further, but there can be no more than vague speculation.

Freedman offers an interesting postscript to Hesse's Maulbronn failure, saying, "The crisis that developed during the months in Maulbronn brought to a head all of [Hesse's] earlier hatreds and fears. It was quite remarkable that in letters home, even in his dealings with most of his classmates, he could suppress so much of the hatred, but it underscores the existence of conflicting impulses functioning side by side" (44). However, Freedman may be stating the case a little too strongly by implying that Hesse felt such hatred at this point in his life. Like any adolescent Hesse was subject to very strong mood changes, stronger than most, in fact, and it would not be long before hatred of the people and the rules controlling him became a dominant factor in his life. Freedman also turns his interpretation into metaphor by calling "the real Maulbronn . . . only a part of the prison; the inferno Hermann Hesse entered in the monastery school was the labyrinth of himself . . . a whole way of life he did not want, a whole future that threatened him" (44). There is truth in this observation.

Returning to Johannes Hesse's previously mentioned letter, its message is again revealing of the elder Hesse's personality and character and gives us insight into the more intimate home atmosphere of the Hesse family. There is no doubt that Johannes Hesse loved his son, but the Christian faith in its Pietist dress stood above all else. Life was to be dedicated to God, and the path was prescribed. The father's letter approaches a hellfire and damnation sermon, which makes clear how confining life was for the Pietist, and the fact that the brief desertion was taken so seriously by the Maulbronn authorities is ample evidence that the official seminary view of life differed little from the father's. But based on what letters and actions have told us about the young Hesse's character and personality, there would have to come a breaking point.

The question as to whether Hermann should remain at the seminary was answered for the Hesses. A long letter from Professor Paulus, the faculty spokesman for the hearing committee, reported that they had found no premeditated plan for the flight—that it had not been an expression of defiance but, rather, an emotional disturbance. Therefore, they were trying to treat him as gently as possible. His punishment would be an eight-hour house arrest. It was also the consensus of the committee that, for two reasons, Hermann should not stay at Maulbronn after finishing the year: first, for his own sake, because he was incapable of sufficient self-discipline to keep his mind and emotions within the limitations necessary for a boy of his age if he were to profit from the education; and second, because of their fear that his continued presence would be a danger to his fellow students (*KuJ I* 189–90).

Hermann wrote to his parents from his "cell" over his bread and water, again in a somewhat distant, objective tone, noting, however, that he was much relieved to have discontinued the violin lessons. He comments, almost in passing, that he had discovered the name of his half-brother Karl Isenberg along with the date, May 28, 1885, on the wall of his "jail" (*KuJ I* 190ff.). We might, on this basis, conjecture that his mother's side of his nature was causing the problems—a point which will be taken up seriously, but in metaphorical guise, later in this study.

It is again of interest to read Grandfather Gundert's account of Hermann's misdeeds: "He left [for recess] with three books, then was struck with a whim to exchange the way back [to class] for another (he is apparently bereft of any sense of direction). I'm afraid he's enjoying being the general topic of conversation" (*KuJ I* 192–3). But, to the old man's credit, when his grandson, whose behavior he had so often mocked in his letters, did arrive home, he treated him like "an egg without a shell." In a 1946 letter to his sister Adele, Hesse recalled, "and what did he say, the feared man, the omniscient one? He looked at me in a friendly manner, saw my pale, anxious face, smiled almost roguishly and spoke the words: 'I hear, Hermann, that you took a little genius-jaunt. . . . ' He didn't say another word about the matter" (*GB III* 321). Despite the kind reception, however, the commentaries in the letters impart a certain disdain for a boy who could not stay on the straight and narrow path determined by his elders.

On March 20, Hermann wrote that his feet were always ice cold but that there was burning deep inside his head, and he quoted from a poem by the poet Herwegh: "I would like to fade away like the evening sun, like the day with its final glow." The same letter reported a major addition to his burdens. His best friend at the seminary, Wilhelm Lang, had been forbidden by his parents to continue the friendship (*KuJ I* 195). The gates were closing all around the young seminarian, and eight days before the spring vacation was to begin, the doctor thought it advisable that Hesse go home because of his constant headaches and inability to sleep (*KuJ I* 197).

After less than a week with his family, Hermann made several firecrackers and, with the apparent approval of his parents and under the supervision of a family friend, went with his younger brother and sister to the top of a small rocky cliff to set them off. The last one failed to explode until he bent over it to find the problem. His eyes were saved by his glasses, but his face was burned, and he had to spend the next week in bed with only his nose and mouth free of bandages.

In his first letter to his parents after returning to Maulbronn, he addressed them with the polite form for *you* (*Sie*) instead of the familiar *thou* (*Du* and *Ihr*), obviously wanting to hurt them and to let them know that they had made a stranger of their son (*KuJ I* 203). An even more distressing letter was sent to Hesse's father by Hermann's uncle, David Gundert. He had received a visit from a Professor Hartmann, whose son was a fellow student of Hermann in Maulbronn and slept next to Hesse in the dormitory. Hermann had repeatedly told the young Hartmann that he would kill him and had actually attacked him physically but was thrown to the floor by others. Lying in his own bed, Hesse told Hartmann that he had to have this diversion to escape his depression. He had a headache that would go away only if he killed someone. When Hartmann responded that his conscience would plague him if he committed murder, Hesse said that he did not believe it. If it did, he would kill himself. He believed in life after death—not heaven and hell but a place where spirits communed, were happy, and understood each other. He did believe in God but not that a relationship existed between man and God. Before going to sleep, the two boys shook hands (*KuJ I* 204–5). If any specific interpretation can be given to this episode, it probably reveals that Hermann had to strike back at something, to make a tangible enemy out of something or someone. The attempt to hurt his parents with the polite and distant form of address belongs to the same behavioral pattern.

On May 7, four days after Hermann's threat to kill his roommate, Marie Hesse had to bring Hermann home from Maulbronn. His fellow students were afraid of him, and several parents had requested that he be removed. Johannes and Marie had been in contact with a Pietist Pastor Blumhardt, whose father had been a faith healer and had treated both physical and spiritual sufferers in a small institution he had established in Bad Boll. The son was now its director and had the same reputation as a healer within the Pietist community. He had agreed to accept Hermann, and he believed in kind treatment and work with the hands, which was "food for the soul" (*KuJ I* 208). Even though Hermann was by now emotionally subdued and amenable to the change, his spirits improved surprisingly quickly. He liked Pastor Blumhardt. Hermann told of his sermons—which should have seemed like heresy to the Pietists, at least if the one described by the new patient was typical: "If many pastors tell us 'you are miserable sinners,' etc! what does it matter? . . . I know that myself, that's not the point of concern, if I have license from God, a message of truth, I can be an adulterer, a Muslim and more worthy than all of Christendom" (*KuJ I* 210).[6]

The sickly youngster experienced a tremendous sense of relief with all responsibilities removed. The latter feeling was tempered only by the thought that Maulbronn tuition had been free, but here his parents had to pay. If it were not for this fact, he said, "I would want to stay forever." Life at the institution was the way he imagined life in the Orient—"only clothes are needed, the rest takes care of itself" (*KuJ I* 211). His daily routine was unregimented: billiards, bowling, walks, eating, sleeping (or not sleeping), listening to music, or playing music (*KuJ I* 213). He even volunteered to work putting papers and records in order. He was invited by and given permission to visit his old idol, Rector Bauer, at nearby Göppingen, which pleased him. Things were going so well that he even recommended that his father come for a rest (*KuJ I* 217).

But on the 20th of June, Hermann wrote a short note to a Herr Brodersen, saying he had borrowed money from him to buy a revolver; several days ago he had made the decision to shoot himself. Herr Brodersen should send this letter to his parents (*KuJ I* 220). The same day Pastor Blumhardt wrote to Hermann's mother to say that her son had disappeared, leaving a suicide threat behind. He returned, however, and Blumhardt looked upon it as a prank, but a sick one. He asked that Hermann be removed and taken to an institution for the retarded and mentally ill in Stetten. Hermann's mother left immediately with her brother, and they found Hermann "like a prisoner, gloomy and disturbed." He did not even greet them (*KuJ I* 222).

Pastor Blumhardt seemed to have forgotten his dictum that patients should be treated kindly. He ranted and raved to the doctor who was called in and insisted that Hermann be taken, unannounced, with "Sack und Pack" to the institution at Stetten; he would not keep him in Boll under any circumstances (*KuJ I* 222). Hesse's mother had no choice, and they arrived at Stetten late that evening. Hermann's immediate reaction was one of panic: "Are you going to lock me up in this prison? I'd rather jump into that well!" But after the director spoke with him, he relaxed somewhat and agreed to stay. His mother left him, herself feeling "broken in body and spirit." His father wrote to him the next day, "It is a new beginning. God hears the cries of the miserable and will not leave us in distress forever" (*KuJ I* 223).

The initial reports were surprisingly optimistic: Hermann was keeping busy and taking walks. His own first letter was amazingly positive. He had spent a pleasant evening with Pastor Schall, the "inspector"; he had visited a class for the first time and hoped to be able to help the teachers. Just a few days later Pastor Schall wrote to the family, saying that Hermann had quickly adapted, was working hard in the garden, and would later replace the teachers to hold review sessions for the students. On his fifteenth birthday, Hermann wrote to the family that he was now "vicaring"—leading discussion sessions—an hour a day (*KuJ I* 226–8).

Only now did the family discover the probable cause of the suicide threat in Bad Boll. Hermann was relatively free to come and go as he pleased, had met a girl, and, although she was twenty-two, had fallen in love and confessed his feelings to her. Her rejection had thrown him into despair. The girl, Eugenia Kolb, was introduced to Hesse by his half brother Theodor Isenberg, who had roomed with the Kolb family for a while. Whether or not she had "toyed" with Hermann, as Grandfather Gundert implies in a letter (*KuJ I* 230), is not certain, but she later wrote Hermann a very understanding letter, without being condescending, stressing that the "first love is never, never the right one" (*KuJ I* 233). In answer to his question, apparently posed after her rejection, as to whether he could come to see her "as a brother," she was most receptive. He was "welcome at any time" (*KuJ I* 234). The rejected suitor could apparently live with this solution, wrote to her several times, and composed and dedicated twenty-three poems to her during the summer that he was institutionalized. The grandfather, in his Greek chorus role, noted that Theodor Isenberg, who took Hermann to the Kolbs', had taken it upon himself to cure Hermann, "naturally by avoiding everything that is Christian or religious, which always repels the youth" (*KuJ I* 235).

By late July, Pastor Schall could write that "Hermann is fresh and happy . . . is keeping his life in order, working hard and sleeping peacefully the whole night" (*KuJ I* 232). He thought the crisis was over. Hermann, himself, had written to his parents asking them to forgive him for all the trouble he had caused, and he spoke of attending a *Gymnasium* after his release. His father replied that he should not be impatient until the "good beginning becomes an established norm." With "nervous, easily moved" people like Hermann and himself, everything depended upon the goodwill becoming "flesh and blood" by means of practice and patience. Then they could talk of finding an appropriate *Gymnasium* (*KuJ I* 232).

Pastor Schall began to question whether all the novels that Hermann was reading might not have caused his confusion. They carried him into quite another world where he lost touch with reality. The pastor was trying to curb this "reading craze" (*KuJ I* 238). When Hermann was released on August 5 and brought home to Calw, the grandfather noted that "his behavior varies, he shows a bit of humility but then puffs himself up again—'Anyone who says I'm crazy is crazy himself'" (*KuJ I* 242). The hoped-for new beginning did not materialize. In her diary, Marie Hesse wrote that everything that could go wrong went wrong. Karl (her eldest son) was home, the children were out of school, and the family had visitor after visitor. It was an unusually hot summer, and it was like living in a dovecote. Hermann was terribly nervous, irritable, and defiant; he argued, would not go on walks, complained of boredom, and would not do what the doctor ordered (*KuJ I* 247). The final blow was the doctor's refusal to sign a health certificate declaring him fit for *Gymnasium* study. His father had to take him back to Stetten on August 22, and he was terribly bitter toward his parents, leaving behind a poem for them to find:

> Farewell to the house of my parents,
> You have thrown me out in shame.
> Adieu to all of my loved? ones.
> From now on I stand alone.
> (*KuJ I* 248)

The month of September was filled with vitriolic letters and recriminations:

What I wouldn't give for death. . . . Miserable, no, cold, I want to be ice-cold to everyone, everyone! You are my jailers. . . . Let me die here . . . or be my parents. The inspector took Turgenev's *Fog* away from me. This miserable life without inspiration, without education, without entertainment is befitting an animal. . . . You would stuff me with your Pietism. . . . They give me speeches: "Turn to God, to Christ, etc.," I *cannot* see anything but delusion in this God and nothing in Christ but a human being, even if you curse me 100 times for it. (*KuJ I* 250–2)

. . . I'll use my last strength to show that I'm not a machine, that you just wind up. . . . I need another atmosphere where I can and want to fulfill my purpose as a human being. (*KuJ I* 261)

. . . Yes, the most materialistic materialism is here. There is no hope, no belief, no love and no being loved, much less any kind of ideal, nothing beautiful, nothing aesthetic, no art, no sensitivity . . . there is, in one word, no spirit here. . . . Is it right to put a young person in an institution for the retarded and the epileptics when he is healthy enough except for slightly bad nerves, to rob him by force of his belief in love and justice and therefore in God? (*KuJ I* 262–3)

. . . But I forget that you are different people, without blemish, without failure, like statues, but just as dead. Yes, you are real, genuine Pietists. . . . You are Christians, and I—only a human being. . . . If you want to write to me again, please no more of your Christ. (*KuJ I* 264–5)

. . . I believe that if the ghost of the dead Christ, of the Jew Jesus, could see what he has created, he would weep. I am a human being, just as well as Jesus, I see the difference between the ideal and life as well as he did, but I'm not so tough as that Jew. (*KuJ I* 266)

. . . Since you are so ready to make sacrifices, may I perhaps ask you for seven marks for the revolver? Since you have brought me to this stage of desperation, you are probably ready to get rid of me. . . . I really should have finished the job in June. (*KuJ I* 268)

. . . "Father" is such a strange word, I don't seem to understand it. It must mean someone whom one can love and who loves with his heart. How I would like to have such a person . . . if I were a Pietist and not a human being, if I turned around every quality and inclination I had, I could get along with you. But I can't and will never live that way, and if I commit a crime, you are guilty right along with me, Mr. Hesse, because you have taken the joy out of my life. Your "Dear Hermann" has become someone else, a world-hater, an orphan whose "parents" live. Don't ever write "Dear Hermann" again, it's nothing but a lie.

H. Hesse, prisoner in the Prison of Stetten (KuJ I 269)

During this period there were no letters from his mother, who had vomiting attacks and often had to take to her bed, but his father tried his best to write consoling letters without preaching, omitting the pietistic admonitions that had always been a part of his earlier advice. He was unrelenting, however, in his insistence that nothing could be done until Hermann learned to control himself. The *Gymnasium* was not out of the question, but he would not be able to attend any school until he accepted the fact that self-control and discipline were needed to get through it (*KuJ I* 267). Pastor Schall, Hermann's immediate supervisor in Stetten, wrote to the father that Hermann "shouldn't believe that he can get through life by playing the violin and writing poems. These are poor excuses for people. . . . I told him what he needs is strict discipline" (*KuJ I* 268–9).

On September 22, the "prisoner" changed the tone of his letter. He had reached the depths of despair—a meaningful phrase he would learn some twenty-five years later in his studies of Jung—and there were only two choices: He could react to the problem in a positive manner, or he could end it all. Despite his many threats of suicide, the fifteen-year-old obviously wanted to live, and his letters had been cries for help as well as condemnations of the world around him, but he now began a gentler approach:

> Please excuse my last letter. . . . I can't run away, where would I go? I can't complain or beg to anyone else, I'm alone, I could make it easy for myself by begging for forgiveness, but I'm not going to, I've done all my atoning here in Stetten. . . . Now that I've lost your love, I feel that I love you very much, but I don't ever want to come home, I can't do it. . . . Wouldn't you perhaps ask Pastor Pfisterer [his "housefather" when the family lived in Basel] if he would take me for the winter? (*KuJ I* 271)
>
> . . . Please write and tell me what I can do to get out, out of here, and to be among people. You will never understand me, but if you have a heart, you have to feel sorry for me, or better, try to help me. (*KuJ I* 272)

The letter was sufficient evidence to make his father believe that there was hope. Arrangements were made with Pastor Pfisterer, to whom Hermann had, in fact, already written, to take him in for a two-and-a-half-week trial period. The reception in Basel at the Pfisterer home was a warm one. Hermann's first letter to his mother reads as if he did not have a worry in the world—he sent greetings from old family friends, had been going on half-day hikes, had visited the art museum, split wood, and closed the letter in English with "also a little money, my darling" (*KuJ I* 280–81).

Pastor Pfisterer's initial letter to Hermann's father was also very promising. He had noticed nothing abnormal. Hermann had been sleeping straight through the night, had a good appetite, and had been carrying on "all kinds of nonsense" with the other boys. The pastor went on to say: "I have the impression that the boy is too advanced for his age. He has a good knowledge of literature, but it goes beyond his years. . . . My Heinrich, who is well gifted and stands at the head of his class in the *Gymnasium,* is like a child beside him, and I'm not sure Hermann's influence is good for him" (*KuJ I* 285).

The pastor's observation is perhaps as revealing as any concerning what lay at the root of Hesse's youthful problems. On the one hand, he was still a child; the "nonsense" that he fell into with the other boys was an expression of a childhood need as well as an outlet for his excessive energy, but he seldom had the opportunity to carry on in this way. On the intellectual side of the coin, he was extremely curious and an avid reader, but this was discouraged by his family and teachers; his artistic and poetic bent was also considered frivolous. His specific goal to be a poet or nothing left him with little patience for the subjects he did not want to study, and his Goethe-like perception of religion (even at age 15)—"Who can say, 'I believe or I don't believe,' feeling is everything"—would in no way fit into the Pietist mold.

His Basel visit, where he was so happy to be part of the family once more, prompted a heartrending prodigal son's return. On October 20, after three happy weeks in Basel, he wrote to his mother:

> Poor mother, forgive, forgive your fallen son, forgive me if you love me, if you believe that there is still a spark of God in me. . . . But your heart, best mother, is a safe haven for me, a harbor, and if anyone can understand me in the slightest, it is you, and you alone know that I can love . . . only now do I see that I am really sick, not only my physical body is suffering, but I'm sick in my innermost being, sick in my heart. . . . I'm afraid of the future. Especially here, where I otherwise am so pleased to be, I feel my sickness with so many healthy boys around me. . . . None of us can forget the past, but we can forgive. Will you, when you are healthy again, write to me like a mother, straight from your heart, will you? (*KuJ I* 287–8)

We do not have his mother's immediate reply, but judging from Hermann's next letter, we can deduce that it was emotional and loving (though she apparently still harked back to the pietistic answer): "Thank you for your letter. I understand it, even the well intentioned sermon! You know that I don't recognize this 'He' to whom I should cry out, but that need not separate us. What you see in that spirit, I see in your love, in all love" (*KuJ I* 289). This is an amazing insight for a fifteen-year-old, and there is a finality in this letter that established the line for Hermann's religious differences with his family. There would never be a genuine closeness among mother, son, and father, but there was a degree of acceptance, a guarded love, and a respect that would be the tone of their relationships from now on.

Pastor Pfisterer, Hermann's "Basel father," found no trace of the so-called "moral insanity." He advised the parents to let Hermann attempt the *Gymnasium* and to "keep the doctors out of it" (*KuJ I* 296). Accordingly, Johannes

Hesse made the necessary arrangements in Cannstatt. Hermann arrived home from Basel on the fourth of November, where he stayed only three days. His behavior was quiet, but according to grandfather Gundert, "he doesn't attempt to approach his father" (*KuJ I* 307). On November 7, he left with his mother for Cannstatt, where a private room was found for him with a Frau von Montigel.

From the beginning his letters were not promising. He was working long and hard but saw little hope. He would have to pass an examination the following summer, and he was deeply worried about this. He requested of his parents that he not be expected to write often. What should he write about? What was interesting to him was not important to them. At the end of a letter on November 25, he remarked, "But I'm falling into a theme that you don't like, that is, I'm saying what I think and what interests me, and that's not advisable" (*KuJ I* 111). He spent the Christmas holidays at home, and his mother could write in her diary that he was "amazingly kind, quiet, and bearable." However, before leaving he told her, "Don't fool yourself about me: I'm still just as sick and unhappy as in Boll and would prefer to die right now" (*KuJ I* 316).

Thus his life was holding together, though barely, but he was in constant depression. He wrote to his mother on January 15–16:

> Turgenev says it produces a pleasant pain to open up scarred wounds again. . . . I like so much to think back on last year, especially Boll, the last place where I felt well for a while. I'm still almost a boy, but since last spring I seem so old, I have experienced so much . . . all my nerves are on edge in feverish agitation; the worst storm is over, but has taken the blossoms from the tree, and now the branches are drooping tiredly. (*KuJ I* 321)

> . . . I had so many happy hours, there was a time when school and the teachers fascinated me, when I sought friends . . . and other times where I hovered in a world of fantasy. Where I saw everything in a better light; all this reached a high point in the sweet-painful feeling of love, in singing and paying court—then the sudden end, desperation, madness, and then the deep, dark, oppressive night. (*KuJ I* 321–2)

His mother continued to beg that he return to the Pietist faith, which upset him, but he did not reply in such hate-filled outbursts as earlier: "If I had all the 'holy spirit' that you wish me to have, I would have been a great Apostle long ago. And your 'God!' He may exist, may even be just what you think He is, but He doesn't interest me. Don't think that you can influence me in this way" (*KuJ I* 323). He put this letter aside, but continued it later in the evening, this time with renewed desperation, telling how he had grabbed several books, not even looking to see what they were, had gone into Stuttgart, and had bought another pistol with the money he got for them. Now he was finishing the letter with the "rusty thing" lying in front of him (*KuJ I* 324). And, just as happened in Stetten, he again surrendered to the desire to live, begging his mother, "Help me!" (*KuJ I* 324). His mother rushed to Cannstatt when she received the letter and found him "ill, irritable, and unhappy." The visit became unbearable, with Hermann shouting at her, and she had no choice but to leave. He did accompany her to the railroad station and was calmer, but his mother could only conclude that "God alone can help" (*KuJ I* 326).

There was a resignation in the young Hesse's reaction to his second threatened suicide. However bitter, it was an admission that he wanted to go on living, even in his misery and desperation. He seemed to perceive that there was a solution somewhere. His landlady wrote, saying that the mother's visit was a "great help" and that Hermann was "back to normal" (*KuJ I* 327). What he really needed was someone to understand him, and even though his mother could not fulfill this wish, he could now believe that she loved him in spite of all their differences. He would no longer accuse his parents of hating him. He could be loved as he was, despite what he was, despite the lack of contact, and this was enough to keep him alive.

At the advice of his professors, Hesse did not take an important examination in March, which meant continuation of the pressure. He was hopelessly depressed but would let his life run down of its own accord now if it so chose: "I think I'm coming to the end, I'm expiring so gradually, I feel so stupid and dull and sick and anxious and without love" (*KuJ I* 335). His uncle David took him to a doctor, who found a slight heart irregularity that was causing too much blood to rush to his head, and this physical explanation seemed to offer a small amount of consolation, but he had dizzy spells in class and continued to think he might die.

When his father wrote, trying to offer some solace by interpreting his depression as *Weltschmerz,* saying that he had experienced the same thing thirty years ago, Hermann replied that this was not the case, he was simply bored and dissatisfied because he could not think of a "single profession . . . that [he] would like" (*KuJ I* 343). But a new note had appeared: "All would be well and good if the world were not so beautiful, or if it were open to me, but I am faced with helping myself with my own strength, and this strength is lessening" (*KuJ I* 343).

For the first time since his depressions began in earnest, he could admit that the world was beautiful—which, as we shall see, would prove the saving grace for Peter Camenzind, the hero of Hesse's first novel just ten years later. But, as would happen in *Demian,* Hesse now tried to escape from turning inward by joining the herd. He met a young, wealthy American who befriended him and had the reputation of leading young boys astray. Hesse started staying out nights and coming home drunk. Now, instead of begging for his mother's love, he could "bear everything but love . . . especially Christian love. If Christ knew what he has brought about he would turn over in his grave. . . . I could have made something of myself if I had been more stupid and not let myself be taken in by religion from the beginning" (*KuJ I* 346).

The landlord informed the parents of Hermann's association with the American family, his drunken arrivals at his room, and his hangovers. His parents made inquiries at another institution at Schönbühl, which was under the supervision of yet another pastor, where children "from better families are sent for correction" (*KuJ I* 353). Hermann's father now laid down the law: If he "does not come home nights and keep to house rules," he would be "sent to the institution" (*KuJ I* 358). This warning and the simultaneous death of grandfather Gundert had a somewhat sobering effect, and L. Geiger, one of the gymnasium instructors, wrote that Hermann had "caused no problems of late" (*KuJ I* 361). The boy found some outlet in his poetry, which he did not often mention in his letters because his parents thought it "frivolous and damaging" (*KuJ I* 363). To show, sarcastically, that his parents' concerns were the least important influences in his life, he wrote: "In the name of all the gods! Don't forget what I wrote about the trousers, the important, light-weight, light-colored summer trousers!" (*KuJ I* 363).

His half brother Theodor Isenberg had become engaged, returned to the Pietist fold, and added his voice to those of the other reformers. But Hermann, following his experience with his wealthy American friend, had now taken a worldly turn. He told his parents that "if you really want to know, my ideal would be 1) to have a millionaire for a father and a few rich uncles, 2) to have more practical gifts, 3) to live and travel as I please. . . . Man lives from bread, not love" (*KuJ I* 371). His mother responded in kind, showing that she had learned to live at least somewhat more positively with their relationship: "Here are a few crumbs [of cake] from father's birthday party for my materialistic son in Cannstatt, he will perhaps like them better than his mother's letters" (*KuJ I* 372).

Despite his troubles, Hermann passed his major tests with flying colors, and as a result he asked if he might study another year and perhaps go into veterinary medicine. A letter to his Uncle David shows the bitterness he felt toward all members of his family for their lack of acceptance of his desire to be a writer: "I once had an ideal . . . but none of you recognized or respected it, so I have lost it. I loved literature, poetry, pantheism, and beauty. It was better to have ideals different from yours than to have none at all. Wasn't the pantheist, the dreamer, closer to you Christians than the atheist, the nihilist? Now I'm my own god, a complete, ready-made egotist" (*KuJ I* 376–7).

A fairly compatible summer vacation was spent with the family, and his behavior during the first month of the new school term in Cannstatt showed improvement. Despite the guardedly optimistic beginning, however, by October his headaches were so bad that he wrote home saying that he could not continue; he asked to come home, to work in the garden (*KuJ I* 395). His father was willing, but in the meantime Hermann should think about the next step: Does he want some kind of an apprenticeship? He should decide on an answer to the question now, an answer that he would not regret later (*KuJ I* 396). The school authorities readily agreed with his decision to drop out, and Hermann arrived in Calw on his mother's birthday, October 18, 1893. His formal schooling was ended. He was slightly over sixteen years old—already, it would seem, with a lifetime of difficulties behind him.

With his patience at an end and with little regard for Hermann's depression and physical problems, his father sent him, only three days after his arrival, to an apprenticeship position in a bookstore, a job his uncle had found for him. The apprenticeship agreement called for Hesse's father to sign his son over to "unconditional obedience to his master, to loyalty, diligence and strictest integrity and to work during the apprenticeship period with all of his strength and will in the interest of the business" (*KuJ I* 400). There was no pay for the job, and when the apprenticeship period was over, Hermann was to be offered an assistant's position in the bookstore in accordance with his abilities. Hermann began work on October 25, 1893, but on November 1, Johannes Hesse began a letter to Dr. Zeller, a physician to whom he now turned for help: "My son Hermann, 16 years of age, appears to be suffering from 'moral insanity,' and last Monday left his apprenticeship position at an Esslingen bookstore which he had just begun. He ran away from the Evangelical Seminary in Maulbronn and then could not endure [his studies at] the Cannstatt Gymnasium" (*KuJ I* 402). Hermann was examined by a doctor and returned home, where, so the family hoped, he would convalesce and recover some state of normalcy. The ailing adolescent turned the next two years of his life into his own spiritual and intellectual apprenticeship period despite both opposition and yet another official apprenticeship, which would begin shortly.

For the first seven months, he helped his father in the printing shop and worked in the garden. He was withdrawn and avoided confrontation with his parents, who by this time were heeding their own advice to leave things in God's hands. There appears to be little evidence that they were trying actively to bring their lonely son back into their church. He was, from all appearances, a stranger in their midst. On January 1, 1894, his mother wrote to his half-brother Karl: "Hermann is being very dear, the poor child. He sings his own poetry at the piano, everything terribly melancholy. Yesterday and today he was out on the lakes for a little while" (*KuJ I* 408).

A voluminous number of letters flowed out of Calw to friends, acquaintances, and former classmates. It was to them that he turned for ties and friendship. His first love, Eugenia Kolb, returned his season's greetings; several friends from Maulbronn renewed his proffered friendship, one of them his former best friend, Wilhelm Lang, whose father had ordered an end to their relationship after Hermann had run away. Perhaps the most significant event of the first several months at home was Hesse's frank, straightforward request in writing to his father that the latter help him financially while he attempted to begin a writing career. Hesse wrote to his father even though they were under the same roof, because any attempt at discussion always ended in argument. He had, so he said, tried to follow his father's plans for him, to become what his parents wanted him to become in the seminary, in the *Gymnasium,* and through an apprenticeship, but he could find no desire, no strength, no courage for any of it. Maybe now, before he ended in an asylum or as a gardener or a cabinet-maker, could he try his own plans? Even if his father called writing a "breadless art," Hermann hoped to make his living from it. To get started he needed someone's help. His parents had already spent a great deal on him, and it would cost them at least another 1,000 marks to make a merchant or something similar out of him. Would they be willing to invest this money in him? If the experiment failed, the worthlessness of his hopes would be proven, and he would "never make another request to do things [his] way" (*KuJ I* 415–6).

His father's answer, also in written form, is not without understanding, but he is unbending and practical: Where will Hermann live and what will his lodging cost? What guarantee is there that he will not once again spend everything on tobacco and drinking and fall into other kinds of debt? Johannes Hesse points out that Hermann's only motivating factor for leaving the seminary, the *Gymnasium,* and the apprenticeship was his disgust for the types of activities they entailed and that the only thing that apparently would not cause him this sense of disgust is a life of pleasure without responsibilities. The choice of regular work, not too strenuous for body and mind, would be the first step toward a return of his health. With his gifts he could become something else later, while practicing a trade or something similar (*KuJ I* 417).

The two letters were the alpha and the omega of the discussion. Hermann obviously felt he would get no further and did not reply. Many years later, in his *Life Story Briefly Told,* he looks back at his failure to gain support for his dream: "A person could become a teacher, pastor, doctor, craftsman, merchant, post-office employee, even musician, painter or architect. For all of these professions there was a path to follow, there were prerequisites, there were schools, instructors for beginners. It was only for the poet that they did not exist! It was permitted to be a poet and it was even considered an honor. But to *become* a poet was impossible, to want to become one was ridiculous and shameful!" (*GS IV* 472).

There was nothing for Hesse to do now but to follow the same path that the protagonists of his novels would take—to listen to the directions given by the "voice within." The decision to show them all appears to have been made with a sense of finality. He would even go about it as his father suggested. On June 5, 1894, his mother reported that "poor Hermann, of his own free will, decided to give up his lazy life style and apprentice himself in Perrot's mechanics work-shop" (*KuJ I* 426), a clock factory, and for the next fifteen months, although very little of his actual work is mentioned in letters to his friends, he considered himself a technician. He even signed several letters during this period "Hermann Hesse, *Techniker,*" an indication of a great need to feel that he finally belonged somewhere, that he had some kind of identity.

His real activity, however, was systematic self-education. His grandfather Gundert's library—thousands of volumes of German literature, philosophy (especially of the seventeenth century), other literatures, history, religion, and more—was now a part of their own household, and Hesse said later that he had read "half the world's literature, studied languages, philosophy and art history," as well as "writing volumes" of his own first literary efforts (*GS IV* 473–4). His letters to friends, in particular Wilhelm Lang and Theodor Rümelin, became pedantic discourses on world literature, especially the state of German literature. The latter, he noted, was in a definite decline. He found little of value in the current naturalistic trends and believed that Ibsen probably would not stand the test of time. Hesse had "little orientation" in Scandinavian literature but was familiar, "in any case, with Lie, Ibsen, Kielland, Paulsen, Strindberg, Winterhjelm, Ettar, Hertz, Hostrup, Bjornson, Bergson, etc." Since Tennyson's death, there had been "little happening" in England (*KuJ I* 462–3). Some of this same erudition was written in a more modest tone to a Professor Kapff, one of his former teachers at the Latin School at Göppingen. Heinrich Heine, Germany's great romantic poet, exiled to France because of his liberal writings, became an ideal. Hesse did battle with the morally bad influence of this "genius" and "almost wish[ed] Heine had never written" (*KuJ I* 429). The fact that Hesse would make this remark is strong psychological evidence of the influence that his parents and his background still had over him. He had long since been reading other authors whose moral influence might be considered just as negative, but Heine was one of those whom Johannes Hesse had always found evil. The father did, in fact, confiscate the Heine books he found in Hermann's desk drawer.

Regardless of the tone of young Hesse's discourses and the obvious attempt to impress his correspondents, there is also a genuineness to his letters. He loved good literature and found meaning in it. He had set himself a task, he had faith in his own judgment, and he was going to prove himself. Many of his letters, especially to his closest friends, contained his own poems. Professor Kapff was positive in his comments on them (*KuJ I* 464), and Hermann's letters gradually became more alive, even cheerful—the first line of one poem read, "May God greet you, you beautiful splendid world"—and he wrote of his new beginnings to Professor Kapff: "Since Cannstatt I've become a new person, more peaceful, clearer in my judgment, more independent; the stupid 'Kneipenleben' [barhopping] isn't to my liking anymore. In my free time I'm completely alone and spend this time almost entirely in studying literature, also its history and a bit of history, art, and philosophy" (*KuJ I* 464–5). And later: "Only now have I gradually found peace and serenity again, I'm emotionally healthy—I don't even want to talk of that insane period full of anger and hate and thoughts of suicide . . . my poetic ego is being edified. The worst 'Sturm und Drang' period has fortunately been overcome" (*KuJ I* 468).

Professor Kapff suggested in passing that Hesse might consider emigration to Brazil, an idea which captured his fancy and became for some time his professed goal. He lamented that his grandfather was no longer living so that he could begin studying Spanish with him. (A later letter does indicate his awareness that Portuguese is spoken in Brazil.) At present he was busy with English, but aside from his classical Greek and Latin, he seemed to have little success with languages. French especially, despite periodic efforts, was "almost as foreign to [him] as Hebrew" (*KuJ I* 500). His later prolonged residence in Italian-speaking Switzerland would make him relatively fluent in at least one other language. He had firmly decided not to try to make his way to a university (this written to a friend, not to his father, who would have agreed wholeheartedly), saying pedantically that there had never been a time when university study was more dispensable than now. Could he have learned more about literature, for example, at a *Gymnasium* than by studying it privately? Certainly not. Knowledge is "in the marketplace, and self study develops one's critical judgment" (*KuJ I* 499).

Hesse's apprenticeship with Perrot eventually came to an end. In a four-line certificate dated September 19, 1895, his master wrote: "I hereby certify that Hermann Hesse served in my workshop from June 1894 until mid September 1895, and acquired knowledge and skills in several areas at my business" (*KuJ I* 511). Although masters were not noted for prolixity and praise when recommending their apprentices, the vagueness and lack of enthusiasm shown by H. Perrot may well indicate that he, like Hesse, considered his protegé's activity to be something less than his primary interest. Hesse felt that the period had not been wasted, however. It had "steadied [his] eye and hand and made a 'practical man' out of [him]"; he was "no longer afraid of work, even physical work and a bit of sweat" (*KuJ II* 10). Ball observes that Hesse's short vagabond novel *Knulp* "could hardly have been produced without this apprenticeship" (43). But because completion of certification as a technician would require several more years, Hesse had talked the matter over with his parents and decided on a simple trade, one that was "more elastic," and this was as a merchant. His father had no quarrel with his going abroad as soon as he could earn his daily bread. Thus his nebulous Brazilian plan was beginning to project itself as a distinct possibility (*KuJ II* 10–11).

Two days after writing about his merchant plans in a letter to Professor Kapff, Hesse saw an advertisement for an apprenticeship in the Heckenhauer bookstore in Tübingen. He applied and was accepted. How he circumvented his ignominious departure from the Esslingen bookstore, as well as all of his previous difficulties, is not known. Very possibly his knowledge of literature and his strong academic training (as far as it went) were more than sufficient to gain him at least a trial period of employment. Hesse would spend nearly four years—from October 1895 to August 1899—in Tübingen, another picturesque city on the edge of the Black Forest. Although the income of an apprentice was meager, indeed, he was approaching independence from his parents. Freedman goes so far as to say, "He had found his own source of 'light'" (56).

He found a large room on the outskirts of the city in a house[7] belonging to a Frau Leopold, who proved to be a mothering sort. Hesse's father laid down a stringent set of rules that were to be followed if he were to approve of the arrangement: Frau Leopold was to be in charge of all finances; Hermann's pocket money of one-and-a-half marks per week would be allocated by her; all bills for shoe repair, etc., would be paid by her, and she had to retain the receipts for the father; all other expenses were to be avoided. In special cases, permission to spend money had to be requested in advance. No debts could be incurred. Smoking was to be kept to a minimum; card playing for money and similar activities were not permitted. Laundry was to be sent home;

papers, pens, etc., were not to be purchased but requested from home (*KuJ II* 18–19).

The Tübingen years proved to be a continuation of the formative months spent in Calw. Hesse was never without a systematic study plan, which he pursued relentlessly after his ten-and-a-half-hour workdays, Saturdays included. He divided literature into periods and movements, and separated out the great individual authors for in-depth study. He also immersed himself in philosophy, history, and art history. His letters to Professor Kapff, even within the first year, became considerably more mature and expressed his rapidly growing knowledge and more refined judgment. From the point of view of faith in his own taste and authority, the letters of the eighteen-year-old apprentice read as though they could have been written by an *Ordinarius* of German literature at a university. Particularly notable are his comments on Schiller and Goethe, especially the latter: reading Schiller, for Hesse, meant to "observe flames reaching out to heaven," but Goethe's creations were "marble images" that the reader could love for their "constant beauty" (*GB I* 10). What the young Hesse discovered and admired most about Goethe was his ability to preserve a peaceful sanctuary within himself. Such a sanctuary was to become Hesse's own goal, and we shall see it as the theme of an imaginative story written at the end of World War I. He saw in Goethe an example of the Olympian who could observe and understand life but, at the same time, remain aloof from it. "For Goethe," he commented, "there was no French Revolution, because he alone stood higher than this highest of red suns of the new era" (*KuJ II* 64). Hesse, too, was striving for emotional distance. We shall see a first attempt to retreat into his own world portrayed in *Peter Camenzind,* and a more intense effort to create an aesthetic haven for himself in *Roßhalde,* but the realities of the war years would mean the end of *l'art pour l'art.* He would gradually discover that he would have to serve as well as observe.

Despite brighter moments, Hesse's *Weltanschauung* a year into the Tübingen apprenticeship was not a positive one, especially his view of European culture. Harking back to his Goethean model, he wrote to Professor Kapff that it was his daily prayer to preserve his own inner world so that he did not fall into ruin and partake of the "same sweet poison" that he saw thousands of others swallowing. Spengler-like, he saw Western civilization in a state of decay, "addicted to morphium" (*GB I* 14). He saw a long period of desolation and barbarism between the collapse of the present way of life and the "new spring," which would come "not from Europe itself but from the periphery" and—here his youthful dream shows itself—"perhaps from Brazil" (*GB I* 15). By present form of life, Hesse was loosely referring to the social problems of industrialization and only somewhat more specifically to the bourgeois values, which he would find to be impossible bedfellows for years to come. His vision is typical of the poet as a young man, but he admits in the same letter, paradoxically, that everyone must "bury his boyhood ideals" sometime (*GB I* 14). He could form his life into a "work of art" through "nature and truth." The society around him, on the other hand, had ever grander and broader plans, thoughts, and perspectives, while humanity, itself, was becoming smaller and smaller (*GB I* 15).

Hesse would dream for a long time of living at an aesthetic distance; he would not give up on the new spring, and he would gradually learn to accept his self-styled position as outsider and lonely seeker after truth. His last letter to Professor Kapff, barely two weeks prior to his move to Tübingen, shows that he was well aware of his individuality:

Already as a boy, more than ever as a boy, I was different from my friends, also lonely, and had sometimes to suffer as a result of it. But precisely what separated me and differentiated me from the others, what made me lonely and often miserable, also raised me up again and again to faith and hope—the dark drive, the longing for and seeking after that which is truly beautiful. And I always return to my belief that the philosophy of aesthetics is the best; at the same time, it seeks and finds beauty and truth, one is in the other. (*KuJ II* 14)

As concerned his religious confrontation, he made a truce of sorts with Christianity during the Tübingen years. His views had changed to the point that he could again "honor, love, and read the Bible." Not surprisingly, he loved the poetic passages the most (*KuJ II* 28). Church services, however, did nothing for him, and he did not go to communion (*KuJ II* 79); he "still [had not] found a God" (*KuJ II* 140). When he wrote to a friend in February of 1897, however, he said that he was not "Godless"; he had a God that was "not dead and not [his] own creation" (*KuJ II* 167). He did not yet explain that his "God" was aestheticism. Despite progress, it seems, Hesse remained emotionally unstable during the Tübingen period, was not sure of the face he wanted to present to the world, and was easily moved to see the negative side of his existence. Foreshadowing a *Steppenwolf* theme of thirty years later, he told his mother that he "avoid[ed] gatherings because his life seem[ed] so dead afterward, so lacking," and he was seized by the "demand to do and to be in daily life what he [did] and what he [was] in his thoughts when he [was] not working" (*KuJ II* 108). His sensitive nature made him take any critical remark about his work personally and too seriously: "They aren't satisfied with me," he wrote home (*KuJ II* 125), even though the store owner, Herr Sonnewald, had written to his father saying he was pleased with Hermann's work, that he showed enthusiasm and interest (*KuJ II* 127). In his diary Hermann wrote on June 9, 1897, "Tomorrow!—that's when my life will be a smoothly flowing river. . . . Tomorrow, the day that will never be today" (*KuJ II* 185).

However, things did not remain as bleak as he liked to paint them in his many moments of self-pity. He developed a small circle of friends—all university students in Tübingen, some of whom he had met at Maulbronn and at the *gymnasium* in Cannstatt. During the winter and spring semesters of 1897–1898, they began meeting regularly, usually at an inn in Kirchheim, a short distance from Tübingen. An oft-published formal photograph shows the five of them as young men of the world, self-assured and posing for posterity, with Hesse recumbent on his elbow on a white fur rug in front of the others, one knee raised with his stylish straw hat perched on top of it. They called themselves the *petit cénacle* (Little Fellowship). Freedman gets to the heart of their collective self-image by labeling them "intellectual iconoclasts" (76). The others, unlike Hesse, knew where they were going professionally, and their self-assurance rubbed off on him. His letters from the one-year period when they were meeting regularly begin to show a confident attitude and a touch of lightheartedness that had not been seen since the early months at Maulbronn. Although the closeness of 1897–1898 could not continue because the *petit cénacle* members began going their separate ways, they met when they could, and in the summer of 1899, the group vacationed for ten days—its final fling together—at an inn called the Crown, in Kirchheim. Julie Hellmann, niece of the owner and apparently very receptive to the competition among members of the group to lavish attention on her, also became one of them—the "soul of the group" according to Faber, one of the members (*KuJ II* 539). She became "Lulu" in Hesse's later fairy tale, a dream princess to whom all pay homage. Hesse wrote nostalgic, impassioned love letters to her for a short time afterwards, and they did not lose track of each other. When Hesse received the Nobel Prize for literature in 1946, he visited her, along with another member of the *cénacle,* Ludwig Finckh.

Another event that helped to encourage the budding writer was a letter from an admirer after he had published his first poems. His fantasy poem, "Chopin's Grand Valse," had so impressed this young woman, Helene Voight, that she wrote him a modest note of praise. An intimate correspondence developed and began to border on the romantic, as indicated in Helene Voight's letter of March 1, 1898, just three months after her first correspondence: "It is so strangely difficult for me to write to you today, although what I have to tell you may not move you in the least. Your letter is dated the twelfth of February, the day on which I lost my young freedom. I am engaged, laughing and crying at the same time" (*KuJ II* 241). Hesse's response likewise shows that an emotional bond had developed: "When I read your letter the first time, I even felt a pang of jealousy; the certainty of your friendship is so dear and present. But I think it can continue because it developed out of our common wandering toward a nostalgic land and from our prayers to common gods" (*KuJ II* 244). The relationship continued on the same spiritually intimate plane for some years, though they never met. Helene Voight-Diederich was, herself, a writer, and her husband, a publisher, would print Hesse's first prose work, *An Hour Beyond Midnight.* A series of fictionalized vignettes out of his childhood and youth, the volume was so entitled because the pieces were written in the dark, early hours of the morning when he could not sleep. Hesse's psychological circumlocutions are evident in one letter to Helene, when he mentions that he is putting together a selection of poems but that getting the manuscript in final form is distressing because of the prospect of writing letters to publishers, calculating everything, etc. When the now newly married friend suggested that she could perhaps talk to her husband about publishing them, Hesse shyly backed away, noting that he was honored with her suggestion but wanted his first publication to "stand on its own feet" (*KuJ II* 273). He underlined the word "first," however, thus leaving the door open to the future, and he remarked in a later letter, "in passing," that the notebook of memories which he had told her about had been started and that he would "be anxious to have [her] see it" (*KuJ II* 287). He did send her the manuscript on February 2, 1899, and her husband agreed to publish an edition of six hundred copies. Hesse asked if the book could be ready by June 14, his father's birthday, and it arrived on the precise day. Again, the deep psychological cleft separating parents and son can be seen in Hermann's peculiarly worded announcement of his gift: "If only I could have found something that you like and could use! Instead of that, a present is coming that you can find little joy in" (*KuJ II* 345). The letter cannot be interpreted as other than a plea for a word of praise and congratulations for this, his first major success. The answer came the following day, not from his father, who was too ill to read the book, but from Hesse's mother. She had not been able to sleep after hastily looking through it. One of his stories he had entitled "The Fever Muse," and his mother told him he should "avoid it [i.e., the muse that moved him to write such things] like a snake; it is the same one that slithered into paradise and still today would like to poison every Love- and Poetry-Paradise" (*KuJ II* 357). She continued:

Oh, my child, flee from it, hate it, it is unclean and has no claim on you, for you are God's property. . . . Pray for "great thoughts and a pure heart." . . . Keep yourself clean. What comes from us, from our mouths and even more from the pen, defiles us—did you think of that? "The King's Celebration" is terrible reading. . . . Child, I am your mother and I love you as no one else can, and I must warn you and speak the truth. My heart rises up against such poison. There is a world of lies, where the base, the animalistic, the impure is considered beautiful. There is a realm of truth, of justice, of freedom, that shows us sin as sin and teaches us to hate it and leads us to divine freedom. Man is called to the sublime, the eternal, the wonderful—does he want to lick the dust? Child of my heart, God help you and bless you and save you! (*KuJ II* 357–8)

She continued the letter the next morning, saying she did not want to send it, but she must: "Some sentences are so indecent that no girl should read them, people talk that way about animals, not about people" (*KuJ II* 359).

Hesse's relationship with his mother would never fully recover. He asked to have his book returned and said he had decided never to answer her letter. If he did, she would be "shocked at how bitter everything in him has become" (*KuJ II* 360). In a second letter the same day, he thanked her for the birthday "goodies" that had been part of his father's birthday celebration, although they were "about the same to the stomach as his godless book is for the spirit" (*KuJ II* 361).

More than twenty years later, Hesse would write to his sister, Marulla: "One of the most depressing and harmful experiences of my youth was a letter from [their mother] in which she discusses my first stories with her prudery and moral fervor. If she had read "Klein und Wagner" [a later short story], she would have known that moralizing drove me along my path" (*KuJ II* 360).

From Tübingen Hesse returned home to Calw before moving to a new position in a Basel bookstore on September 15, 1899. As usual, he looked optimistically forward to change. "Just think," he wrote to Helene Voight-Diederich, "to Basel! . . . my favorite city, my city of cities . . . the home of Burckhardt and Böcklin.[8] I also spent the longest and most wonderful part of my childhood in Basel, which has almost more enchantment for me than Burckhardt and Böcklin" (*GB I* 59).

Aside from looking forward to Basel, he was also pining for his "fairy tale princess," Julie Hellmann, with whom he had ostensibly fallen madly in love during the ten days in Kirchheim with the *petit cénacle*. He wrote to her: "Didn't you see how my hand and voice trembled when I said goodbye to you? . . . I get up in the morning and am unconsolable because I won't be seeing you all day . . . you torture me, you don't know what pains of love and jealousy oppress me constantly. . . . I must tell you that you are my princess and the jewel of my dreams" (*GB I* 61). Hesse was aware that he was not going to pursue his princess. More than a love letter to Julie Hellmann alone, the letter was an expression of Hesse's need to find someone to love: "You can believe me, I won't force myself on you. . . . I only want you to know about it and accept me as your love-slave" (*GB I* 62). The fantasy eventually passed, replaced by the reality of his new work in Basel. He was a *Sortimentsgehilfe,* a jack-of-all-jobs in the Reich bookstore. His first apartment was shared with a young architect named Henrich Jennen who had just won the design competition for an addition to the city hall in Basel. Jennen was much more outgoing and social than Hesse and prompted him to join in making the rounds of various taverns and wine houses. Hesse apparently wrote to his parents of his tippling, and although his mother's comments are not available, the son's response to a letter makes it clear that she again warned him not to be led astray. Hesse reported that she would be pleased because he would be moving away from the "monster" Jennen shortly (*GB I* 72).

The four-year Basel period, from September 1899 to October 1903, provided a series of experiences in the later formative years of the maturing young man. Freedman calls him "a man poised on the edge of achievement when he arrive[d] in the city" (87). Of special importance is the influence of Jakob Burckhardt, the historian of world fame who had died just prior to Hesse's arrival. He would continue to be *the* historian for Hesse, who would pay tribute to him as Father Jakobus in his final novel. Hesse, in fact, ranked him as one of the three major influences on his life, along with the Christian and international spirit of his family and the great Chinese philosophers.[9]

Although his letters often express contradictory states of mind, Hesse's life took on a new independence. Some of the most edifying and perhaps positive experiences were a result of his visits to the Wackernagel family. Dr. Rudolf Wackernagel was a government archivist and historian, whom Hesse's father knew and who opened his house to the young bookseller. Hesse soon called it his second home. Despite his professed dislike for gatherings and parties, he spent much of his free time with the Wackernagels, who socialized with many friends in the university community and whose house was a haven for other, younger Basel intellectuals. There were also museums, and Hesse began to fill in his gaps of knowledge of art history with a systematic study prompted by visits to local galleries and their displays of Böcklin and Holbein.

Frau Wackernagel was a well-educated woman, and Hesse soon credited his many conversations with her for his new optimistic outlook on life. Roles seemed almost reversed, as he lectured his father on the positive aspects of the present era. Johannes Hesse had sent him a copy of a lecture he had given in which he had warned against the "sceptical, corrupted present age" (*GB I* 96). His "more enlightened" son pointed out that the seventeenth and eighteenth centuries had been "more godless" than the present. In contrast, the present age was in "unpious revolution" against superficial traditions, and all save the completely obdurate were filled with a powerful "longing for God." The "much maligned literature and art of our day" [which, a short time earlier, he had been maligning himself] is, to be sure, more subjective but shows more faith and enthusiasm for salvation than it did at that time. Moreover, the age is not only mission-minded and printing Bibles, but its thinkers are returning to Buddha, Christ, and the Neoplatonists. . . ." The era was "indeed striving to find ideals. If the philosophers and thinkers of earlier centuries were using the Bible as a playground for their dialectic or warily avoiding it, at present they are arguing seriously about the Bible and the person of Christ" (*GB I* 96–7).

In what could be little more than an attempt to "get back" at his father, Hesse called Catholicism a "shining example" of the folk religions, adding that whoever had ears for it could "hear God's word just as well in a mass as in a Bach chord or a [Protestant] sermon" (*GB I* 97). They should not feel sorry for the Catholics because they were not reading the Bible, which was so full of entanglements, because "we ourselves" disregard and fear everything that does not come "literally from Luther or the consistories [the Pietist councils]." Hesse's use of "we" is strong psychological evidence that his ties to Pietism were deep indeed. Although he had outwardly disengaged himself from it, he could not escape the feeling that he was still of part of the community. Hesse ends his discourse with the comment that "our era does not take second place to any of the earlier golden ages as regards seriousness and good will" (*GB I* 97). Other letters written within the same time period show extreme contradictions vis-à-vis his commentary to his father and, thus, underscore Hesse's emotional need to oppose him. To a newly acquired Italian friend, for example, he had written several months earlier, "My way of life, my way of looking [at it], of thinking, of enjoying myself, is almost without connection to the life of my time. . . . As a poet I cannot find the right relationship to the present day and the people" (*GB I* 87–8). Just three days before writing the above letter to his father, Hesse wrote to another friend, "I have one eternal and unfulfilled desire—to live an independent, private life, even if a very modest one. I would spend my life in out-of-the-way Italian nests, take long hikes and feel myself completely and comfortably separated from all the humbug of modern life" (*GB I* 93).

Hesse also said he was completely disinterested in politics and had "never read a newspaper" (*GB I* 94). To a new-found acquaintance, fellow aspiring writer Stefan Zweig, he wrote that his "heart has never belonged to people, but to nature and books." In the same letter he noted that he "like[d] to associate with children, farmers, sailors, etc., and [was] always ready to go drinking in a sailors' hangout" (*GB I* 95). This quotation gives the impression that Hesse felt himself close to "the people," but from childhood on, he retained a sense of elitism, to some extent unintended but, nonetheless, a part of his character. In describing his walk to the bookstore in Tübingen, for instance, he described the slum area that he walked through with thorough disdain for the "drunken men, the skinny, sloppy women, and the dirty insolent children"(*KuJ II* 27). Despite the fact that he had enjoyed his second home with the Wackernagels, among the professors and young intellectuals, he wrote to Alfons Paquet, another new friend, that he had "never sympathized with students. Scholars as well as students are abominations to me"—also "musicians, actors, and men of letters." The only ones he liked were the "creative artists, especially the painters" (*GB I* 99).

It is difficult to make sense of the contradictions and inconsistencies that occur in Hesse's various letters during this early Basel period. The most logical conclusion is a simple explanation, namely that his life was still in limbo, despite a certain external stability that was setting in. His poorly controlled arguments with his father seem to have been for the sake of disagreement only. His general dislike of "functioning" intellectuals was jealousy. They did not look at him as their equal—recognition that he badly needed. His relationships with individual intellectuals, however, could be quite positive. He was, we may recall, very grateful to Professor Kapff, who corresponded with him in Tübingen. And the *petit cénacle* group, of which he was the only nonstudent, was one of his most positive experiences. If Hesse got along well with the "lower classes," it was because he stood a step above them. In other words, he was still far from possessing a stable mental attitude, although he was able to live in the world, carry on his work, and make a favorable impression.

His relationship with his parents was riddled with complexities—guilt feelings, feelings of superiority, recognition of their genuine love for him, but bitterness that they could not approve of his life and his dreams. And he could never forgive their moralizing. Freedman calls his attitude toward them his "insulation from their world" (99). His mother's death on April 24, 1902, did nothing to simplify his feelings. Letters written after her condemnation of his first book are studies in mood contrasts. Part of each is inflamed with a barely controlled bitterness, but then a curtain is drawn, and loving son writes to loving mother. Hesse's unwillingness to make the short journey for his mother's funeral would bother his conscience most of his life and reveals how deep the emotional split had become. Nor was a real closeness with his father ever reestablished.

But a new love would now change the direction of Hesse's life. A romantic inclination toward a certain Elizabeth Laroche, a young woman whom he had met and admired at the Wackernagel home, collapsed when Elizabeth decided to marry someone else. Hesse then turned his attentions to Maria Bernoulli, a woman nine years his senior who even bore a slight physical resemblance to his mother, if several pictures of her in later years are any indication. Maria and her sister operated a photography studio in Basel. Hesse first mentions her in a letter, calling her "an artist" (*GB I* 100). The relationship developed into more than friendship when a mutual friend, another artist named Fräulein Gundrun, left for Italy and wanted companions for the trip. Her friend Maria decided to go at the last minute and coaxed Hesse into joining them. The journey enlivened the acquaintanceship and would shortly lead to marriage, which at first would prove to be a romantic dream come true but eventually would turn into tragedy. Back in Basel, he was "strolling along the path of amour," on his arm, in the moonlight, a "small, dark, wild sweetheart" (*GB I* 104). He wrote to a friend that "marriage, of course, is out of the question" but that, nonetheless, for the present he was "as gallant and full of passion as any Romeo," and he even advises his friend to follow in his footsteps—"Don't think about it, act! It makes you years younger and worlds richer" (*GB I* 104). Two months later he was considering the possibility of marriage, though admitting that he had a "certain fear of it" (*GB I* 105). Hesse describes his bride-to-be as "no silly little Gretchen"[10] but at least "my equal in education, experience and intelligence"(*GB I* 106). Hesse continued to have mixed emotions, and in the end he surrendered to what he felt was a mistake—"My whole nature tells me to stay single"—by rationalizing that "tragedy belongs to love and life in general; without pain, deep and heartfelt experiences are not possible" (*GB I* 106). This utterance was to prove prophetic.

Maria's father did not approve of the match, since he considered Hesse's future uncertain at best (*GB I* 108), but despite the protest, the couple became engaged in the spring of 1903. And fate was about to start smiling financially upon Hesse. He did not have as much faith in his ability to write prose as to write lyric poetry, but practice and posterity would reverse this judgment. He was awaiting the reception of his first novel, *Peter Camenzind,* which was to appear in book form in 1904. Also, the big opportunity he had been waiting for suddenly presented itself. The Fischer Publishing House, a major firm, offered him a five-year contract upon the recommendation of a Swiss poet, Paul Ilg.

Hesse, gambling on his ability, resigned his position at the bookstore after signing the contract on June 10, 1903. Leaving his fiancée in Basel, he returned to Calw, where he immediately began work on his second novel, *Beneath the Wheel,* a bitter critique of adult hypocrisy and of the educational system that had cast him out.

Peter Camenzind did not disappoint him. It ran to three editions and earned him 2,500 marks in early royalties. Thus, the marriage could take place on August 2, 1904, in Basel. A new chapter in Hesse's life was opening, and small signs of recognition were beginning to show themselves. He was invited to give a public reading from his works, but he expressed anxiety because he was just a "poet of forest and field" (*GB I* 114) and could not bring himself to dress formally for the occasion. He gave advice to another aspiring writer who was impatient with his rejections—"How many poems did I get back unopened or with negative comments from editors?" (*GB I* 112). He had a long meeting with his publisher, Fischer, during a three-week visit to Munich and was introduced to Thomas Mann, another young writer who had just taken a giant step into literary history with his novel *Buddenbrooks.* Hesse was also being overwhelmed with correspondence and was on the editorial board of several journals. A small monograph on Boccaccio was published by Schuster and Loeffler in Berlin in April 1904 and another on St. Francis of Assisi later in the same year. It appeared that Hermann Hesse had arrived, which makes this an appropriate point in time to interrupt the biography and turn attention to his first two novels, *Peter Camenzind* and *Beneath the Wheel.* The financial success of the former had made his marriage possible, and its content will help us to understand the dream that prompted his move to the rustic village of Gaienhofen. The latter work, written in the few months preceding his marriage, is an outpouring of oppressive memories—a much-needed purgative.

CHAPTER TWO

Peter Camenzind

An Idyll Pursued

Prior to *Peter Camenzind,* Hesse's published writings had been somewhat of a potpourri: a collection of poems, "Romantische Lieder" ("Romantic Songs") in 1899, followed closely by *Eine Stunde hinter Mitternacht (An Hour beyond Midnight),* a series of prose vignettes, and *Hinterlassene Schriften und Gedichte von Hermann Lauscher (Posthumous Writings and Poems of Hermann Lauscher)* in 1901. He first mentions a novel in progress in a letter of October 19, 1902, noting that he had been working on it for almost a year and that, if he continued at the present pace, it could be completed in perhaps ten or twelve years (*GB I* 91). But the struggling author obviously found sudden inspiration when the well-known Fischer publishing firm invited him to submit a manuscript. *Peter Camenzind* was published by Fischer in January, 1904. It is a first-person narrative that carries the protagonist's life into perhaps his later thirties, which means that the twenty-six-year-old Hesse was writing well beyond his own life experience, projecting his own fictional image into the future.

The tale begins in the Swiss mountain village of Nimikon, where about two-thirds of the families are named Camenzind. Peter is an only child and is led into academic pathways by the local pastor, who recognizes his intelligence. Peter's Uncle Konrad is the village eccentric, bristling with ideas and projects that keep the populace both amazed and amused. When he rigs up the first sailboat to be seen on their mountain lake, he is cheered as it disappears in full sail around a point but becomes the butt of jokes when he struggles home at midnight soaking wet and without his boat. As a boy, Peter is led silently to the haymow for a weekly strapping. Neither father nor son knows why, but Peter later compares the punishment to the thunderstorms that nature periodically sends into our lives for no apparent reason. One night he experiences his sickly mother's death, sitting beside her and holding her hand while she silently and uncomplainingly passes away.

At the pastor's insistence, he is sent to the university in Zurich, where he meets Richard, a music student whose piano playing causes Peter to discover the "magic of music, the most feminine and sweetest of the arts"[1] (*GS I* 256). Through Richard he is introduced to artists, writers, and other intellectuals at various salons and gatherings. Peter reads voraciously and, within the span of several years, becomes a well-educated man. Richard secretly takes one of his friend's stories to a publisher, and after its immediate success, Peter finds it relatively easy to make his way as a freelance writer. He falls in love with an Italian painter, Erminia Aglietti, and romantically rows her out onto a lake to declare his love, but before he can make his own feelings known, she tells him that she is in love with someone else. A second, and deeper, love for a girl named Elizabeth also goes astray. Alone once more, he turns to his work, which even takes him to Paris for an extended period.

St. Francis of Assisi becomes Peter's idol, and he tries to emulate the saint's love for the world but nearly fails his first major test when a crippled brother of friends comes to live in their house and proves a barrier to the friendship. Peter realizes that Francis would not have avoided such a creature, befriends him, and eventually devotes himself to caring for him, sharing the handicapped Boppi's love of nature and animals. Boppi's death leaves him with a profound sense of the real values of life, which he finds more apparent among the *Volk* than in the salons of artists and intellectuals. Peter feels that much of art and many so-called artists are shallow. His own projected literary effort, if he continues his major work at all, will be profound, its theme derived from his understanding of nature which reflects the mysteries of the universe and which can be the key to human understanding—a motif that would continue to make its presence felt in Hesse's writings.

By now his father is elderly, and Peter returns to Nimikon, taking over the household and again becoming a part of the community. When the book ends, he is about to buy the village inn, which his father has frequented all his life. Peter has decided to preserve the sacred locale as the heart of the community and to prevent outsiders from destroying the romantic idyll that Nimikon represents for him. Here, within the confines of a natural, simple life, its cycles reflected in the surrounding alpine nature, is where Camenzind/Hesse expects to find peace and meaning. The protagonist can, indeed, be identified with his creator at this point, for when the novel was finished, Hesse said he found the conclusion its best part (*GB I* 111).

This first novel, a realistic, straightforward narrative that culminates in an idyllic, back-to-nature dream was in vogue at the time, especially among young readers. Stelzig calls the denouement "grist to the mill of popular taste" (95), and Freedman notes that the book appealed to the "counter-culture of nature, sainthood, and dream [which] had been created precisely in response to the pressures of the new age that had begun to close in on them in the empire of Wilhem II" (109). Hesse *had* arrived and was prepared to believe that he could become his own Camenzind creation.[2] His dream is left hovering eternally on the last page of the novel. We can also find, in simplified form, stylistic techniques and thematic substance that will be replayed time and again in Hesse's prose. Readers may, in fact, be surprised at how firm the foundation of his spiritual reality was, even in this early period.[3]

Hesse's admiration for St. Francis of Assisi is the best starting point from which to analyze the novel and seek out the Hesse reflection behind it. At the same time that he was working on *Peter Camenzind,* as noted earlier, Hesse was also involved with a biography of the saint, who is easy to love and to idolize. He was born into a wealthy Italian family and, as a youth, led a dissolute life but, after several years of debauchery, stripped himself naked in front of his father, literally giving up all worldly possessions to begin life anew. In a dream (dream messages will become a favorite stylistic device for Hesse), he was directed by God to restore the Church of St. Damian, where the Franciscan Order and the Order of the Poor Clares would be founded (and both names that will have meaning when we progress to the novel *Demian*). Francis called everyone and everything in the world his brother or sister and was so at one with nature that birds would sit on his head and shoulders and eat from his hand. Hesse's idolization of St. Francis and the Boppi episode reflect the legacy of simple purity and love that lay at the roots of Pietism, which, as Hesse perceived it in practice, had become absorbed in legalism and sectarian narrowness. Hesse, like his Peter Camenzind, wanted to be a gentle, caring soul, but he, too, had a difficult time loving people. Boulby also emphasizes this thematic aspect: "On a windy night Peter will go out into the storm to visit a solitary tree to see how it is faring, but he has no love for his own kind" (28). Hesse saw the living solution to his problem personified in St. Francis and made the attempt in *Peter Camenzind* to equate the vicissitudes of human nature, which Francis could accept, with those of nature itself, which Hesse could accept. As a frame of reference to provide a symbiosis of the two worlds, he created a metaphor that would change little, if at all, in future writings. The amazing first sentence of *Peter Camenzind*—"In the beginning was the myth"—is, in fact, the threshold to Hesse's *Journey to the East.* The biblical source of the sentence is readily recognized, but it is also an allusion to Goethe, who, in his *Faust,* had translated the Greek (rendered in English as "In the beginning was the word") as "In the beginning was the deed [Tat]."

But what did Hesse mean by *myth*? He begins his explanation in *Peter Camenzind* by saying that, just as God had written his poetry in the souls of the East Indians (*Inder*), the Greeks, and the Germanic peoples, and struggled to make Himself understood to them, He continues to write His poetry anew every day in the soul of every child (219)—i.e., children are natural participants in the mythical vision of life; they do not have to name lakes and mountains and trees as do adults, who have lost the magic. Thus, the word *myth* to Hesse meant and continued to mean the divine poetry expressed by life itself. Hans Jürgen Lüthi reads basically the same meaning into Hesse's Alpine myth, saying, "Camenzind greedily peers into the abyss of his own being and into the abyss of nature, listening to its thousand voices and recognizing the voice of God within them" (14). If, as children, we understood the whisperings, we must struggle to regain and renew the magic as we grow older, a metaphorical message that Hesse portrays in an alpine legend of the clouds, "The Story of the Snow Princess," which he tells in the early pages of *Peter Camenzind.* The princess—a cloud appearing from on high with her retinue—seeks to settle over the mountain tops and into the valleys, but the northwest wind is jealous and attacks her, sometimes driving her back. The young Camenzind equates the clouds with man's dreams; they are symbols of wanderings, the souls of humankind hovering between time and eternity. The princess is patient, however, waits high above, and eventually returns, winning the battle with the wind and enveloping the landscape in fog until she can renew it with a covering of fresh, new snow. When the fog lifts, the world is once again purified and glistening (231–2). But, alas, rebirth is not permanent. The struggle of the Snow Princess against the resistance of the wind—i.e., humankind's struggle to rejuvenate the magic of its relationship to life—will be repeated time and again in various metaphorical guises in Hesse's novels, culminating in the *Natur* and *Geist* struggle in *The Glass Bead Game.* To love this game of life, to love it all, as did St. Francis, was for Hesse "nothing less than a return to the beginning of creation and a passionate greeting from God's paradise."[4]

Hesse's protagonists will reach their higher levels of understanding by listening to their inner voices, but relationships with other characters will also play significant roles. The more profound the lessons to be learned, the more mysterious the relationships may be, as we shall see in *Demian* and *Steppenwolf,* but we should not overlook that the basic stylistic patterns are present in *Peter Camenzind.* Even if the two secondary characters, Richard and Elizabeth, are very real, they nonetheless foreshadow more abstract characterizations in later novels. Richard is Peter's friend and tutor—a close male-to-male relationship, which will occur repeatedly in Hesse's prose and which has led to various critical suggestions of homosexual connotations. Stelzig, for example, notes that Peter is "so taken with Richard that he is jealous of his relationship with women. The episode in which the two friends bathe in the river . . . is colored by homoerotic sentiment . . ." (91).[5] Such close relationships will often result in confused interpretations, especially the correlation of narrative and metaphorical roles.

Peter is sent off to be educated, and since Hesse himself lacked university experience, it is not difficult to see that the student Richard was given the task of introducing Peter to this "big world." Hesse is doing little more than distancing himself from a situation with which he was not familiar, and, although we still have virtually no firsthand account of university life, Richard is at least its representative. We see the trace of disdain that Hesse would always harbor for this structured "mind-side" of life in Richard's surprise at Peter's ignorance of Nietzsche and Peter's angry response in asking how many glaciers Richard has climbed (259). Richard's unnecessary death just weeks after his departure is meant to signify that he has fulfilled his role in Peter's life—i.e., the latter has acquired what he could from Richard and is now an educated man.[6]

A second relationship of importance in Peter's life is with Elizabeth; eventually he will fall in love with her. She seeks him out as he sits alone at a gathering of Zurich intellectuals after he has already established a certain reputation. She recognizes him as a poet, not because he is the writer Peter Camenzind but because she perceives that he understands and loves nature. Shortly after their meeting, Peter remarks, "At that time my joy in the silence of nature and my relationship to [Elizabeth] began to change. . . . I saw again and again the forests and mountains, meadows and fruit trees and bushes . . . waiting for something. Perhaps for me, but in any case for love. And I *began* [emphasis provided] to love these things" (308).

Hesse's intended purpose for this new relationship is clear, once we know the novel, but he does a poor job of constructing the metaphor. He obviously wants Peter to learn how to love humankind, and learning to love Elizabeth is a first step, as Boulby, too, points out: "Peter even dreams . . . of finding in her a bridge to take him back to other human beings" (23). But Hesse should not have mentioned Peter's "changing relationship to nature." It does not change. Hesse appears to have forgotten that he has built Peter's entire character around his love for, and understanding of, nature. Thematically, then, the Elizabeth episode is a failure. She does contribute to the external narrative but is probably little more than a reflection of Hesse's experience with Elizabeth Laroche, the encounter in the Wackernagel salon in Basel. Ball strongly implies this: "They were whispering in Basel . . . that the model [for Elizabeth] had been a Fräulein Laroche" (74). The episode may reflect Hesse's ambivalent feelings toward his impending marriage, as well.

A third feminine companion should not be overlooked. While visiting in Assisi, Peter spends an extended time at a *pensione,* an inn, owned by a simple vegetable seller some years his senior. She falls in love with him, and he becomes very close to several villagers who gather at her *pensione* every evening. He learns what it is like to be loved but not to love in return. He tells her and the group, after recounting his early love story with Erminia (and keeping his deeper love for Elizabeth a secret), that he will not love again, that he now loves St. Francis, who has taught him to love all people (323), which statement may also be an unintentional or psychological expression of fear of marriage. Since the roles of the female characters are not stylistic and thematic successes in *Peter Camenzind* (in fact Hesse will always have trouble portraying feminine characters convincingly at the narrative level of his novels), it is better to postpone comment on their future metaphorical roles. Peter's statement "And God touched me with his soft, feminine hand" (300) must also await meaningful interpretation until other "feminine" hands are found in *Demian*. In any case, if Peter fails to learn to love humankind through Elizabeth, he at least makes strong inroads through his tender care of the crippled Boppi.

Peter's dream, once he has learned to love his fellow humans sufficiently, is to teach others the same lesson through his "great work of art." He wants to teach his readers to "listen to the heartbeat of the earth, to participate in all of life and, in the pressures of their individual little fates, not to forget that we are not gods and have not created ourselves, but are, rather, children and a part of the earth and the cosmic whole" (328). Echoing St. Francis, he continues: "And above all I wanted to place the beautiful secret of love in your [he suddenly switches to direct address] hearts. I hoped to teach you to be just brothers to all living things and to become so full of love, that you wouldn't even fear sorrow and death, but receive them earnestly and sisterly when they came to you as sisters" (329). The basic thematic similarities of this first novel to future works indicate clearly that Hesse's philosophy of life was all but etched in stone, however naively and simplistically, when he wrote *Peter Camenzind.* He would need only to bring it to higher levels in subsequent novels. The dream that Hesse/Camenzind portrays at this time belongs to the young and idealistic. The older author knew he would not change the world with a literary masterpiece, as Peter Camenzind hoped to do.

Before we end the discussion of *Peter Camenzind,* a few words should be said of Peter's parents. His mother is little more than a vague presence, and it will be recalled that Marie Hesse's reaction to *An Hour beyond Midnight* created a bitterness in her son that he could never overcome. His guilt feelings for not attending her funeral are sublimated in *Peter Camenzind,* where the boy discovers in the night that his mother is dying, sits at her bedside holding her hand, closes her eyes when she is gone, and only then awakens his father who is asleep beside her. The scene is a quiet, personal tribute to love even if there is outwardly no final communication. Stelzig calls the death "a confessional fiction, not of what was but . . . of what might or should have been" (93). Stelzig is also on the right track when he says that "the emotional charge attaching to the relationship is channeled into and expressed through the lyrical bonding with nature" (93).

Johannes Hesse's lack of understanding for his son is probably reflected in the periodic and undeserved thrashings meted out to Peter. The abyss separating both fathers from both sons is apparent, but when Freedman states that the ending of *Peter Camenzind*—his return to the village to become a respected member of the community—is an "offer of reconciliation to Hesse's own father" (116), he is only partially right. The dichotomy in the relationship remains. Peter is returning on his own terms and takes charge of the household. Camenzind's father is a heavy drinker, whereas Johannes Hesse looked upon the body as "a temple of the Holy Spirit" into which such poison as alcohol should not enter (*KuJ I* 132). Freedman may be stretching the alcohol motif a bit when he equates "Camenzind's love for wine" (which he passes on to his son) with Johannes Hesse's "legacies of headaches and anxieties" (113). Johannes was also a pious, learned man, whereas Herr Camenzind is spiritually and intellectually simplistic. A biblical allusion attests to his limited existence. Instead of "In my father's house are many mansions," Peter writes "My father's little house was bordered by a tiny fenced-in garden" (227). There is also a hint of retaliation in Peter's guardianship of his father, for it is the son who now displays the paternalistic attitude and appears to enjoy controlling the keys to the wine cellar.

With our retrospective vision of the young Hesse at the time he produced *Peter Camenzind,* we can see that his basic nature was kind and sensitive, even if these qualities had often been obscured and repressed by the problems of his teenage years—the expectations of his parents, of school, and of society. Injustices he suffered, real or imaginary, caused him to act uncaringly at times, but this was not his nature. He honestly admired the goodness of his parents and wanted to be a kind human being. Francis of Assisi offered him the first fully good and, more importantly, fully natural model and ideal. If his parents, the Bible, Pietism, and society were full of contradictions, St. Francis was not. By the time he was completing his novel, Hesse appears to have decided to emulate his saint as best he could and lead a simple life, which would now include Maria Bernoulli. If he has left a wife out of Peter's Nimikon future, it is probably a calculated choice. We do know that Maria's father was against the marriage, and Hesse perhaps avoided a conclusion that would have allowed a direct comparison to his personal situation.

The content, structure, and style of *Peter Camenzind* are deceptively uncomplicated, but the themes and stylistic techniques foreshadow the maturer writer: the outsider-protagonist, new beginnings, nature imagery, the role of death, the role of art, and disdain for the out-of-touch intellectuals. A most important stylistic device—the metaphorical treatment of character relationships, be they male-male or male-female—has its beginnings in the Richard friendship and the ill-formed Elizabeth episode. And Hesse's deep admiration for St. Francis's service to humankind should be remembered.

CHAPTER THREE

Beneath the Wheel

Burning Memories

Hesse's second novel has proven to be a better survivor than his first, although as creative literature, *Peter Camenzind* is more imaginative and typically Hesse than *Beneath the Wheel*.[1] If the youthful naiveté of the former has relegated it to a secondary position among Hesse's works, *Beneath the Wheel* is more memorable reading because of its controversial theme: it is a caustic attack against German education and the adult world's hypocritical treatment of children,[2] chronicling in fictionalized form Hesse's adolescent sufferings and venting his long-smoldering emotions with a vengeance. He accuses the educational system in particular, and the adult world in general, of cruelty to children, of ridiculing their innocence, and of attempting to break their wills. Hugo Ball points out that Hesse's young life had gone well prior to the state examination and the first sojourn in Maulbronn but that, after Maulbronn, it was as though "the devil were loose" (43).

The novel was written in late 1903 and early 1904 in Calw,[3] where Hesse was awaiting the reception of *Peter Camenzind*. If we judge from a letter to Stefan Zweig, alone, memories of youthful difficulties had been forgotten: "I've been sitting in my old home town in the Black Forest for a short time, where I plan to stay at least through the winter. My very comfortable old room with its windows overlooking the scenes of my boyhood pranks . . . has a very scholarly and industrious look about it with the desk and a lot of books, and it already has a strong smell of tobacco." He hopes to "work very hard this winter, at least a novel or so" (*GBI* 108). Nevertheless, the work that he produced indicates that old, burning memories had to be purged. Calw was the site of adolescent failures and many battles of wills with his parents.

The novel begins with a description of the protagonist's father, Joseph Giebenrath, a colorless everyman who shows the expected respect for the church and the authorities, as well as blind obedience to the unspoken commandments of bourgeois well-being. He is a Philistine of the first order, whose intellectual demands are satisfied by the daily paper, an occasional amateur theater performance, and the circus. He is a middleman of some sort with a certain business acumen, but he is distrustful of anyone who might be considered superior to him and instinctively hostile toward anything intellectual or sophisticated (*GS I* 375–6). Frau Giebenrath is long since deceased.

Despite his own nondescript profile, Joseph Giebenrath has fathered a son, Hans, the likes of which has not appeared in the little Swabian town in its eight or nine centuries of existence. His genius is recognized by the teachers, the principal, and the pastor as well as by his fellow students. All know that he is assured of a career, behind either a pulpit or a lectern. But admittance to this secure future must be gained by passing the dreaded state examination, which grants tuition, room, and board at the seminary in Maulbronn and, subsequent to a successful performance at this level, similar privileges at the college in Tübingen. To ensure that Hans, the school's only candidate for this examination, will represent them well, the principal gives him an extra hour of Greek instruction daily; the pastor gives him another in Latin and religion; and twice a week the mathematics teacher holds a special session for him. To keep a balance between intellect and spirit, Hans attends confirmation class for an hour in the morning before school, where, however, he secretly prepares for his academic day rather than paying attention to his catechism. Evenings are spent on homework, and the day of rest on strongly recommended extra readings. He is, of course, reminded that everything should be done in moderation; one or two walks each week in the fresh air will work miracles. Hans is torn by ambivalence. The attention paid him by the teachers and pastor fills him with pride, but he longs for his childhood, as well. In a dramatic backyard scene, he smashes a water wheel and rabbit hutch that he had built with his one friend, August, as if the destruction can rid him of desires for those happier childhood days.

A strong contrast to the other secondary figures is presented in the character of the shoemaker Flaig, a devout Pietist. He is genuinely interested in Hans's welfare, warns him against the "worldly pastor who doesn't even believe in God," and, by implication, warns him against losing touch with his spirituality by falling victim to intellectual pride. Hans has guilt feelings toward this simple man whom he admires but now avoids and reluctantly makes fun of because his schoolmates do. Hesse's treatment of Flaig is interesting because he represents much of what Hesse rebelled against—the fundamentalist religion of the Pietists. While Hesse does not attack doctrine in this novel—aside from portraying its proponent, Flaig, as a simple man—the ambivalence that is apparent in Hans's positive attitude toward this guileless, God-fearing shoemaker and the implied negative attitude toward his conservative faith is representative of Hesse's attitude toward his parents. If he can respect their spiritual integrity, he cannot equate it with their tightly packaged Christianity. It is tempting to think that Hesse was fully aware of the dichotomy he was portraying in Flaig, but at this point in his development it is more of a deep psychological reluctance, or even an emotional inability, to separate the well-intentioned person from his simplistic piety. And perhaps Hans's father is incredibly *un*passionate in subtle comparison to Johannes Hesse who could or would not respect his son's artistic passions.[4] Whatever the intention, Hesse's father cannot be recognized as a single character in the novel, but respect for his integrity is portrayed in the shoemaker. Conversely, Hans's "supporters"—the teachers, the principal, the pastor—are all cut from one cloth. They may appear to be helping Hans, but their cumulative efforts and ulterior motives can all be summarized in the pastor's comment to his wife on the day that Hans begins his exams in Stuttgart: "He is going to become something special, he will make his mark, and then it will have done no harm that I came to his aid with the Latin lessons" (390).

As mentioned earlier, Hesse's treatment of Hans's success in the state examination is also interesting. Whereas Hesse himself had stood twenty-eighth in the rankings, he places Hans second. As many of his early letters show (e.g., his flowery exhibition of literary knowledge in his commentaries to friends while at the Tübingen bookstore), the young Hesse did have his intellectual pride, and he appears to have been bolstering his own ego in the portrait of Hans Giebenrath. It is to his credit, however, that he is conscious of the character flaw, evident in his ironic portrayal of Hans, the conquering hero, feeling his great superiority over the ordinary people: "He had surpassed them, they now stood beneath him. They had plagued him enough because he . . . made no friendships and had found no pleasure in their roughhousing and games. So now they could watch his progress, these dachshunds and dummies. He despised them so much that he stopped whistling for a moment to distort his lips" (406). At this point in the novel, it appears that Hesse is placing a fair share of the blame for Hans's ultimate demise squarely on the latter's own shoulders because of his pride and superiority, but the outcome of the book will make it clear that others had instilled the pride in him.

Hans is permitted to miss the last few days of the school year because of his Stuttgart performance. He returns to nature—fishing, swimming, dozing in the sun—but his pleasures are short-lived. The pastor, the teachers, and the principal are soon "helping" him to prepare for the rigors of Maulbronn with hours of summer tutoring, and Hans's nervousness and sleeplessness return. But he thinks he must be grateful, and in due time, brimming with academic knowledge, he is delivered to the Protestant theological seminary. It is not Hans, but the narrator/Hesse who comments as the boys are unpacking, with proud parents looking on, that it had not occurred to a single one of the mothers or fathers that they were selling their sons for the sake of financial advantage

(432). "It will be . . . possible for several years to make it appear in all seriousness that the study of Hebrew and Greek, as well as lesser subjects, is the goal
of life for these youths. The great thirst of the young souls can be slaked by
turning them to pure and ideal studies and pleasures" (426). The rector at Hans's
school at home had introduced this theme earlier: "It is [the rector's] duty and
his profession for which he is responsible to the state, to tame and weed out the
wild forces and natural passions of the young boys and in their place to plant
quiet, moderate and state-recognized ideals. . . . There was something in
[Giebenrath], something wild, unruly, uncultured that first had to be broken, a
dangerous flame that had to be extinguished and stamped out" (418).

Hans, for the first several months, is a model pupil, one of the "strivers,"
pleasing in the eyes of his masters. But at this point, we are introduced to the
secret hero of the novel—Hermann Heilner is Hans Giebenrath's alter ego and
an early prose example of this *Doppelgänger* motif which will occur so often
in Hesse's novels and which will become a highly polished, stylistic device
after he becomes familiar with Jungian psychology.

Heilner is a "light-hearted genius," sure of himself, has his own values,
and cannot be coerced into studying for the sake of class ranking. He is a lonely
outsider, but when Hans chances upon him sitting by a pond writing poetry, an
unlikely friendship develops between the grade-conscious striver and the free
spirit, much to the detriment of Hans's scholastic performance. Hermann lures
him away from his studies, the results are soon evident, and the teachers change
their attitudes toward the former star pupil. When Heilner chases a classmate
through the hallways because he refuses to stop scraping on the violin, the chase
ends before the headmaster's door, where the victim pounds to seek refuge. Just
as the door opens, Heilner catches up with his quarry and delivers a kick that
sends him sprawling into the sacred chambers. Heilner is severely chastised
and ostracized by all, including Hans, who nevertheless suffers emotionally for
his cowardice. The headmaster calls him in for a conference following the incident and warns him about the negative influence of the likes of Hermann Heilner;
if one does not heed one's duties and responsibilities, one may well be crushed
"beneath the wheel" (hence the title of the novel). But when another classmate,
nicknamed "Hindu," accidentally falls through the ice of a pond and drowns,
the death makes Hans aware of how transient and precious life is and that its
real values, one of which is genuine friendship, should be respected. The close
ties with Heilner are resumed, and Hans's studies again suffer a decline. Heilner
is expelled after wandering off for a day, and we know only of his later life that
"if he did not become a hero, he did become a man" (484).

Hans's depression and severe treatment from the masters cause a fainting spell, and the authorities of the seminary advise that he be sent home, where he is now a pariah. His teachers, the pastor, and the rector avoid him, not understanding what could have happened after all the attention and privileges they had lavished upon him. They will not be associated with his failure. Only Flaig shows sympathy and understanding; Hans's father is at a loss for explanation.

Summer becomes autumn, the prelude to death for all that has flourished, and Hans too wants to die away with the rest of nature. It is the time for the apple harvest and for making cider, and the occasion is an annual festival for the small town. Even Hans's troubles cannot keep him from nostalgic wanderings among the baskets of apples, the cider presses, and the happy people. Several proffered ciders lighten his mood, and when he greets the astonished Flaig with a joyful voice, he is invited to help at his press, a common enough invitation to older children. Flaig's niece from Heilbronn, an eighteen- or nineteen-year-old named Emma, is there, and her playful eyes indicate that she is a "woman of the world," not one whose life is centered around Pietist Bible studies. With none-too-subtle, Eve-like charm, she offers an apple to all the boys who pass by, and when Flaig leaves the two of them alone to work the press, Emma's teasing manner awakens thoughts in Hans that he has scarcely dared to think before. That night he is drawn back to Flaig's house, where stands in the darkness behind a fence; when Emma notices him, she comes out and stands silently in front of him. "Would you like to kiss me?" she asks, and when Hans cannot answer, she pulls him toward her and then leaves him clutching the fence, suggesting that he come back the following evening. When he does, she leads him into a darkened stairwell and urges him on until the quavering boy must beg permission to go home. The next day when he returns to Flaig's cider press, he learns that Emma has gone back to Heilbronn with the morning train; she did not even take him seriously.

In the meantime, arrangements have been made for Hans to become an apprentice in a machine shop. He will work with his old friend August. Hans, whose dreams had placed him far above all of his "stupid classmates," is now to become the lowliest of apprentices. On his way home from his first day of labor, a former classmate calls him a "State-Exam-Mechanic" as Hans passes by in his ill-fitting uniform.

August has just finished his year of apprenticeship and will receive his first wages on Saturday. He invites Hans to join him and two others to celebrate the occasion on a Sunday excursion to the next town. Hans reluctantly agrees, somehow setting his sore muscles into motion. Before long, he too is caught up in the festive mood and the tall tales of the journeyman worker who is one of their number—stories of conquests, outwitting unjust masters, and victorious brawls with journeymen in other trades. The Sunday escapade is filled with local color—the long walk to the neighboring village, Sunday merry-making in the taverns, and flirtations with the innkeepers' daughters. Hans feels that this life is not all bad; it is good to celebrate a well-earned Sunday, to be a part of the working world, to laugh, to tell jokes, to know that one belongs, and to have friends. But as the day wears on, he cannot keep pace, songs become melancholy, the strong beer is having its effect, and Hans tells the others he must go home. He lies down under an apple tree and feels ashamed. He is broken and miserable. He breaks out in "Ach, du Lieber Augustin," and stops with the line "Alles ist hin"—everything is gone. An hour later he pulls himself up and starts the long walk home, but he never arrives. The following day his body is found in the river, and he is once again a celebrity. The teachers, the principal, the pastor, and other important personages all come to his funeral, and the principal remarks, "He could have made something out of himself. Isn't it a pity that we so often have such bad luck with the best ones?" As Flaig watches these dignitaries leave the cemetery, he says to Hans's father: "There go several of the gentlemen who helped him get where he is" (546).

The phrase "beneath the wheel" may well be taken from Hindu ceremonies, where devotees, in religious fervor, would sometimes throw themselves beneath the wheel of the huge moving statues of Shiva. Boulby suggests another source—a popular novel of the time, Emil Strau 's *Freund Hain* (*Friend Death*), in which the protagonist decides to kill himself as a consequence of the tortuous educational system, regretting only the effect on his mother: "Would it not be ten times worse for her to have to watch all the wheels gradually pass over my living body?"(123).[5] But regardless of the origin of Hesse's image, there is bitter irony in his choice of these words for his title. The headmaster at Maulbronn had warned his fourteen-year-old pupil not to let up in his diligence, or he would be crushed, whereas Hans is crushed precisely because he had not let up. And if we look to the Hindu analogy, we see that the devotee is driven to be crushed out of ecstasy, while the headmaster's warning is a threat as to what will happen to Hans if he succumbs to the least of his feelings.

This, Hesse's second novel, is only peripherally within the thematic continuum that began with *Peter Camenzind* and that would continue in subsequent works. Only the weakly implied Heilner success story pulls it somewhat into line. The narrative amounts to more of an "I'll show you all" statement to those who knew him, written when he felt himself on the verge of success in his quest to become a writer. The denouement stands in contrast to the ending of *Peter Camenzind,* where the hero has returned to his village to lead a Rousseauean existence and play a quietly paternal role in the lives of the simple people, to minister to them in the unlikely position of innkeeper, so that they can continue their close-to-nature lives. If Hesse was inspired by St. Francis's life while writing *Camenzind,* it was Nemesis, the god of vengeance, who moved him to compose *Beneath the Wheel.* Although he had written occasional apologetic letters to his parents for the troubles he had caused them, the novel gives little indication that he accepted any blame for his traumatic adolescent difficulties. Even Hans's pride and feelings of superiority are treated with caustic irony and implied to be the fault of his mentors.

The name Giebenrath was appropriated from a bakery shop owner next door to the Calw Publishing House but is very apt for Hesse's purposes, for it derives from the words *give* and *advice,* from which we can infer that Hans was too trusting and malleable to believe that he should not acquiesce to every demand made upon him by his elders. In short, the novel's theme and tone reveal the full strength of the bitterness Hesse felt, and the work is first and foremost a catharsis, which concept Boulby supports, calling *Beneath the Wheel* "the most pessimistic novel Hesse ever wrote" (52); he then adds, "for it alone [of all Hesse's novels] denies completely the inward way" (52). The latter statement seems to overlook the importance of Hermann Heilner.

Hesse's failure to mention Giebenrath's deceased mother in any detail suggests a psychological inability to deal with his relationship to his own mother and especially with her death. The father character is a petty, insignificant man but cannot be directly compared with Johannes Hesse. The strictness and self-consciousness of the teachers and the headmaster are Johannes's traits, but so too is the genuine concern of the Pietist Flaig. There is, in fact, abundant evidence of a petty, vengeful spirit directed against the discipline associated with the father concept, and, though it will soften, it will continue to be a major focus in Hesse's novels (e.g., twenty years later, in *Narcissus and Goldmund,* Goldmund's father will be portrayed as a narrow-minded Christian who abandons his son to a cloister expecting him to atone for the "sins" of his mother). The various father-like roles played by the several figures in *Beneath the Wheel,* and especially the duality motif shared by Hans and Hermann Heilner, are stylistic features that will develop rapidly and become trademarks of Hesse's prose, unfolding in psychological intricacy, as mentioned, following Hesse's introduction to Jung. The use of initials and names—the *H*ans, *H*ermann, and *H*eilner that relate to Hesse's own—serves to hint that the author is freely associating himself with his protagonists. The source of names will also remain a challenge in subsequent works—many traced and interpreted by Joseph Mileck[6]—and they will continue to give critical license to seek out the fictional borderlines that both join Hesse with and separate him from his characters.[7] In some instances, they may allude to acquaintances or historical figures.

Although the reader does not know whether Hans Giebenrath eventually died by stumbling into the water or committed suicide out of despair, the message remains the same: a young, promising life has been ruined and sacrificed.

CHAPTER FOUR

Gaienhofen and Bern

Idylls and Realities

Nimikon had been the imaginary village where Peter Camenzind had grown up and to which, after years of testing the waters in the outside world, he had returned, convinced that the Rousseauean or Tolstoyan life was what humankind was intended to live. Hesse and his new bride wanted to pursue the same dream. After an unsuccessful search of the area around Basel, Mia (as Maria was called) had found their Nimikon, an even smaller village named Gaienhofen. It lay on the German shore of the Untersee, a smaller lake connected to the Bodensee, or Lake Constance, which forms a part of the border between Germany and Switzerland. They had rented one-half of a primitive, ancient farmhouse that was built on the side of a hill. The large living room and Hesse's study looked out onto the lake. There was no indoor plumbing, and water had to be carried from a well. Hesse had cached away 2,500 marks in royalties from *Peter Camenzind,* which, he calculated, would keep them for two years even without additional income. Thus, the newlyweds settled in. "The gypsy life is over," said Hesse (*GS I* 126). His suddenly acquired fame—in the form of letters, requests, and invitations—that had been plaguing him in Calw after the appearance of his novel had subsided somewhat, and his father-in-law's attitude seemed to be mellowing after the hurried, secret wedding while Herr Bernoulli was away. Maria, however, became ill less than a month after arriving in Gaienhofen and had to return to Basel for several weeks to recover, so the newlyweds suffered an almost immediate separation. Hesse got their estate in order and took up a task that would prove a mainstay of their financial support for years to come as well as a subject of continual complaint—reviewing books. In May 1906, he and fellow writers Albert Langen, Ludwig Thoma, and Kurt Kran began to publish a journal, initially entitled *Süddeutschland* (*South Germany*) but later renamed *März* (*March*). Hesse remained a co-editor until 1912, reviewing prose works of his own preference. He had his own criteria for selecting the books, and, though they were relatively broad, he was quite particular, accepting only those that he felt made a positive contribution. Such limitation is interesting, for it conforms to the criteria that his parents used for their church press and their moralizing, which so irritated Hesse.

Of his co-editors, Ludwig Thoma would live on in literary history because of his short stories of Bavarian country life—*Lausbuben Geschichten* (*Rascal Stories*)—colorful satires in which city ways and sophistication come out second best in contests with the homespun realities of peasant life. Thoma was also associated with the satirical journal *Simplicissimus* and once had to spend six weeks in jail for insulting the membership of "morality clubs." Hesse enjoyed making fun of his co-editor's arrest in a letter. After noting that he, himself, had spent three nights in Fasching celebration out of frustration over his writing, he adds, "and meanwhile you are atoning for your Godlessness in prison. If you were a saint, surely an angel of the Lord would come and free you. But you can't expect that. If only some prince, upon the occasion of a silver wedding and double marriage ceremony, would grant you a pardon, but then you aren't criminal enough to warrant that. . . . The Middle Ages had so many beautiful and positive aspects, it's a pity that only the churches and the prisons have survived" (*GB I* 135). The outwardly flippant tone of the letter shows that Hesse had a sense of humor, a characteristic for which critics do not give him sufficient credit. If he does not openly express sympathy for Thoma, neither does he look upon the incarceration as a disgrace. Both men knew what would happen when they chipped away at the righteous and the facades of false piety and morality. Hesse had learned as a child in school how closely and powerfully the teachers and authorities united to hold their establishment together, and we have seen how he vented his wrath on the subject in *Beneath the Wheel.*

For the time being, Hesse was coping well, and life was kind. His friendship with Ludwig Finckh—"Ugel" (one of the members of the *petit cénacle*)—had continued, and Hesse convinced him that he, too, should move to Gaienhofen. His old friend helped to keep Hesse's spirits up and brought him into more social contact than Hesse would have managed by himself. Another writer, Wilhelm Schäfer, also lived in the area and arranged gatherings of south-German intellectuals, which Hesse attended with Finckh's encouragement. A wedge would come into the friendship with Finckh when the latter joined forces with those who were ringing the bells of war in 1914, but for now, he and Finckh remained the closest of friends. And an intimate friend or two were what Hesse needed badly throughout his life—one reason why friendships, especially male friendships, play a major role in his novels.

But Hesse's basic nature remained that of the outsider. Finckh tells how, when a group of four ascetics[1] happened through Gaienhofen, Hesse was at once "fire and flame," dropping everything and disappearing with them for four weeks. When he returned, he had lost considerable weight, was deeply tanned, and wanted to eat only vegetables and fruit.

After three years in their farmhouse, the Hesses decided to build their own home with a sweeping view of the lake, just a few minutes' walk from the village. A reconciled father Bernoulli would loan them the bulk of the money without interest, and even before construction began, Hesse was looking at the investment as an early inheritance. Although they were now "settling for life" (*GS IV* 625), they would remain for scarcely five years. Such luxuries as a bathtub and running water seemed more like necessities now, since one son, Bruno, was already two years old. The large lot provided a sweeping panorama of the Untersee, the church tower in Constance, and a background of Alps. There was even a darkroom in the basement for Mia. The tile stove in Hesse's study proved not such a technological advancement as expected. When the *Föhn* (a warming wind) came, gas collected in the stove and it exploded, sending smoke and soot throughout the house and requiring a two-hour trip into the city to fetch the repairman. This happened three or four times, and it is a measure of Hesse's never-ending problem with nerves that he admitted to packing his bags immediately and departing for Munich, leaving the mess for the maid and his wife to contend with. It seems that he had chosen to forget the practical skills he had learned as an apprentice in the machine shop.

The desire for a garden and yard was also a motivating factor in leaving the old farmhouse. Gardening would always remain a leisure-time activity for Hesse, although he likened it to slave labor. His favorite picture of himself shows him sitting in his garden, an old straw hat on his head, burning branches, cuttings, and leaves. Besides vegetables, strawberries, and raspberries, Hesse planted hundreds of sunflowers on both sides of the garden pathway, with small, colorful flowers at their base. Thus were the physical surroundings of the growing Hesse family. A second son, Heiner, was born on the first of March, 1909, and a third, Martin, on July 26, 1911.

Hesse kept himself very busy, leaving most of the child care to his wife and their maid. In addition to the constant book reviews, he continued his own writing. *Diesseits* (*This Side*), a series of sketches, appeared in 1907 and was highly successful—not that the sketches were great literature, but he was now a known author. A short artist-novel entitled *Gertrud* appeared in 1910,[2] and already we see the germs of marital problems that the artist suffered, a theme that would take on a more personal nature in *Roßhalde*.

These first three Gaienhofen years, however, were relatively good ones, as should be expected of a new marriage and blossoming professional success. Mileck calls them "boisterously happy" (*Critics* 7), but this may be putting it a bit too strongly. Hesse's letters had indicated a fear of marriage before it took place, and there was a sense of separation almost from the beginning. Hugo

Ball quotes from a Hesse sketch of 1907 (the year they were building their new house): "'I still hear, as I did in the most pressing years of my youth, the voice of life calling and warning within me, and I don't intend to be unfaithful to it'" (95). It was also in 1907 that Hesse wrote his *Knulp,* the vagabond story that expressed his own wishful thinking to be so free. He was gone from home on trips for five full months in 1909, and he commented to his friend Hausmann that his personal life had little to do with his work—it was a shadow in his life, and shortly his relationship to family was limited to "earning enough money" (*GB I* 210). He would "give [his] left hand if [he] could again be a happy bachelor with an extra pair of boots, twenty books, and a box full of [his] secret poems" (*GB I* 194).

Just six weeks after their third son was born, he left on a real "journey to the East" with an artist friend, Hans Sturzenegger—to Singapore, Sumatra, Kuala Lumpur, Ceylon (Sri Lanka), and lower India. He delved into his English grammar books in preparation, and when Martin was born, he wrote to his father, "We have got a little boy the day before yesterday" (*GB I* 195).

The four-month trip was not so fulfilling as expected. Only the Chinese impressed him. The majority of the other peoples that he encountered—the Malays, Javanese, Tamils, Singhalese, and Japanese—he called "poor remnants of an old paradise-civilization" who were being corrupted and eaten up by the West. They were "dear, good-willed, clever and gifted natural creatures that our [Western] culture is destroying. If the whites could bear the climate better and raise their children here, there would be no more Indians" (*GB I* 202). He had gone "to see the primeval forests, stroke crocodiles, catch butterflies" but found something more beautiful—"the Chinese cities of lower India, the first real people of culture that he had come across" (*GB I* 204). By comparison he found his homeland coarse and grey but was happy to return.

Hesse's interest in India was obviously spiced by his parents' and grandfather's tales of their missionary experiences and by their many visitors from the East. He did not like most of what he had gone to see—the simple, close-to-nature life was too close. Like other Westerners, he suffered from constant stomach problems and the heat. Hugo Ball remarks that he did not seem to know why he went: "Maybe to see his mother's birthplace [which he did not], maybe to refute the Indian dreams of his family life. Maybe to free himself of the last torturous connection to his father and mother. . . . Maybe, too, the poet sees his Indian dream-suffering as a cause of the dissonance in his marriage" (106). If we can believe the fictionalized account (to be discussed in the chapter on *Roßhalde*), he wanted to get away to put his thoughts in order. He would tell his friend Ludwig Thoma when he returned that "things in my private life that

65

are not harmonious drove me away, and I can see in better perspective now" (*GB I* 204). What Hesse did learn, however, even if he made many of his observations from his first-class accommodations, was that "not only are the East and West, not only Europe and Asia one, but . . . there is a commonality and brotherhood above and beyond this,—mankind" (*GS III* 855). This is an insight that harks back to St. Francis, but it would be years before this observation, so significant to the theme of his mature writing, can be meaningfully internalized.

The first major change that his journey may have influenced was a move. Mia, too, was ready; the idyllic dream was over. They had both exhausted Gaienhofen and felt the need to be near more people, according to Hesse's final analysis (*GB I* 515). When the move would take place, and to where, was not certain for some time. Mia did not want to be in Germany, nor did Hesse want to return to the Stuttgart area to bring back memories of the problem years. Both were fond of Bern, but neither was ready to move into a city; this would be forsaking their ideals. But the question was soon answered for them. Hesse had had a good friend, the painter Albert Welti, who lived in an old country house with a large garden some distance from the city of Bern. Such a house was what they both wanted, and as fate would have it, both Welti and his wife died, one after the other, just as the Hesses had determined to move. At first they were reluctant to rent because of the circumstances, but nothing else appeared, and they made the move, even inheriting the Weltis' dog. The house had originally been built in the seventeenth century, with a number of additions and remodelings having taken place over the years. It was half-primitive, half-patrician, surrounded by ancient trees and an orchard, and shaded by a single giant elm. It was full of crevices and corners, in part cozy, in part spooky. There was also a small tenant farmhouse on the property, and here they could get "milk for the table" and "manure for the garden" (*GS IV* 628). Behind the house stood a stone fountain, and a vine-covered veranda on the south side overlooked forested hills and the mountains. Despite the picturesque setting, a shadow hung over the move from the beginning. Several years later Mia would tell Hesse that she had been afraid and depressed in the house, and he, too, began to feel the pressures that were to change and destroy life as he had felt about it until now. His novel *Roßhalde* would fictionalize the breakup of their marriage, which was slowly gaining momentum, presenting Hesse's own point of view and including a somewhat feeble attempt to see Mia's side of the troubled union.

CHAPTER FIVE

Roβhalde

An Idyll Ends

Between the publication of *Peter Camenzind* and *Roβhalde* lay ten years of marriage for the Hesses, what Stelzig calls a "decade of domestic—and domesticated—fiction" (107). The dream of a Tolstoyan life, of a return to the good earth in a Nimikon of their own making, was not to be. Hesse's letters, even in the beginning of the Gaienhofen years, say far less about Mia than one would expect in a new marriage, and it was inevitable that two such temperamental people would find the confines of wedlock cloying.

Roβhalde is Hesse's attempt to analyze his marriage problem or, as he somewhat equivocally rationalized in a letter to his father, "the problem of the artist and marriage in general":

> The novel has given me considerable difficulty, and is at least a provisional solution to the most troublesome problem that concerns me in a practical sense. For the unhappy marriage that the book deals with is not at all based on a wrong choice, but on something deeper, on the problem of the "artist-marriage" in general, on the question, whether an artist or thinker, a man who not only wants to view and portray life instinctively, but above all as objectively as possible—if such a person is capable of marriage at all. I don't have an answer, but my relationship to the problem has been presented as precisely as possible; a matter has been brought to a close in the book, which I hope will have a different ending in life. (*GB I* 242).[1]

We find nothing of Mia's reaction to the novel in correspondence but can readily infer that its theme would leave little doubt in her mind that the marriage was emotionally, if not legally, ended. Even if Hesse can say that he "hopes to end the matter differently from its ending in the novel," the thematic treatment of marriage had to have had a devastating impact on Mia. Her complete mental collapse less than two years later is ample testimony that there is considerable truth—as well as psychological fiction—behind this piece of early work.

Hesse was not hard put financially during the Gaienhofen and early Bern years (until the war began eroding his income), so it was not money worries that weighed on his mind. He admits as much by making the protagonist of the novel, Johann Veraguth, a famous painter living on a gracious estate called *Roßhalde,* although the artist himself lives simply enough and alone in his studio. His wife, Adele, occupies the villa with their younger son, Pierre, who enjoys the freedom to wander as he pleases from one parent's world to the other (a situation that will metaphorically expand in *Demian* into symbolic "mother-father worlds"). There is also an older son, Albert, who despises his father. Young Pierre is the result of a temporary period of renewed intimacy that the couple experienced when Albert became seriously ill for a short time. Hesse tries hard to focus on the nature of the artist per se in the novel, not just on his personal difficulties. He burdens his protagonist with an imperative: the calling of the artist demands that he commit himself fully to his work, and this commitment ordains the conquering of any obstacles that may be placed in his path. It is Pierre who symbolizes these external and emotional barriers, for Veraguth loves him more than anything else in the world. Pierre is lovingly drawn as a beautiful child with a St. Francis-like relationship to life around him. He speaks to nature and it to him; the gardens of *Roßhalde* with their birds and flowers are as much a part of his life as the relationship with his mother and father. Childhood in the novel is portrayed as the magic age of life— the time of innocence when we do not yet question the meaning and purpose of being; we simply feel ourselves to be a part of it. This point is stressed early in the novel, when we meet Veraguth the painter in his studio. He is completing a painting of a dying fish lying on the bottom of a fisherman's boat, and he asks his servant, Robert, to tell him if he has captured its mouth properly. Robert, he says, will know better than the artist himself because the servant had often fished as a child. Implicit in this scene is Veraguth's dream to recapture this magic kingdom of youth. If only he can again learn to see the world through the eyes of a child, he can become one of the "kings of nature" through his painting. The reader is to understand that complete surrender to his calling will give the artist access to this ethereal realm, where he can again feel himself a natural part of creation but at a higher level of understanding than in childhood. This enhanced sensitivity, in turn, will permit him to recreate his feelings and his visions in his art. The love that Veraguth feels for Pierre and his marital confinement, in general, prevent his complete submission to this imperative, and in a dream Pierre beckons to him, as if to symbolize the hold he has on his father or, perhaps, an invitation to return to that childlike state himself.

Veraguth cannot interpret the vision alone, it seems, but he will have help. An old school friend, Otto Burkhardt, now a rich and successful planter in India, returns for a visit and is able to give Johann Veraguth a tantalizing picture of the East (perhaps, too, an opportunity for "rebirth," should we choose to think that Hesse is purposely using the name of Burkhardt as an allusion to the Renaissance historian who had influenced him significantly): "Throw everything away, and you'll suddenly see the world waiting for you again with a hundred beautiful things. You . . . have lost the connection to life" (*GS II* 531). When Johannes asks him if he must give up Pierre, Burkhardt tells him that he must: "You have to . . . wash yourself clean of everything in your past, otherwise you'll never again be able to look freely and clearly at the world" (532). In order to make his point and tempt his friend into agreement, Burkhardt has brought dozens of pictures from his Indian world—a natural world when compared with Europe and, of course, an Eastern world. Veraguth is convinced. But the scene portrays not only artistic enticement; it breathes escapism as well. Hesse/Veraguth's desire to flee from the claims of family life is at least as strong as the call to surrender himself to his envisioned artistic mission: "It was not only the shimmer of tropical seas. . . . It was more the distance and quiet of a world in which suffering, worries, and battles . . . would become alien, far and pale" (504).

The augured separation from Pierre, as well as the isolation of Veraguth and Adele from each other, are symbolized in a painting that Veraguth completes after Burkhardt's departure. The features of Pierre are easily recognized in the likeness of a beautiful child at play, but the figures of a man and a woman in the background do not resemble either parent. While Pierre appears to be bathed in light, "death and the most bitter coolness" emanate from the same light as it engulfs the parents (549). Later, in both *Narcissus and Goldmund* and *Journey to the East,* Hesse will make the statement that the artist's creation is more important than the artist, that the child is more important than the mother. But Hesse's thinking has not yet progressed to this point. Pierre, the "creation," is the center of focus in the painting for another reason. He is beautiful and innocent in order to emphasize the love that Veraguth feels for him, even though the denouement of the novel will leave no doubt that Hesse's artistic calling—or "artistic ego"—is more important than any creation at this time.

Simply abandoning Pierre to his mother will not fulfill the demands being made on Veraguth. The older son, home for a visit, takes his brother for a carriage ride, and after their return Pierre becomes sick. His illness proves to be meningitis, and the parents are forced to watch helplessly as he dies a painful death. And after it occurs, Veraguth "drinks his cup of suffering to the dregs" by painting his son on his death bed. This, Hesse would tell us, is what it means for the artist to give his life to his art. Only if he can accept the worst anguish the world has to offer him can he truly be free to surrender himself to his creative nature. Only then can he open himself to the world as the childlike observer. This dream-to-reality sequence is portrayed with consummate subtlety in the novel. During Burkhardt's visit, Veraguth leads his friend to a corner of his estate to show him a scene he intends to paint. A tunnel-like, beech-lined path opens onto a moss-covered bench, beyond it an opening into a valley surrounded by hills. The scene is to "fade away into eternity," and Pierre is to be seated on the bench as the visual focal point, drawing the viewer's eye into the romantic landscape in the background— i.e., the child is a bridge into that infinite natural world that Veraguth so wants to be a part of. As the boy lies dying, however, Veraguth wanders to the scene and sits down on the very bench where he was to have painted his son[2]—an early example of symbolic transference of qualities from one character to another, barely touched upon in the Peter-Richard relationship in *Peter Camenzind,* though developed somewhat more fully by the Giebenrath-Heilner kiss that brought Hans into his friend's world in *Beneath the Wheel.* This stylistic technique, in variant forms, will become a trademark of Hesse's novels. Here, in *Roßhalde,* he implies that Pierre's relationship with nature and eternity can be returned to his father.

Veraguth apparently will meet the challenge. When the novel ends, he is shown walking alone through the park-like grounds of *Roßhalde,* and the narrator tells us:

> What remained to him was his art, of which he had never been so certain as now. He was left with the consolation of the outsider, to whom it is not given to delve into life and drink of it for himself; he was left with the strange, cool, but nonetheless intractable passion for seeing and observing, and with the secretly proud ability to take part in the process of creation. . . . Now he stood belatedly impoverished in the bright sunlight and was determined not to lose another precious moment of it. (633)

There is abundant psychological evidence that this conclusion is little more than bravado as it relates to Hesse, himself. Minutes earlier the sky had been "full of approaching rain clouds," and the phrases "imperturbable loneliness" and "cold desire to create" are also hardly faith-inspiring. In short, the *Roßhalde* story expresses a wish, but little more, on Hesse's part that he could devote his life so completely to becoming an artist-king.

It is obvious that Hesse wanted to feel himself at least partially removed from his subject matter and think of his novel as treating the problem of the artist and marriage, reaching beyond his own emotional bondage. It is possible that he actually intended the name Veraguth to convey a sense of irony to the reader—that he, Hesse himself, could be more aloof and objective than this self-centered, "very good" artist, that he could "solve the problem differently," as he had said to his father. But there is no feeling of a stylistic lightness, no sense of the author's conscious ironic distance in *Roβhalde*. The name Veraguth conveys a sense of hubris rather than irony when the story ends. Now he will become the great and dedicated artist that fate has intended him to be. He will become a "king of nature"; he has sacrificed everything. But his dedication is really no more than escape from the world of reality into the world of art for art's sake or, more precisely, art for the artist's sake. Veraguth shows no desire to move back and forth between the two realms, as will Hesse's later creation, Siddhartha, in his symbolic ferryman role. Nor has he yet clearly delineated the artistic-intellectual relationship that will drive Goldmund's creative genius.

If Hesse had wanted to paint an objective picture of the artist, his finished portrait is that of a particular artist who feels very sorry for himself,[3] for the Veraguth veneer easily peels away to reveal a rather pathetic Hermann Hesse underneath. The ending of the novel is really an omen of demise for Hesse's aesthete-god rather than an omen of its phoenix-like rebirth. The family problem is his own; the same feeling of separation and isolation that Veraguth suffers emanates from Hesse's letters of the time. It is not stated with clarity in either place. If Hesse was, in fact, trying to be objective in his description of the difficulties that exist between Veraguth and Adele, he failed. Veraguth can only condemn his wife for not responding to his needs and being his helpmeet, and in the defining passage of the marital difficulties, the reader finds little reason to be sympathetic toward the artist: "I always demanded of Adele that she give me what she didn't have to give. She had never had a lively nature; she was serious and melancholy, I should have known that from the beginning. She could never call a spade a spade and help herself through anything with humor and lightheartedness. . . . She had no way to respond to my claims and moods, my longings and my sudden disappointments, with anything other than silence and patience . . . if I tried to carry her along in a moment of a happy mood, it didn't work" (521). Veraguth gives no evidence in the book, save in the attempted light-hearted conversation with Burkhardt, that he himself could ever possess a sense of *Schwung und Humor.* Ball seems almost cruel to Mia or, ostensibly, to Veraguth's wife, Adele, in his analysis of the relationship in *Roβhalde,* saying, "The tension between wife and husband is an unbridgeable

gap between becoming, between rest and motion, between harmony and dissonance" (99). Put in its best light, Ball's comment means that Mia/Adele was not
the enabler that the artist Hesse/Veraguth needed.

There is a touch of irony in the novel's outcome which is more than likely
unintentional. Whereas Veraguth had surrendered everything to gain a new lease
on his artistic calling, he is remembered by posterity not for what he produced
after his departure from *Roßhalde* but primarily because of the painting of Pierre
and his estranged parents. It was in the critics' eyes "painfully filled with soul"
(549). In other words, Hesse carelessly tells us that Johann Veraguth, in fact,
did his best work at *Roßhalde,* at least in the eyes of the critics, while lamenting
his lack of freedom to commit himself solely to his art. The protagonist's longing for artistic greatness is, in fact, his only real objective; he has not given
meaningful thought to the purpose of his art. He will be no freer with these
egotistical restraints imposed upon him than he was with the restraints of family. Hesse will not acquire the ability to step back and see the frailty of his
Roßhalde mindset until he is deeply involved in the tragic and demoralizing
atmosphere of the war, which now looms on the horizon. We shall see a significant transformation expressed in the essays and the few creative works that he
was able to produce during the war period.

CHAPTER SIX

World War I

The Awakening

While the estrangement of husband and wife was gradually becoming reality in the Hesses' personal lives, the European world was moving toward war. Although living in Switzerland, Hesse was still a German citizen, and this situation, which opened the door for charges of cowardice and draft-dodging, made him defensive. To prove that he was not hiding and shirking his duty, Hesse attempted to report for active service several times but was turned down because of poor health and his age.

The first of his wartime essays,[1] "O Freunde, Nicht diese Töne" ("Oh Friends, Not these Tones") (*GS VII* 44–9), the title taken from Schiller's celebrated "Ode to Joy," given lasting life in the fourth movement of Beethoven's Ninth Symphony, is directed more against the artists and intellectuals who have abandoned their universal vision in favor of German nationalism than against the war per se. Nonetheless, he assures his readers, "I am a German, and my sympathies belong to Germany" (45) and "I am the last person who would deny his fatherland at this time"(47). He ends the essay with a plea to all who sit at their desks and write. They should preserve the peace, build bridges, not use their pens to destroy the foundations of a future Europe. Needless to say, the essay was not well received in a Germany where talk of war filled the air.

Hesse's activities during the conflict proved his German loyalties—as he understood them—and they took the form of sympathy for the common soldiers who may or may not have wanted to be on the battlefield. More importantly, however, they were universal, humanitarian efforts to remind those same German soldiers that there was a higher life and higher meaning beyond battlefield and fatherland. He spent long, arduous hours for nearly four years editing and publishing inexpensive editions of German classics of his own choosing for shipment to prisoners of war in France and England. He sent Christmas packages, as well, and his office in Bern, opened and operated in cooperation with the German embassy, also served as a liaison for prisoners and their families. Although he had a coworker, a Professor Richard Woltereck, Hesse appeared to do the yeoman's share of the labor for the entire period until all the German prisoners were returned home in 1919. By this time, he was mentally and emotionally exhausted, his financial resources depleted, and his family separated. Despite the chaos on every side, he would credit the long ordeal for his awakening. Mileck summarizes his experiences by saying that it took the war to "startle him from his retreat, to make him acutely conscious of the plight of our Western world and persuade him finally to examine the political field." Insightfully, Mileck adds, "His subsequent expostulations were not those of a zealous reformer of political and social institutions, but those of a contrite humanitarian" (*Critics* 44). We shall see Hesse's thoughts moving in this direction in the following selected writings.

One of his most interesting creative efforts is a fantasy, ostensibly a dream, that he had had eight weeks before the outbreak of hostilities. He entitled it "Dream of the Gods" (*GS III* 927–31), but he is supposedly writing it ten years after the war has ended. The narrator is walking alone, everything is growing dark, and he wonders why. Entering the single lighted building, he finds many people sitting in a huge hall. On the stage is a Priest of Knowledge. Around him are images of many gods, and the priest picks them up one at a time, beginning with the God of War, to explain their origins. They all began their existences at different times and under different circumstances because of the needs and desires of the people who did not yet understand the unity of the world. The priest explains each god, telling why each, in time, became dispensable. Even birth and death have been dispensed with, because humankind has recognized that there are no individual powers and properties, neither in the human soul nor within the earth—only the give and take of a single universal force, a unity that will later be portrayed in the river symbol in *Siddhartha,* alluded to by "the immortals" in *Steppenwolf,* and symbolically "traced to its sources" by Joseph Knecht in *The Glass Bead Game.* Determining the essence of this force is humankind's great assignment.

Suddenly, the hall begins to grow dark, a storm breaks out, and the walls begin to crumble. The narrator escapes the collapsing building and finds a childhood friend who had long ago committed suicide. The latter is laughing and dancing amid the destruction and points to a crumbling palace. He tells his old friend that it is all right, that new and better ones can be built. Out of the chaos, the God of War takes shape in a cloud-like configuration, hovering over a mountaintop, and all the other gods and goddesses come running to him. People gather and kneel before them.

The dream expresses a vision that humankind is capable of recognizing itself as inseparable from a single universal spirit. Moving ourselves in this direction is the task of the Priests of Knowledge—i.e., figures we will later encounter as the Cains, the Steppenwolves, the artists, and their immortal forebears—but, unfortunately, humankind chooses to succumb to the easier entice-ments of worshiping lesser gods. Now the God of War dominates, but a new world can be born out of war. Hesse's vision of the "give and take of a single force in the world" (929) is the essence of the dream and will become the broad frame of reference toward which his thematic continuum will build when he can again take up his pen. The dream story shows that, intellectually, Hesse had already developed his concept of universal oneness—art was no longer his god—and was ready to enter a much more mature stage of writing as early as 1914.

An extension of his concept of a single universal force is found in "A Bit of Diary" (*GS VII* 143–9), written in 1918. Here the narrator/Hesse is again dreaming, this time about the duality of life, of suffering and heal-ing. He hears two voices, the first a louder voice closer to his conscious-ness, the voice of the authorities. It is the compounded voices of Moses, of parents, of prophets, of school, of Kant and Fichte. Collectively, they be-come one and prompt him to react to the sufferings by resisting them, by taking measures to do away with them. The second voice is distant, com-ing out of the darkness, out of the unconscious, and it tells him to accept the suffering and to nurture strengths to overcome it. If we do not flee from suffering (as Siddhartha will also tell us), it is not suffering; death is not death. Then, slowly, the voices are heard in concert. The combined voices are, at the same time, both masculine and feminine—a metaphor to remember—and together they produce a harmonious polyphony as the whole world turns beautifully and passionately, even though its axles creak and smoke (a meta-phor to be repeated in *Siddhartha*). Everything he has loved has been taken away—his children, even his poems, his art. But the saint can close his eyes and smile; there is no resistance, only acceptance. What was lost is not lost but becomes a part of him, changed but not destroyed.

Hesse wrote this essay as the war was drawing to a close, and we see reflected in it his decision to leave his family, the loss of his aesthetic dream, and his willingness to suffer life's afflictions. By extending the metaphor of the dream, we can see that it will apply to the suffering caused by the war. If we accept the creaking and smoldering of the world turning, it does not destroy but simply belongs; life is still beautiful. This is one of Hesse's most significant images, and to understand it is to understand why Hesse's vision is hard to accept, for which of us can live in the shadows of suffering and death and find them beautiful shadows of life? This is the truth of *becoming* for Hesse, but he sees humankind as still too far removed to understand and accept it. And, unfortunately, the lesser gods with authoritative doctrines tempt us with lesser solutions.

Hesse admits to a flight from life in the essay "Zuflucht" ("Refuge") (*GS VII* 62–8), written in 1917. To live comfortably in a little house, high on the hill overlooking a southern sea, had been a test. But a Bible verse led him to understand that this was not meant to be his real home: "The Kingdom of God is within you" (67) suddenly made sense to him—that God speaks from within each and every human being. Home is the source of the voice. Just as Luther's revelation, that God's grace was greater than any sin he could commit or even imagine, permitted his rebirth, so did this revelation not only lead Hesse out of his aesthetic refuge but also free him from the authoritative God who spoke through his pietistic parents when he was a child. This inner voice takes on a new dimension and will overlap with his Jungian insights, all of which will shortly join forces and pour forth in *Demian.*

"Von der Seele" ("Concerning the Soul") (*GS VII* 68–78) is an essay written in 1917. We begin our lives, according to Hesse, with a primitive, childlike soul, and most remain at this level. But those who long to understand what life really means will reach a stage of "pure observation," which permits them to love the world and everyone in it, good as well as evil, God and the devil, heaven and hell, without desiring anything in it for reasons of greed. This would shortly become the message of the god Abraxas in *Demian.* It is interesting to note that Heinrich Böll, another Nobel Laureate, used virtually the same phraseology—love without desire—as the focal point of his novel *Der Zug war pünktlich* (*The Train was on Time*), which brought him to fame following World War II. He, like Hesse, was sometimes criticized as simplistically moralistic.

In a short satirical fantasy, "If the War Lasts Two More Years" (*GS VII* 83–91), written late in 1917, the narrator, a writer named Emil Sinclair, has taken a "temporary absence from life." When circumstances are too bad, he simply leaves the temporal sphere to wander through history or through the cosmos (as will those who journey to the East). When he returns this time, it is 1920, and the war is still going on—now all over the world. He is arrested for going on a walk without permission and puts authorities into a state of shock when they discover he has no identification, no card showing his permission to exist, without which, of course, he cannot get a license to die. A captain, who recognizes him as the writer Sinclair, explains that they owe their strong sense of order and discipline to the war. Everyone is a soldier or a civil servant, and this gives them all a sense of purpose and belonging. Sinclair repeats the magic charm that permits him to stop his heartbeat, exits his body, which he leaves behind a bush, and continues his otherworldly journey, not giving too much thought to returning.

This brief fantasy was written while Hesse was struggling with the novel *Demian,* which was to mark a new stage of his work. He had, accordingly, selected a pen name, Emil Sinclair, under which "If the War Lasts Two More Years" also appeared. The message should not be interpreted to mean that Hesse was encouraging others to drop out. On the contrary, it implies that those who are capable of vision must continue to promote humanity, regardless of the madness around them; the real meaning of life is not found in the viscissitudes of daily ups and downs but in the realm of the spirit—the Goethean sanctuary—even while the turning world creaks and groans. T. S. Eliot expressed the same message with his phrase "Teach us to care and not to care."

Another open letter is entitled "Christmas, 1917" (*GS VII* 91–4). In a sad, again ironic tone, Hesse notes how nice it is to celebrate Christmas, when, once a year, we express love and faith. The fact that we do not do it every day of the year is, of course, to be blamed on the political and economic involvements—the state is guilty; the military is guilty. But this is not the truth, he continues. We, ourselves, are to blame for the desolation of our lives, for hunger, for evil, and for sadness. It does not matter whether we take up the teachings of Jesus, Lao Tse, the Vedas, or Goethe—all of their teachings meet in the concept of eternal humanity. There are thousands of proclaimers, but only one religion. The voice of God did not come from Sinai, does not come from the Bible. The essence of love, of beauty, of sanctity is not in Christianity, not in antiquity, not in Goethe or Tolstoy, but in the individual human being. It is the teaching of the Kingdom of Heaven that we carry within ourselves. This theme will become vintage Hesse.

One of the better-known short stories to emerge from Hesse's pen during the war years is "The European" (*GS VII* 104–12), a futuristic vision written in 1918. Hesse portrays the end of civilization because of the war. But God, spectator to the folly, has decided to give his foolish creation another chance and has flooded the earth as in the Noah story. The last European is afloat on a raft nearing the end of his strength when he is rescued by Noah, himself, in a replay of the biblical epic. All species of animals and races are represented in pairs on the ark, save the lone European male, who now moves among these "lesser peoples" appearing aloof and superior. As life goes on aboard the vessel, Noah decides that the various pairs should show what each will contribute to the new beginning when the waters subside. The European scoffs openly at the simple talents and skills of the primitive couples and is finally the only one left who has not shown what he has to contribute. His gift is of a higher nature, he explains—the gift of intellect and reason. "What is this?" the others all want to know. It is not something that can be shown, the highly civilized man explains in quiet exasperation. "I store images of the external world in my head and form new images and new orders from them. I can create the whole world anew in my brain" (109).

Poor Noah, however, is confused. Why should the world that God has created be created anew? The others applaud Noah's question, and the European becomes increasingly agitated, saying his intellect is for the purpose of solving large problems upon which the happiness of humankind depends. The audience is quite pleased with this, for humankind should be happy, and they want him to demonstrate his prowess. But again he must disappoint them, for he must have something specific to work on. The others finally decide that he is being humorous; maybe he is meant to amuse. But they continue to brood over this puzzling, irritable man and ask Noah if he should really be involved in the founding of the new civilization. Noah does not understand him, either, but notes that he is the only one among them without a mate. God is perhaps giving him a warning. If he wants to continue at all, he must mix with the other races, share in their natural cultures. The following morning, in the east, the peak of a mountain is visible.

The simple tale is a strong criticism of the superior—and masculine—European whose Western culture has already destroyed the world. The story can easily be seen as a forecast of Castalia's failure in *The Glass Bead Game,* where there is also no feminine component to life in the province. The lone European is obviously being instructed to look back into history and rediscover where reason and intellect began to oppose and attempt to control nature rather than to enable humankind to live in harmony with it (a theme to be dealt with in "The Rainmaker" some fifteen years later). Postwar Europe is analogous to the mountaintop reappearing after the destruction. How will it rebuild itself? Will it continue along its masculine path, or will it incorporate the simpler, nurturing, feminine values that can still be learned from the "primitives?"

In "War and Peace" (*GS VII* 117–20), written in the summer of 1918, shortly before the November armistice, Hesse notes that, to many, war is a natural condition whereas peace is more difficult, something we can only seek. "Thou shalt not kill" expresses an old ideal, but if humankind is capable of obeying such a commandment, it is marked as something special in nature. Humans are a creation *im Werden* (in a state of becoming), a blueprint for the future, of nature's longing for new forms and possibilities. "Thou shalt not kill," Hesse continues, is not simply a commandment meaning that we should not harm or destroy others. They and I are one. My life *is* my relationship to the world and to others. Peace will come, killing will cease, only when we realize that all of life is within us. The secret magic, the secret holiness, that everyone carries with him is called *atman* by the East Indians, *Tao* by the Chinese, and *grace* by the Christians. Wherever this highest knowledge is found, a barrier is crossed, enemies become brothers, death becomes birth, scorn becomes honor. This short essay again shows how Hesse can perceive all of creation and being in a single image without the need to separate its offspring into nationalities, religious denominations, isms, or even individuals.

"Fantasies" (*GS VII* 150–6), another 1918 essay, records Hesse's thoughts as he weeds his garden: What is the difference between the normal person and the thinker? Normal people, he muses, are the conservatives; they like things to be healthy; they like to preserve and protect things the way they are. A normal lizard would never have the idea of flying; a normal monkey would never think of leaving the trees and walking upright on the ground. The first monkey to have this idea had to be a monkey with imagination, an outsider. The label *gifted* or *fantasist* implies toying, testing, experimenting with problems. Such people may go insane, but they might also invent wings. Thus the task of the thinker is to ensure that the idea of an ideal humankind be preserved and pursued. The ongoing life of humankind plays between the two poles. It is the writer's function to join them, to pursue ideas, to create ideals, and to dream.

At this point in his reverie, Hesse realizes that he is only trying to justify his own existence, for how seldom it is that he is able to realize any of his noble ideals. But he dreams on—what is the ideal person? It is, he concludes, a normal person who would voluntarily pursue the necessity to dream and create without feeling the curse of those who are born to it. When it became apparent that a new demand from the world of the ideal was needed, he would not fight it but would go along with it. He could change himself easily; he could even die easily—a point to recall when we encounter the unexpected death of Joseph Knecht at the conclusion of *The Glass Bead Game*. Hesse must admit, however, that he himself does not like to change, that he does not want to die, even though he knows very well that every death is also a birth. He is happy to interrupt his thoughts when the postman arrives.

Hesse's little fantasy shows that he sees himself as one of the cursed born to be a thinker. He finds it no easier to live his vision voluntarily than the normal person finds it easy to accept changes forced upon him. The only difference between them is that one is guided from without, the other from within. A visionary must follow the latter imperative, however uncomfortable. As we shall see, Hesse will create just such an ideal according to this formula in the person of his last protagonist, Joseph Knecht.

In an analytical essay entitled "*The Brothers Karamazov* or the Decline of Europe" (*GS VII* 161–78), written in 1919, Hesse compares the chaos of postwar Europe with the convulsive collapse of Dostoevsky's Karamazov family. He sees western Europe suffering a demise, struggling toward a new beginning, and he calls it "a going home to the mother, a return to Asia, to the sources" (162). Old Father Zosima, as a visionary, can see that there is both good and evil in the Karamazovs but can love and bless the degenerate old father just as easily as he can love and bless the saintly youngest son, Alyosha. But it is Dmitri who becomes, in Hesse's eyes, a new ideal, possessed of amoral thinking *and* sensitivity, God *and* the devil. Hesse says that all four of the Karamazovs make up the Russian man. But it is Dmitri who balances the combined qualities of all—what Hesse had just learned from his Jungian experience to call *individuation*—and acts according to the promptings of an inner voice. By analogy, Hesse is saying that Europe should now renew itself in the same way. By recalling this analysis of Dmitri, we shall see in the next chapter how Hesse has constructed his Demian, who, in turn, will provide a role model for Sinclair.

Another essay relates Hesse's "Thoughts on Dostoevsky's *Idiot*" (*GS VII* 178–88). He compares Prince Muishkin to Christ. When Hesse thinks of Christ, the first image that comes to mind is that of Christ in the Garden of Gethsemane, where he is struggling with the fear of pain and death on the one hand and anticipating his higher rebirth on the other. The conflict is a difficult one, and when he looks to his disciples for support, they are asleep; he is totally alone. This is the one feature that Hesse finds Dostoevsky's idiot to have in common with Christ: he, too, is alone. Renewal of the soul demands magic thinking—acceptance of the chaos and return to the unknown, to the animal, to all beginnings. It demands that we not become animals but that we reorient ourselves, seek the roots of being and of forgotten instincts, which we must constantly reappraise in order to move ourselves along the path of *becoming*.

Hesse's analogy is obviously intended to portray Christ's dual nature—his human fear of death and the concomitant divine longing to return to the Father—as a metaphor for the struggles of resurrection for all of humankind. The message of rebirth is a theme that Hesse will continually stress—that we experience chaos, tragedy, and depression whenever we are caught up in the crudeness of life but that we can be renewed by it and reborn at a higher level of understanding. At death, just as did Christ, we will enter into the ultimate rebirth—returning spiritually to the Father and fulfilling our earthly assignment of returning to the Mother, as Hesse will express it in *Narcissus and Goldmund*. Only at death can the father/mother polarities become one, become a union of apparent opposites. And every life/death, like Christ's, should serve humankind, however majestically or humbly, as will the death of Hesse's final hero, Joseph Knecht.

The short essay "Eigensinn" (*GS VII* 194–200) was written in 1919 and extols the virtues of the word itself, which has many nuances: stubbornness, willfulness, obstinacy, self-will. Within the context of the essay, the word translates best as self-will. Hesse praises it because it exemplifies his own spirit and driving force—as he interprets it.[2] Jesus, too, was self-willed, Hesse asserts. By way of explanation, he points out that every stone, flower, tree, and animal has its own self-will, meaning that all develop according to an inner law, with the result that the earth is rich, beautiful, and good. Only two cursed creatures, he continues, do not follow the eternal calling and thus do not grow, live, and die as the deep, inborn self-will commands. They are humans and their domestic animals. Those who do follow their inner commands are usually outcasts; sometimes they are stoned to death, but later they may be recognized as heroes and emancipators. The antithesis of self-will, *Herdensinn* (the will of the herd), on the other hand, demands subordination and adjustment. If the majority of the people were self-willed, Hesse asserts, the world would be different, but they are few, and it is for these few that he writes, placing on them the responsibility for moving humankind into its fated future.

"Zarathustra's Return: A Word to the German Youth" (*GS VII* 200–31) is the longest of the essays written during World War I. Rumor has it that Zarathustra (or Zoroaster, the Persian prophet who taught that life was a continual struggle between the good spirit and evil spirit) has returned. His former students, home now from the war, find him in a crowd, smiling as he listens to a speaker trying to move the masses to follow him. The students approach their former master and ask him to give them direction. He makes light of the lost war, the want, the groping for direction, calling it all "theater." They are upset and angry with him,[3] but he reminds them that he is not a teacher; he is a human being, he is "you and I." He has only learned to be Zarathustra, and they should learn to be themselves. Humanity has been given one gift—to recognize its fate. Just as the body of a child grows in its mother, fate is intended to grow in every human being. He who looks to external forces for his fate is lost. The Germans are attempting to blame the enemy for their pains and problems. Should they not consider that the pain is in themselves, not out there? They ask what they should do. Zarathustra distinguishes between *Tun* (doing) and *Tat* (deed). Doing is what they carry on with—business, politics, meetings—to keep busy, to avoid their fate. Deeds will never be done by anyone who has to ask "What should I do?" The deed is done because the inner voice demands that it be done. It is painful to be alone, so we seek company; it is painful to hear the demands of our inner voice, so we make noises with machines and hammers. When this is not sufficient, we create enemies—all this because we are fleeing from ourselves. If we listen to the inner voice, we will suffer, and only in this suffering will we learn our fate. The school for suffering is loneliness—the path that humankind fears more than any other. The path to the self is never completed unless it be in death, when one "dies his own death."[4]

Most people do not want to taste loneliness, Zarathustra continues, but prefer to stay with the herd. Loneliness comes only to those who have the "magic stone" in them that attracts fate (what we shall shortly discover as the "mark of Cain" in *Demian*). They must recognize that they can belong to an empire without borders, to the Kingdom of God, as their fathers call it. World improvement is a concept that angers the prophet. The world is not here to be improved. Nor are we here to improve ourselves. We are here to be ourselves. Only if we are will the world become a better place; it will be rich and beautiful. If the world has ever been improved by humankind, it has been so because of those who were themselves. In farewell, Zarathustra tells his listeners that there is a hidden being in each of them, still sleeping the sleep of a child. In each of them is a call and a cast of nature. There is a bird in every breast. If it is silent, then there is something wrong. But when it speaks and sings, humans should follow its voice—a metaphor that will reappear in *Siddhartha*.

Zarathustra is significant in thematic terms because in it Hesse delineates the preprogrammed inner voice, the voice of God which will lead people to their particular fates if they choose to listen for it and follow it. Those who do will be lonely; their lives will be difficult. Most will follow the herd; only the few will be faithful and saved, a Hesse concept no different from Goethe's God-given formula in *Faust:* "Wer immer strebend sich bemüht, den können wir erlösen" ("He who continually strives can be saved").

Last but not least of the wartime writings is "Thou Shalt Not Kill" (*GS VII* 235–9), written in 1919. Here Hesse reminds his readers that the evolution from apes to cultured beings is a long, slow process; we must admit that we stand much closer to apes than to real human beings. Every follower of Lao Tse, every disciple of Jesus, every follower of St. Francis of Assisi was much further along hundreds of years ago. In order to improve, we must live in faith. The future, faith, and thought are always right. These are the motors that fuel the world.

Hesse tells of a missionary who tried to convince African tribesmen that they should plant coconut palms. The tribesmen refused, laughing, even though they knew that the trees would ultimately bear fruit. That a person should do something now and be rewarded only years later they found ridiculous. Hesse goes on to say that the poets, the prophets, the fools, and the dreamers of the future are the ones who plant trees for later: "Our task as human beings is this:

within our own unique, personal lives to move one step further along the path from animal to human being" (239).

The collective content of the wartime writings provides at least a three-fold forecast of themes to come. First, Hesse has been able to decide that life, itself, is positive and worth living despite the outer chaos of war and personal crises. He has seen the world unrelentingly worshiping its false gods and yet has been able to work among them and retain his own faith. Second, he has come to recognize that Hermann Hesse the poet cannot change the world or even institutions but that he can change himself and that he can, perhaps, serve like-minded individuals through his writing just as he has served individuals with his actions during the war. What he writes from now on will be directed at the individual.[5] He will not preach (at least he will not consider it preaching)—a lesson learned from his family—but will reach out to a select spiritual brotherhood whose members can distinguish God from lesser gods. Finally, Hesse has broken through to his longed-for Olympic vision of an eternal humanity—a single, spiritual force behind the dualities of earthly life—and he stresses the dedication that it will entail to understand and unite them. He will spell out this vision—in stages—in terms of Christianity and war in *Demian,* in a Buddhistic-Hinduistic setting in *Siddhartha,* in terms of the world of the senses and the world of the mind in both *Der Steppenwolf* and *Narcissus and Goldmund,* in the gentle irony of a prodigal son story in *Journey to the East,* and in full, conscious application of his ideal man concept in *The Glass Bead Game.*

CHAPTER SEVEN

Demian

Rebirth

Demian is the work that promoted Hesse to world literature status and introduced his inner voice as a stylistic device. By mid–World War I, he was no longer simply seeking to pour himself into art, as had Veraguth, but had attained an Olympian view of what the role of art and that of the artist should be. He called the artists the "feelers and advance guards of humanity who sense the new becoming" (das neue Werdende) (*GB I* 343). He knew this, he thought, because he "ha[d] been living in business, politics, activity and organization for fourteen months" (*GB I* 341)—what most are wont to call the real world. But Hesse takes issue: those who live for their spiritual vision live in the real world. To Carl Selig he would write several years later that "our [the poets'] reality is likely more genuine, in any case I prefer it immeasurably, to that of the people who belong to 'the world.' Without contact with the beyond of 'the world,' this world would be useless" (*GB II* 61).

If a few short years earlier Hesse had thought that solving his marriage crisis would grant him freedom, he learned during the war that life's hurdles were far more numerous and complex. The death of his father in March of 1916 brought his distress to a breaking point, and in April he entered a private clinic, Sonnematt, near Lucerne. As has often been noted, his treatment by Dr. Joseph Lang and, through him, the acquaintance with Jungian psychology were the keys that enabled him to put his life—and life itself—into new perspective. We shall see in *Demian* that, by novel's end, Hesse has created his own mythology, in which Stelzig sees little clarity, calling it "so syncretic—a quilt patched together from several of the leading world's faiths—as to preclude any systematic formulation or even dogma other than that of *Eigensinn* [self-will] itself" (71). In regard to this time in Hesse's life, Stelzig appears to be right, but a later Hesse statement, "I myself believe that the decisive characteristic of my life and my work is the religious impulse" (*VII* 497), means, it would seem, that we should expect to find clarity in his religious message. His writing will, indeed, gradually unveil a "systematic formulation" of belief.

A strong religious impulse, primarily Christian, displays itself immediately in the introduction to *Demian,* where biblical diction abounds: God, divine, spirit, savior, crucified. And there are other allusions with religious connotations as well: the word *eggshells* foreshadows the bird-egg imagery that is to become a central symbol of rebirth and regeneration. A Faustian essence is apparent in the sentence, "Every human being, as long as he lives and fulfills the will of nature, [is] worthy of every attention." The Jungian medium (which Stelzig rightly calls the "dominant note . . . in the composition of *Demian*" [141]) is indicated in the sentence, "The life of every person is a path to himself." The mythical, gnostic, and biblical Eve/mother symbol is alluded to: ". . . all have the same origins, their mothers." The Nietzschean concept of man as a bridge to the future is apparent in the statement that "everyone is an attempt on the part of nature to create humankind." And the image "in everyone a savior is crucified" points directly, via the most dominant Christian symbol, to Hesse/Sinclair's "mythological Christianity" (*GS III* 101–2). Ten years after writing *Demian,* Hesse stated: "At the base of my soul I am a Christian . . . as concerns the spiritual and moralistic attitude, to be sure, not, however, according to the content of my creed" (*GB II* 225).

The religious tone is set early in the narrative, when the young Sinclair's growing awareness of two worlds is introduced—worlds which Ziolkowski says "can be reduced roughly to something approximating the traditional Christian dichotomy of good and evil" (*Novels* 96). Freedman says, "The first world came to be that of the spirit; the second world remained that of the senses" (27). Freedman's view illustrates why so much difficulty has been encountered in Hesse's "two worlds" metaphor. As will be brought out in detail in the discussion of *The Glass Bead Game,* Hesse intends us to understand that the world of the spirit lies beyond the sense/mind duality. Sinclair, himself, describes one world as *das Vaterhaus,* a world of "duty and guilt, bad conscience and confession, forgiveness and good intentions, love and honor, the word of the Bible and wisdom" (l03). The parallels within the sentence indicate a simplistic, dual-level perception of life, with established borders that Sinclair does not have to cross, for, at this point in his young life, the "father world" houses both mother and father (l03). Sinclair can have security and fulfillment in his father's house, but this is a child's understanding. It incorporates only the nurturing aspect of the mother, and it does not doubt the authoritative role of the father. The boy does not yet relate the concept of mother to other feminine attributes, those of the dark world, which is still vague and frightening to the ten-year-old—a world of servant girls and working boys, ghost stories, scandals—"a colorful flood of monstrous, alluring, terrible, puzzling things" (104). But as the narrative progresses, we shall find this simple duality gradually becoming a broad and complex masculine/feminine, father/mother metaphor.

To begin the transition, we see Sinclair's fall from grace, humorously precipitated by extending the metaphor from Genesis—he does not eat of the forbidden fruit but steals entire baskets of imaginary apples,[1] an act that propels the ten-year-old Eden-dweller out of paradise. Although Eve's absence is conspicuous, the reader will, in retrospect, recognize the daring theft as a response to feminine temptation. At this stage of the narrative, we are aware only that Sinclair's ego tempts him to invent the tale that places him in the power of evil: "My sin was that I had given the devil my hand"(114). The Satan reference is to Franz Kromer, the older boy to whom Sinclair has told the stolen-apple story to impress his friends. In fact, Kromer repeatedly presents a reptilian image as he slips into the doorway behind Sinclair, hisses at him, spits through his teeth, and ultimately slithers away. The name Kromer is one of the few among significant Hesse characters whose origins are obscure. Mileck comments, "Without assistance from Hesse himself, it is far too brash to attempt to account for the name Franz Kromer" ("Names" 172). He is probably right, but one speculation is worthy of consideration. There was an actual Franz Krommer, a Czech violinist (1759–1831), director of the ballet orchestra at the Hoftheater in Vienna and later director of chamber music and court composer to the Habsburgs. For present purposes, it is of note that his compositions for violins were still commonly used for violin lessons at the end of the nineteenth century. The young Hermann Hesse had serious and unexplained difficulties with his violin teacher, as mentioned in the Maulbronn chapter, and he might have chosen the name Franz Kromer in remembrance of the torment he had undergone, whatever its nature.

In any case, in order to make his blackmail demands, Kromer leads his victim to a construction site, which symbolizes the beginning of a new stage in Sinclair's life. He is being led into the other world, where his existence suddenly seems as totally insecure as it had seemed protected at home, in the *Vaterhaus*. Kromer torments him for several weeks, in dreams as well as in reality. One dream, especially, is a revelation of Sinclair's slowly surfacing demonic nature, which Hesse represents in Jungian terms: "What was once Franz Kromer was now a part of myself" (144). In the dream, in a reversal of the Abraham story, Kromer tries to force Sinclair to kill his father, thus providing a narrative transition for the appearance of Sinclair's new friend and savior, Demian. He is an older boy who wears a sign of mourning on his sleeve, obviously for his father, an image which will shortly take on the biblical proportions of the Old Testament authority figure from whom, by implication, Demian has freed himself and from whom Sinclair is just beginning to struggle (unconsciously at this point) to liberate himself.

Critics have written much about the figure of Demian in Hesse literature,[2] and his most obvious role is apparent in the name itself—the mythological *daemon* or *daimon,* meaning spirit or divinity, and sometimes cast as the inner-self, sometimes as a superhuman being who helps or harms humans, hence the ever-present connotation of temptation, danger, or evil. The concept is also found in gnosticism, where such a figure is a *Soter,* or savior—primal man who sets himself and his initiates free.[3] Hesse, however, was deeply involved with Jungian studies at this time, and his primary model is undoubtedly the Jungian archetypal self—the end product of the individuation process, which term we must understand if *Demian* (and later *Steppenwolf*) is to make sense. Carl Gustav Jung dissected the human psyche into component parts. The outer layer, the face that we expose to the world, is the "conscious ego." Behind this mask is our "personal unconscious," a reservoir of our own "feeling-toned complexes,"[4] which influence our behavior and actions. At a much lower level is the "collective unconscious," a reservoir of "superpersonal" experiences that form our "psychic foundation" (Jung 53) as a species. Both levels direct our lives and actions as we unconsciously react to instincts, emotions, and past experiences that a given life situation may evoke. We must seek out and understand these forces if we are to be in control of our lives. Jung calls the discovery and balancing process "individuation" (Jung 3).

But how do we reach into our unconscious? Dreams, visions, and flashes of insight open some of the doors for us, but Jung perceives additional bridges called the *anima* and the *animus*—the former meaning the "woman in a man" and the latter the "man in a woman" (Jung 19). If we do not recognize our duality, we cannot lead balanced lives. The *anima* and *animus* are frequently projected as real people, whose insights—really our own—enable Jungian "archetypes"—"patterns common to the whole of humanity" (Jung 80)—to step forth. These, too, may be projected as real people. Jung calls the *anima,* itself, an archetype—a "life behind consciousness" (Jung 76). Another archetype is the "wise old man"; another a "shadow"—our "negated ego-personality" (Jung 173), which may force our negative impulses into action because we are frightened, angry, covetous, etc. When we meet with our shadow and reach the depths of despair, we must make choices: either learn from the experience and rise above it or succumb and lead our lives at unfulfilling and less meaningful levels, which is detrimental to ourselves, to society, and to the development of a higher humanity. Thus, within the individuation process that is about to take place, we can see Demian as Sinclair's "archetypal self," the mirror reflection of the Sinclair he wants to become, is supposed to become.

The names Demian and Sinclair, in addition to their Jungian implications, incorporate yet another meaning, one which links them to Christianity and which, thus far, appears to have been overlooked in Hesse criticism. As is well known, Hesse had long admired St. Francis of Assisi and had even published a short biography of him in 1904. Francis began his mission after hearing a voice from the cross in the Church of St. Damiano calling to him: "Seest not that my house is in ruins? Go and restore it for me."[5] In commenting on St. Francis's thoughts toward his new church in the Assisi biography, Hesse wrote: "He saw a community growing around him just as if he had torn it away from the church, which he nonetheless honored as a *mother* [emphasis provided]" (48). Hesse honors this feminine spirit, which he finds the Christian Church to have ignored, in the choice of the name Sinclair, clearly reminiscent of the founder of the Order of St. Clare, who was inspired by Francis. She and her sisters became an integral part of the Franciscan order. Regardless of the eclectic connotations, this mysterious Demian will express himself to Sinclair as an inner voice.

The final situation involving Kromer, Sinclair, and Demian is an excellent example of what Jung provided for Hesse's narrative technique: the tormentor—whom we now recognize as Sinclair's "negative ego-personality"— has ordered his victim to "bring his sister next time," and Sinclair, only vaguely aware of the secret, forbidden things that older boys and girls do, can think of no greater sin. In Jungian terms, he finds himself at the depths of despair, which Jung calls the meeting with one's own shadow (Jung 74). There are two choices now, and Sinclair's love and respect for his sister outweigh his fear of Kromer: "My decision never to do that immediately stood firm" (133). It is at this juncture that Demian arrives and "guesses" the whole story, and Kromer is mysteriously dispatched—the first time that Hesse makes significant use of the mysterious event in his major prose works. By not explaining in precise, objective terms how the tables were turned, Hesse is attempting to direct the reader to the metaphorical meaning of the episode; we do not need a logical explanation. It simply means that Sinclair has placed the entire Kromer situation in proper perspective in his own mind for the first time—can make only one decision—and his tormentor backs down. Just as Harry Haller will "kill" Hermine, in the later novel *Der Steppenwolf,* when he no longer needs her, so too does Sinclair rid himself of Kromer when he can no longer tolerate his demands. (Note that a variation of this stylistic technique, without the element of mystery, was used to separate Pierre from Veraguth in *Roßhalde.*)

It is helpful to point out that this act occurs after Demian has interpreted the Cain story for Sinclair—a stronger man had slain a weaker man, and people feared him because of it, but, unwilling to admit their fears or kill him for his crime, they said, "God has marked him" (126). Hesse thus implies that a seed was planted by the story, which then nourishes Sinclair's newly discovered resolve and inner strength. His sign—even if borne by his externalized *daimon* at this point—causes Kromer to flee.

The Kromer episode has dramatized Sinclair's first step into the dark world, but as might be expected, the adventure has been too much, and Sinclair retreats to his father's house, confessing all to his parents. When he later asks his father about the Cain and Abel interpretation, the father replies that "[this] stupid story is nothing more than the devil's attempt to destroy our faith. For if one believes that Cain was just and Abel unjust, then it follows that God has erred, that the God of the Bible is not the right and only God, but a false one" (142). The father is playing the role of spokesman for conservative church doctrine and establishing borderlines that Sinclair must eventually cross.

The next episode in Sinclair's life is covered in the chapter entitled "Der Schächer" ("The Thief") and is a reference to one of the thieves who died on a cross next to Jesus. Demian respects this thief, who did not repent at the last moment but had the courage to die as he had chosen to live. As in the Cain story, determining one's own path in life and accepting responsibility for the consequences are the issues.

The years Sinclair spends in confirmation classes coincide with his years of puberty. The *Urtrieb* (primal drive) of awakening sexuality is, thus, stressed as a parallel to the awakening of reason—an excellent example of Hesse's division of life, itself, into the senses (the feminine realm) and the mind (the masculine realm). The parents try to ignore the former: "They helped only, with inexhaustible effort, in my hopeless attempts to deny reality and to go on living in a child's world that was becoming more and more unreal and false" (*GS III* 144). The church does the same for his awakening reason. Sinclair finds himself unable to accept many confirmation teachings as an act of faith; he must think critically about them and is urged on by Demian, who is in the same class. He reenters Sinclair's life as the dark world is again making its presence felt, this time as it relates to the inherent dangers of challenging traditional pietist/ religious teachings.

Before the relationship of the two youths becomes close once more, Sinclair notices Demian standing in front of the former's house, sketching the coat of arms with the bird over the doorway (145–6), thus reintroducing the motif that had been briefly mentioned in the introduction. The reader should recall that the house had once been part of a cloister, and the escaping bird hints that freedom from the confines of narrow Christianity is possible.

During the confirmation classes, notes Sinclair, concepts that the Pastor discusses "lay far away from me in a silent holy unreality" (148). Simultaneously, a feeling of closeness to Demian awakens, and when the pastor discusses the Cain and Abel story, Demian turns to look at Sinclair, who now becomes alert, recalling what Demian had told him earlier—that "it wasn't true the way he was teaching it, that it was possible to criticize it" (148). Sinclair draws closer to his inner self as he has the thought: "At that moment there was again a connection between myself and Demian" (148). The association becomes ever stronger as Demian moves from seat to seat in the classroom until he is sitting next to Sinclair. Johanna Neuer rightfully describes the ever-closer relationship as "the growth of Demian with himself [Sinclair]."[6] The amusing incidents of Max Demian causing other students to look around, to scratch their heads, etc., are simply meant to show that the inner self causes most everyone to twitch occasionally when challenged to think for himself, but how many are "Cain enough" to take serious notice?

A second significant conversation in the chapter concerns the story of a moth which Demian tells. A certain species produces only one female for every five hundred males, but the males can locate the female up to two hours away. Demian explains by saying that "if an animal or person turns his entire attention and his entire will to a specific task, he will achieve it." He digresses, however, to explain that the moth could not, for instance, fly to a star because it seeks only that which has "purpose and value" (152). The metaphor illustrates, in terms of Sinclair's desire to follow the urgings of his inner nature, that primitive instincts are always with us, but they should be obeyed only if they have purpose and value. It is the task of the masculine, or mind-side, of life to make this judgment.

Hesse makes a point of stressing that Sinclair does not laugh at the concept of the trinity and the virgin birth as do some of the other boys, even though they accept it. He still has, as before his confirmation, the deepest reverence for religion, itself, but must interpret doctrine for himself. This confession indicates that the now-mature Hesse need not hate Christianity any longer, as he had once expressed to his mother that "your God . . . may well exist . . . but he doesn't interest me" (*KuJ I* 323). His professed respect for religious belief per se in *Demian* is evidence that he is not condemning what he finds to be the real core of Christianity—its spirituality and ethic—but rather is challenging theologians to listen for God's voice, not to each other, and to recognize the metaphorical message as the essence of mysterious events.

Demian describes the biblical God to Sinclair as "the good, the noble, the fatherly, the beautiful, and even the pinnacle, the sentimental," but, he adds, "the world consists of other things too. And this is all simply attributed to the devil." We must, he goes on, "honor and consider everything sacred, the entire world" (156). Sinclair, in Jungian reflection, notes: "What Demian said about God and the devil, about the official divine world and the deadly silent devilish world, were precisely my thoughts, my own myth" (157).

When the final communion for the group is held, Sinclair states: "I was not ready now to be accepted into the church, but into something quite different, into an order of thought and personality that had to exist somewhere on earth, and I considered my friend to be its representative or messenger" (159–60). We now see clearly that Demian is his archetypal model, or, as Ziolkowski labels him in his book *Transfigurations of Jesus,* a Christ figure, and Sokel has para-doxically called him the "anti-Christian Christ figure,"[7] to which Hesse would readily agree. As he will tell us in *Siddhartha,* "for every truth, the opposite is just as true" (*GS III* 725).

However, if Sinclair has found a spiritual guide, his God is still in hiding, and he must continue his pilgrimage. The next episode finds Sinclair at board-ing school, and to indicate that the search does not end with a single episode of insight, Hesse permits his protagonist to give in to his lesser self once again, to fall into a life of dissipation, another "meeting with his shadow" and what Demian later describes in Nietzschean terms as a "last attempt to join the herd." In order to redirect Sinclair onto a positive path, a Jungian anima figure—a bridge to the unconscious—enters the scene. When, in the depths of despair, Sinclair sees a girl walking in a park, he is entranced and calls her "Beatrice" and is moved by her beauty and innocence to reform himself. The girl is an obvious allusion to Dante's Beatrice, and we see, as Sinclair prepares to move on to a higher stage of life, that the feminine realm has implications of beauty, inspiration, and pu-rity; it is not only dark, seductive, and dangerous. He is slowly beginning to realize that both feminine allure and feminine purity are part of the mother world.

When Sinclair attempts to paint the girl's face (Hesse himself had just be-gun painting as a form of relaxation), it becomes a mixture of feminine and masculine features: it is Demian; it is his own face, his *Inneres,* his fate; it looks at him like a mother. "It was the one who knew all" (181). The entire spectrum of the Jungian individuation process and the collective unconscious is visible here, including the archetypal mother image. Sinclair's own features represent the ego, or persona, and all elements are struggling to merge into a meaningful whole.

At this juncture it is clear that Sinclair's secret voice has gained domi-nance; he will not again flee to his father's house, but he still does not know how to balance the two worlds. The Jungian integration of personality is not complete, and he longs for guidance, for Demian. The path to be taken is indicated when he dreams of Demian and the bird and coat of arms above the door-way to his family home. In the dream, Demian forces him to swallow the im-age—to interpret or internalize its meaning for himself—and Sinclair feels the bird coming to life within him. He awakens to paint this image but cannot re-member it exactly. He knows only that the bird is sitting on something—a flower or basket or nest—but when the painting is finished, he has shown the bird breaking out of a globe as if out of a giant egg (183). Thus the egg and globe are one, and, as we shall soon see, Hesse is not only implying that Sinclair must be reborn by breaking free of his confining childhood world but is also expanding the image into global terms. It will shortly relate to societal rebirth, specifically Germany's, after the war.

Sinclair sends his painting to Demian's former address, and somewhat later a note inexplicably appears in his notebook (another mysterious event): "The bird is fighting its way out of the egg. The egg is the world. Whoever would be born must destroy a world. The bird flies to God. The god's name is Abraxas" (185). Thus the image takes on religious significance in the form of the gnostic god.[8] But how did the note find its way into Sinclair's notebook? Ziolkowski tries to provide a realistic explanation for its appearance: "Although Hesse, typically, leaves this point quite vague, it is implied that the note was put there by the practice teacher . . . who has just come from the university and probably knew Demian there" (*Novels* 92). As noted, we misunderstand Hesse's intent if we feel it necessary to provide a realistic explanation, which he obviously avoids. Again, as previously occurred in Kromer's mysterious flight, he is drawing our attention to the importance of the symbolic content. In effect, Hesse is stylisti-cally illustrating a message of his novel: Mystery is best explained by meta-phor.

In any event, seconds after Sinclair has discovered and read the note, his instructor coincidentally explains the god Abraxas—"a godhead who had the symbolic assignment of uniting the divine and the satanic" (186). Sinclair has found his God! And significantly enough, he (via his *daemon*) has been able to interpret the vision himself; the instructor's explanation is but a narrative-level reification of a Jungian "flash of insight," stimulated by the bird dream.

Even after this moment of enlightenment, Sinclair's lack of direction re-mains a problem: "There was only one thing I couldn't do: tear out the deeply hidden goal and paint my future as others did, who knew precisely that they wanted to become a professor or judge, doctor or artist" (189). (This statement can justifiably be considered Hesse's recognition of his false dream in *Roßhalde*— that devoting himself to art had to be his goal.) Thus, Sinclair must continue his journey but soon has the help of yet another figure who assumes a temporary guiding role. He is an organist friend, Pistorius, whom Sinclair discovers playing Bach in a small church. Later, after listening to him a number of times, Sinclair describes his music as "not pious like the parishioners and pastors, but pious with careful devotion to a world of feeling that stood above all denominations" (192). The implication raises traditional church music above its ritual function within a Christian setting to give it universality; the symbolic role of music will continue to grow in importance in Hesse's thematic continuum.

Sinclair's new friend soon elaborates on just such religious universality with the statement: "Every religion is beautiful. Religion is soul, it makes no difference whether one takes Christian communion or makes a pilgrimage to Mecca. . . . Christ is for me not a person, but a Heros, a mythos" (204). This sentence, once more, emphasizes Hesse's already deeply rooted vision that all religions have developed out of myth—metaphors to explain the mystery of man's place in the universe. Reducing the mystery to a particular myth, isolating it from others, he thus implies, will give it limitations and foster prejudice and self-righteousness.

Before Pistorius departs, he will have played a threefold role in Sinclair's life. First, he has stressed the universality of all religious faiths; then, as an Abraxas disciple, he has helped Sinclair to understand good and evil in a single world; and finally—and most importantly—he has served as a warning, this last function resulting from an incident that occurs when he and Sinclair are talking quietly one evening as they lie before the fire. Sinclair suddenly sees an image of a sparrow hawk—the bird he had painted breaking out of the egg— shoot upward in the flames. At the same moment, he remarks almost casually to Pistorius, "What you are saying is so, so damned antiquarian" (217). Pistorius admits to being a "backwards seeker, a romantic." He knows intellectually what life should be, but he has not had the courage to follow the path he has discovered. As Sinclair did after his venture with Kromer, Pistorius has returned to live in his father's house. He represents a lesser Demian—only the masculine aspect of the archetypal self—and reflects Hesse's personal recognition that he cannot live in an ivory tower as had always been his temptation. Sinclair has now filled in the masculine side of the equation, but the bird image in the fire symbolizes the need for the daring feminine counterpart.

Somewhat earlier Sinclair had had another dream in which he embraced his mother, but she was, at the same time, someone else: "The embrace was divine worship and wrongdoing" (188). The mother image takes on new proportions here; she is spiritual and holy, but the embrace also encompasses the sensual, erotic, even oedipal.[9] In other words, we inherit all of these qualities because we are born both of the earth and of the spirit; they all belong to life. Sinclair later recaptures the vision of the embrace and tries to paint it. As he stands before the image, the words spoken by Jacob to the angel occur to him: "I will not leave you until you bless me" (211). In other words, the Sinclair-mother embrace is analogous to the Jacob-angel struggle. Just as Jacob saw God's face, so has Sinclair now seen the face of his God. The image becomes "woman . . . man . . . girl . . . animal"—that is, God himself is telling Sinclair that he is more than God the Father; he does encompass the Abraxas qualities. When Sinclair awakens in the night, the painting has literally vanished. He has only the vaguest idea that he may have burned it (212). Thus, once more, we are directed to look to the symbolic meaning: Sinclair's understanding is complete; he has internalized the image "as if it had become nothing but [him]self" (212).

To illustrate his new Demian-like status, Sinclair is mysteriously drawn into the night through winding, dark streets until he comes to a construction site similar to the one that Kromer had led him to. Here he finds Knauer, a younger boy who had previously sought Sinclair out, thinking to recognize in him a spiritist, someone who could advise him, because his sexual urges were over-powering his will to stay on "the higher spiritual path" (209). Sinclair had coldly told him that continence was not all that important, and Knauer, in total despair, is about to hang himself, presumably following a visit to a prostitute, since Sinclair's call has taken him through the red-light district (212). In Demian-like fashion, Sinclair gives him a brief lecture: "We are not swine . . . as you think, we are human beings. We create gods and struggle with them, and they bless us" (214). Sinclair now knows and espouses, as Demian had before him, that everyone, Knauer included, must find God in his own way. Everyone's God is one God, despite His myriad voices, and he who listens for the voice and battles his way to Him will be blessed. Just as long ago Demian had guessed Sinclair's problem with Kromer, now it is Sinclair's turn to rescue another budding Cain. He is Knauer's momentary *daemon.*

It still remains for Sinclair to know more intimately the feminine side of the God that he has embraced. When he returns home on vacation he sees for the first time a picture of Demian's mother—this is the dream vision he had painted and been carrying with him! He searches everywhere for her, but to no avail. (Hesse will display the same subtle irony when he shows Govinda's wandering search in *Siddhartha* and H.H.'s search for Leo in *Journey to the East;* all will fail in their external searches.) However, when Sinclair arrives in the university city—the city of "H.," no less—where he will begin classes, he encounters Demian, and in his mother's house—no longer the cloying father-house of his childhood—hangs the sketch of the bird he had sent to Demian. Freedom and rebirth are possible within this house.

Frau Eva, as she is now characterized for the first time, nourishes her small circle, of which Sinclair says, "Our task was to represent an island in the world, perhaps a model . . . to bring the message that there was another possibility for living life" (236). Hesse's use of "another possibility" is interesting. He does not inform us of the nature of the opposing possibility, but his remark can be interpreted as psychological evidence that he is drawing the contrast between Sinclair's new life and his childhood; he has reached a higher stage of development, one which can accommodate both the mother world and the father world.

Hesse now expands the theme of individual rebirth to societal rebirth. Sinclair has again dreamed of his bird; this time it is breaking out of a cloud, and the vision has appeared to Demian and Frau Eva, as well. She interprets the dream as a foreshadowing of the coming war, but of great interest is the overpowering erotic longing that Sinclair feels for Frau Eva on the day that hostilities are breaking out. Frau Eva feels his call but does not respond. It parallels the lustful call for war felt by society, which also should have gone unanswered, and we are once again reminded of the story of the moth and the essay "Self-Will." We should respond only to those urges that have purpose and value.

Both Demian and Sinclair are involved in the fighting, and one night, as Sinclair is standing guard, another vision occurs to him: a city in the clouds from which millions of people are streaming. A God-like figure with the features of Frau Eva stands among them, and the people disappear into her. She cries out in pain, as though giving birth, and the stars spring out of her forehead, just as Athena, the one-time Goddess of War who evolved into the Goddess of Wisdom, sprang from the forehead of Zeus. In other words, there can be rebirth following the horrors of war. (Ziolkowsky rightly points out the similarity of the dream to *Revelations,* but Neuer misses the point of the metaphor, vaguely describing Sinclair's final vision of Frau Eva as "the beginning and end of mankind" [14]). One of the stars explodes over Sinclair, and when he awakens he is wounded and lying in a cellar, a stall, on a bed of straw. Next to him lies Demian, also wounded, and he kisses Sinclair for his mother, symbolizing Sinclair's acceptance into the brotherhood, or, in Jungian terms, the union of individuation. Stelzig calls the kiss only an "odd consummation" (149), but it means that Sinclair is now a whole, healthy person in the Jungian sense. Frau Eva and Demian will always be with him, as Demian's final statement affirms: "When you call me, I won't come anymore riding crudely on a horse or on a train. You'll have to listen within, then you will notice that I am inside you" (256).

Every reader will recognize *Demian* as a positive philosophy of life, and we must pay tribute to an author who could write such an affirmation of faith while his private world and the world around him were being reduced to ruins. On January 1, 1917, Hesse had written to his friend Hans Sturzenegger: "It has been clear to me for a long time that my attitude (even within my official activities) can one day lead to a break with my homeland, my position, family, name, etc., and I'm determined to let it happen" (*GB I* 343). This is not the Johann Veraguth of *Roßhalde,* who wanted to escape wife and family to pursue a personal dream. Hesse has sacrificed his own mental health to give solace and aid to German prisoners of war; he has watched the complete mental breakdown of his wife and the breakup of his family; he has lost his financial security; he has made hosts of enemies and learned to accept abuse for his attitude toward war; and he has envisioned that real life lies beyond all of this.

Far from being a flight into fantasy, *Demian* depicts Hesse's first independent steps along the spiritual path that he created out of the chaos both of his life and of war. Dr. Lang had opened a door that enabled Hesse to understand the nature and complexities of the human being and of human society, which had left him a lonely outsider. A large part of his personal dilemma, as we can determine from the strong religious theme in *Demian,* was the childhood bonding with the Pietism of his family. He now feels free to let Christianity speak in symbols, just as he has learned to let other religions, as well as philosophy and literature, speak in their symbols. Stelzig points out that there are even more features to the eclectic maze through which *Demian* has taken the reader: the "confluences of the conceptual world of the German Romantics and of the traditional dialectical thinking culminating in Hegel; of Nietzschean ideas of Christian as well as Gnostic motifs and of assorted other strands from Socrates to Dostoevsky, Bachofen and Freud" (141–2).

Hesse has harvested what interested him from these many sources, as will remain his practice, and has ignored what does not. He has added a feminine content to the masculine Christianity, which theme, in various guises, will appear in much of his work yet to come. He has rediscovered God after losing faith in the authoritative figure at the heart of his parents' Pietism. If his gnostic model, the god Abraxas, is unacceptable to traditional Christianity, it is nevertheless one that has had significant influence. Gilles Quispel, professor of early church history, says in his Hesse study: "Why should gnosticism be scorned?" and goes on to note that the German Idealism of Schelling and Hegel was the gnosis of the nineteenth century, that Goethe was influenced by it, and that Freud based his writings on gnosticism; he even charges that Martin Buber (who criticized Jung for his heretical views based on gnosticism) had been a gnostic before he "hid his thoughts under the terminology of Existentialism." Quispel concludes his view by saying, "This should show us that every gnostic is in good company. Gnosticism is a splendid word, not a derogatory term" (244).

Perhaps the most controversial statement concerning Christianity which Hesse makes in *Demian* is his alteration of *the* Christ into *a* Christ. The mystery of being could be meaningful to Hesse, so it appears, only if there is a Christ in everyone (recall that Sinclair is reborn on a bed of straw in a stable), as Hesse notes in several passages: "The spirit has manifested itself in everyone, the creature suffers in everyone, a savior is crucified in everyone" (102). "He who desires nothing but his fate . . . stands completely alone and has the cold cosmos around him—that is Jesus in the Garden of Gesthemane" (222). "That which nature wants of man is written in the individual, in you, in me. It was written in Jesus, it was written in Nietzsche" (229). *Demian,* accordingly, can be seen as a discerning and serious challenge, not only to Christianity but to any religious confession that considers its prescriptive doctrines to be the only approach to God.[10] Volker Michels recognized this incumbent plea for religious tolerance by entitling a Hesse paper "Gegen den Nationalismus der Konfessionen" ("Against Denominational Nationalism") (147). Hesse sees the very act of labeling faiths as establishing barriers between one religion and every other, because few adherents will recognize their pathway as *a* pathway rather than as the *only* pathway. He will make the same criticism within a Buddhism/Hinduism framework in his next novel, *Siddhartha,* when he notes that "a true seeker could accept no teaching . . . he who has found, however, could approve of every teaching, every path, every god, nothing more separated him from the thousands of others who lived in the eternal, who breathed the divine" (*GS III* 701). Both works preach a bold gospel that God is to be sought only within the self. And these myriad inner voices, however paradoxical it may seem, are one. If obeyed, the voice will enable the masculine component of life to interpret and evaluate the feminine urges and instincts in every breast and to synthesize the whole. And, according to Hesse, this inner voice of the individual speaks in the universal tongue of all creeds, however deeply it may lie hidden beneath their doctrines.

97

CHAPTER EIGHT

Siddhartha

The Vision

Hesse's Sinclair exemplified a youthful search-for-self in a western European, typically German, environment. Pietistic Christianity served as the basic metaphor for an oppressive masculine world, from which Sinclair had to escape in order to find his own meaningful relationship to life. Helene Welti apparently commented to Hesse that she found Sinclair's search to be prompted by egoism, and Hesse's answer permits us to understand the difference between his writing following his awakening during the war years and the art-for-artist's-sake dream of Johann Veraguth. His own search, he feels, is humankind's search; his innermost being is everyman's innermost being: "This 'I' is not the individual person as he feels and appears to himself, it is rather the innermost, the essential core of every soul, which the East Indians call 'Atman' and which is divine and eternal. Whoever finds this I, be it through Buddha or the Vedas or Lao Tse or Christ, is, in his innermost being, one with the all, with God . . . this innermost essence is the same for all men; it is God, it is 'meaning'" (*GB I* 445).

Siddhartha was to become an Indian Sinclair, or, as Mileck called him, "an Indian in disguise . . . his story is one of a westerner with a western ideal."[1] Rose, in apparent agreement, says that the book helped the West "to understand that God had revealed himself to mankind in different ways" (75). When he was thirty, Hesse had called himself a Buddhist (*Werkgeschichte* 88), but this, too, proved limiting, and *Siddhartha* was, as Milek notes, his expression of "liberation from Brahmanism, Hinduism, and Buddhism" (*HHudR* 102). *Demian,* likewise, had been an expression of liberation from doctrinal Christianity. Hesse was well read and knowledgeable in every major religion,[2] as a child had "breathed in and absorbed the spirit of India just as deeply as Christianity" (*GS VII* 371), but he found in Eastern thought "more room for his imagination," something that was lacking in "oppressive Christianity," where he had "never had any kind of religious experience in his youth" (*GS VII* 372). Nonetheless, he could later say that Christianity had played a "commanding role" in his life—not a "church Christianity," however, but a "mythical Christianity," which could live "not without conflicts, but at least without war alongside a more Indic-Asiatic–colored faith, where the only dogma is the concept of unity" (*GS VII* 373). *Siddhartha* will portray this unity.

In the 1932 essay entitled "A Bit of Theology" (*GS VII* 388–402), Hesse divided the process of becoming a person into three stages (and here we see the influence of Jung): first, innocence; then, despair; and, finally, downfall or salvation. To Hesse these stages were universal, regardless of culture or civilization. In retrospect, we can easily see how Sinclair fits into the pattern: his fall from innocence in the Kromer episode, his despair as a student, which nearly resulted in his downfall, and then his gradual struggle to pull his life together on a higher plane—his salvation. Hesse will follow the same model in *Siddhartha,* although he will begin with the age of innocence all but over for his protagonist. In the novel, we shall see that Buddhist and Hindu thought play metaphorically, though less obviously, the same roles as the church in *Demian,* as Rose also notes: "the pious Hindu path" is "comparable to Protestant Pietism" (68–9). The Pietists teach surrender to the will of God; the Buddhists, especially as Hesse sees them, teach escape from the world of appearances and the senses. We shall see that this doctrine ends in renunciation—and near failure—for Siddhartha just as confirmation ended in renunciation—and near failure—for Sinclair. Both works propound the now-familiar Hesse conviction that religion in doctrinal form, be it Christianity, Buddhism, or Hinduism, builds barriers. Humankind—past, present, and future—is one. Every spiritual search confirms the perception of a "basic problem," each search expressing it in "analogous symbols" and recognizing that "something is intended for it" (*GS VII* 390). Religious communities, therefore, separate themselves from each other not only through doctrines but also with their symbols. Dogma, as expressed in any particular religion, is to Hesse "tied to time" and can never be more than a stage in humankind's development which will someday be overcome and surpassed (*GS VII* 391).

Siddhartha was begun in December of 1919 in Montagnola, and the first part flowed quickly from Hesse's pen. Here, he was dealing with the struggling and suffering Siddhartha, but when it came to portraying the victor and affirmer of life, Hesse could not continue. He had experienced the trials and tribulations of Johann Veraguth's marriage and artistic ambitions and expressed this in *Roβhalde;* the soul-searching of the World War I period had provided him with the *Demian* decision to bear his mark of Cain and not to let concern about the future destroy him. But the future had been left open in those two tales, and Hesse wanted to place his Siddhartha within an all-encompassing, closed framework. This was no easy task.

The novel is set some six centuries before the birth of Christ, in ancient India at the time of Gotama Buddha, whose eightfold path has since guided the faithful toward *Nirvana*. Siddhartha is a young Brahmin, handsome, learned, and a prince among his caste members. Everyone knows that he is destined for greatness (i.e., he already "bears the mark of Cain," so this story begins where *Demian* ended). But there is dissatisfaction in Siddhartha's breast. He suspects that his father and the other erudite Brahmins have learned everything to perfection from the holy books, but he wonders where are those who have succeeded in living the wisdom that "your soul is the entire world" and not just "knowing" that it is true (*GS III* 620)?

One evening after meditation, Siddhartha announces to his friend Govinda that he will join a group of Samanas, wandering mendicant priests, who have just passed through their city. Govinda is frightened because he knows that Siddhartha is taking his first step into the world and that he must follow him. When Siddhartha, as a dutiful son, requests permission to join the Samanas, his father says he does not want to hear the question a second time, but Siddhartha does not move. The father cannot sleep and gets up every hour to find Siddhartha standing with crossed arms in the darkness. Just before dawn the father asks him why he is waiting. "You know why," Siddhartha answers. "You will get tired." "I will get tired." "You will fall asleep." "I will not fall asleep." "You will die." "I will die." "You would rather die than obey your father?" "Siddhartha has always obeyed his father." "Then you will give up your intention." "Siddhartha will do what his father tells him to do" (624). And so, reluctantly, his father gives permission and asks that Siddhartha return home to teach his father of the art of bliss if he finds it in the forest—an admission that Siddhartha was right; his father's gods are only objects of veneration, not living companions. Siddhartha's farewell to his mother is carried out as the father instructs him, but *mother* is little more than a word in the book, an interesting departure from the significant role of Frau Eva in *Demian* and evidence that Hesse has a purpose in focusing attention on Siddhartha's origins within the masculine priestly class. As we shall see, however, the feminine world will play its role as well.

Once he has joined the Samanas, Siddhartha's only goal is to "become empty" of everything—wishes, dreams, joy, and passion—little different from the goal that his Pietist parents had demanded of Hesse when he was a child. After every impulse in his heart has been destroyed, then his innermost being will surely awaken, so Siddhartha reasons. He becomes a protegé of the eldest Samana, but the deepest secret remains hidden, and Siddhartha eventually realizes that destroying the will is not the answer. After he and Govinda have been with the Samanas for three years, a rumor reaches them that an enlightened one, a Buddha, has appeared, someone who has overcome the suffering of the world and has brought his chain of *karma,* of rebirth, to an end. Govinda is ready to try this new master, and Siddhartha agrees that they should seek him out, although he has lost faith in teachers (634). The Samana elder is angry when Siddhartha announces their departure, but the young disciple stares him down, and the old man silently backs away and blesses him—an explicit example of the stronger will asserting itself over the weaker (the same motif expressed in the Sinclair-Kromer confrontation). It is interesting to note that Hesse portrays the elder Samana as full of scorn for the so-called Enlightened One, again making the point that dedication to a particular formula for salvation—what the ascetic practices—creates self-righteousness.

Siddhartha and Govinda find the Buddha and listen to his teachings. So impressed is Govinda that he immediately asks to become a disciple, assuming that Siddhartha will follow. But the next morning, when Siddhartha unexpectedly meets Gotama in the grove, he boldly speaks to him about his doctrine, praising his victory in finding the unbroken chain of being, of cause and effect (634). But for Siddhartha, himself, the unity is imperfect. The message cannot contain for Siddhartha or for others the secret of what the Enlightened One, himself, experienced that enabled *his* life to fall into place (643). Here we see why, in *Demian,* Hesse found a Christ in everyone and, now in *Siddhartha,* he finds a Buddha in everyone. There can be no formula for salvation or enlightenment. And, true to his own awakening during the war years, Hesse cannot believe in *Nirvana* if it means separation from the suffering of life. His God incorporates and blesses the earthly life as well as the spiritual. By leaving the Buddha, Siddhartha is rejecting the prescribed formula that this religion offers, just as, in *Demian,* Sinclair rejected the absolutes of Christianity.

When Siddhartha leaves the grove, he is through with teachers and teaching: "I want to learn from myself . . . I want to get to know myself, the secret that is Siddhartha" (646). He feels as though he is seeing the world for the first time, a puzzling and magic world, and in its midst is he, Siddhartha, the awakening one—not the Enlightened One—on the path to himself. His first impulse is to return home to his father—as did Pistorius—but then he realizes that his home, too, is a part of the past. He suddenly knows he is completely alone, and a shudder runs through him—the "last shudder of his awakening, the last pain of birth" (649). This is hardly true, and again we see that Hesse's mellifluous style sometimes oversteps thematic content.

This is the end of Part One of the book, which Hesse had little difficulty putting to paper, but now the words stop coming, and he is forced to lay the manuscript aside. Gradually the rest of the book takes shape, and finally Siddhartha can set off to find Siddhartha. Küng labels Hesse's study of Lao Tse "the liberating experience that permitted him to finish the book" (*HHudR* 63).

The first chapter of Part Two is entitled "Kamala," which is the name of a courtesan. We shall also meet a wealthy businessman, Kamaswami. As a proper noun, the root word *kama* signifies the Hindu god of love and desire; thus, we are informed that Siddhartha will seek meaning in the world of the senses. As he spends the first night of his new life in the hut of a ferryman, he dreams of his friend Govinda, the ultimate follower, who asks him in imitation of Christ, "Why hast thou forsaken me?" Then Govinda changes into a woman, and Siddhartha lies suckling at her breast. In a description reminiscent of Sinclair's painting of his dream figure, Siddhartha finds that "she tasted of woman and man, of sun and forest, of animal, of flower, of every fruit, of every desire" (652). Ziolkowski sees this dream as a "transition from Siddhartha's previous ascetic life, personified by Govinda, to his new life in the arms of Kamala" (*Novels* 160). Boulby, in like manner, calls the dream "the characteristic transition from male to female" (14). Both critics are struggling to make the point that Siddhartha will leave his masculine world and embark on a quest through a world of darkness with the same feminine attributes of seduction and danger that Sinclair had to face.

At the edge of a village, his first temptation appears in the form of a young woman who attempts to seduce him. Though he is sorely tempted, his inner voice tells him "no"—there is a difference between obeying one's inner voice and succumbing to impulse, as Demian had discussed with Sinclair. But the next woman Siddhartha sees as he enters the city offers an acceptable temptation—she is Kamala, a beautiful, elegant courtesan, and as her sedan chair is carried past the curious Samana, she returns his smile, and his first worldly goal is clear. After a bath in the river and a haircut and shave from a friendly barber, Siddhartha returns to Kamala. She is amused that a Samana should come out of the forest and ask to be taught the art of love. Even though she is willing to exchange a kiss for a poem, he will learn no more until he can return wearing fine clothes and bearing gifts. Despite her apparent amusement, however, she recommends this potential lover to her friend Kamaswami, a wealthy businessman, but insists that he become his equal, not his servant.

Thus begins Siddhartha's life in the city among the "*Kindermenschen,*" as the next chapter is entitled—what Demian, via Nietzsche, had called "the herd." In Kamaswami's employ, Siddhartha soon becomes a wealthy man and enjoys the intimate company of Kamala. At first it is all a game; he feels superior to those who pursue worldly pleasures and riches, but gradually he, too, falls under the spell of possessions. Perhaps some twenty years after his arrival, he notices that Kamala's face is betraying wrinkles, his own hair showing traces of grey, and Hesse, using one of his favorite stylistic techniques—the dream—directs Siddhartha to his next stage of existence. He dreams of a rare songbird that Kamala keeps in a cage; one morning he finds it dead, and as he throws it out into the street, it is as though he is discarding all that is good and of value in his life. When he awakens he feels death in his heart. The inner voice that had always prompted him to go on—to become a Samana, to turn away from the Buddha and face the unknown—has been silent for a long time. He leaves the city in despair, without informing anyone of his departure. When Kamala is told of his disappearance, she frees her song bird from its golden cage, and we become aware that the bird, the song in Siddhartha's breast, is not dead but will seek him out. From this day forward, Kamala accepts no more lovers and discovers that she is pregnant with Siddhartha's child.

Siddhartha's aimless wandering takes him back to the river that he had crossed with the ferryman. As he is about to let himself slip into the water and end his useless life, the sacred word *om* reverberates within him, and his slumbering spirit awakens; the little bird has found him. He recognizes the folly of his contemplated suicide, lies down in the grass, and falls asleep.[3] When he awakens, he finds his old friend Govinda sitting beside him. He had come upon the richly dressed, sleeping merchant, he explains, and sat down beside him to protect him from snakes. After Siddhartha has thanked him for his intended kindness, and as the monk is about to take his leave, Siddhartha says, "Farewell, Govinda," stopping him in his tracks. With humorous irony, Hesse has Govinda, the follower, explain his journey: "I'm not going anywhere. We monks are always underway . . . we travel from place to place, live according to the rules, spread our teachings, accept alms and move on" (686). Boulby interprets this episode to mean that "the woman Kamala has only given place to the man Govinda . . . [who] is now a symbol for humanity, the object of a new kind of love. Now at last Siddhartha can really love" (146). The message seems much simpler: Govinda portrays the eternal searcher who will never find what he is looking for because he cannot recognize what stands directly before him. Thus is the life of the intrepid follower.

Siddhartha smiles after his departing friend and, when he looks at the river, finds it smiling back at him. The thought formulates itself that he will stay by this river, which will gradually become the dominant symbol and central metaphor of the novel. The same ferryman who brought him across the river years ago now rows him back again. Vasudeva recalls the Samana who had slept in his hut and invites him to share it once more. That evening, when Siddhartha tells the old ferryman his story, Vasudeva knows that the river has spoken to his guest and grants his request to stay with him and be his assistant. Hesse notes that Vasudeva's greatest virtue is the art of listening, and when Siddhartha says, "I will learn it from you" (696), Vasudeva replies: "You will learn it, but not from me. The river has taught me. . . . It knows everything. . . . You will also learn the other thing from it" (697). When Siddhartha asks what "the other thing" is, Vasudeva's answer indicates that he must wait for this message: "I can't tell you what 'the other thing' is, my friend. . . . I am not a scholar. . . . I only understand listening and being pious. . . . I am only a ferryman, and my work is to take people across the river. I have taken many across, thousands, and to all of them my river is an obstacle on their travels. . . . But for a few among the thousands, four or five, the river ceased to be an obstacle, they heard a voice . . . and the river became sacred to them, as it has to me" (697).

Just as *Demian* pointed out that there are few Cains in the world, so too does *Siddhartha* tell us that few people care enough about the meaning of life to look for the symbols of meaning that surround them. The voice of the river thus becomes synonymous with humanity's inner voice, which most ignore. The flowing water separates the polarities of life. Siddhartha first lived on one side, where he tried to discover the way to the spirit through the mind, in the teachings of the Vedas and the Brahmin elders, from the ascetic Samanas, and by listening to the wisdom of the Buddha. Then he crossed the river to reach the city, where he gave himself over to worldly pleasures and values; the two worlds are but a variation of the worlds of light and darkness in *Demian.* Now Siddhartha will begin to discover what it means to travel back and forth between them, and—the all important lesson—he will listen while so doing.

Siddhartha's first lesson from the river is that there is no such thing as time, and when he asks Vasudeva if he has learned this secret as well, the old ferryman smiles broadly and comments: "Yes . . . this is what you mean: the river is the same everywhere, at its source, at the mouth, at the waterfall, by the ferry, where the current is rapid, in the sea, in the mountains . . . and that for it there is only the present, no shadow of the future" (698).

The metaphor is central to Hesse's theology. It differs from Buddha's teaching that we can escape the suffering of the world and the necessity of rebirth in the chain of *karma,* and it differs from the Christian message of reaping the rewards of salvation in another world. In short, it expresses all of being as an eternal present: "Nothing was, nothing will be, everything is, everything has being and presence" (698). Siddhartha is excited with the discovery and realizes that all suffering, all self-torment, anxiety, all difficulties, all hostility are anchored in time, and all will disappear when time is overcome, when time can be thought away.

Some time later Vasudeva smiles even more broadly when Siddhartha says to him, "Isn't it true, my friend, that the river has . . . very many voices. Doesn't it have the voice of a king and a warrior and a stone and a night-bird and of someone giving birth and someone sighing. . . . And do you know which word it speaks when you are able to hear all its ten-thousand voices at once?" Vasudeva, still smiling, bends forward and whispers *"Om"* in Siddhartha's ear (699). But now the river's message must be made reality for Siddhartha.

News that the Buddha is dying sweeps through the land, and pilgrims by the hundreds begin flocking to pay him homage. Among them is Kamala and with her a son, an unwilling traveler who longs for the comforts of his home. A short distance from the river, she stops to rest and is bitten by a poisonous snake.[4] Vasudeva hears the boy's cry for help, carries Kamala to the ferry, and brings her across the river to their hut. Siddhartha recognizes her immediately and also realizes that the boy is his son. She lives long enough to speak to Siddhartha and to know that she does not have to see the Buddha to fulfill her wish of seeing an enlightened one—Siddhartha is no different. (The name, in fact, means "one who has reached the goal." It was also the name of Gotama Buddha.) And he indeed feels himself blessed, for now he has a son.

The young Siddhartha, however, finds little satisfaction living with the two old "banana eaters." His father cannot convince him that fine clothes, a soft bed, and servants have little meaning. Vasudeva reminds Siddhartha that his own father had not been able to prevent him from joining the Samanas or from learning the lessons of worldliness in the city. One morning the boy is gone. As happened to Johann Veraguth in *Roβhalde,* Siddhartha, too, must give up that which he loves more than anything, and we recall his earlier conversation with Kamala when he had said that they were unlike the other *Kindermenschen* because they could not love (672). Now he has learned what it means to love. Only now does he realize what his goal has always been: "nothing but a readiness of the soul, an ability, a secret art of being able, at any moment, in the middle of life, to feel and inhale the thought of oneness" (716).[5] And one day as he crosses the river, the water laughs at him for letting the wound burn so deeply, and that night he tells Vasudeva all that he has felt, and Vasudeva seems to absorb all of his sorrows. It is at this point that Siddhartha realizes that Vasudeva is no less enlightened than the Buddha.[6] The old ferryman invites him to listen more closely to the river. As they sit on the bank, all the images of his life dance before him. He hears voices of joy and sorrow, good and evil, laughter and mourning—thousands of voices—and if he does not let himself be caught up by any single voice, he hears only the single word *"om"* (720). In this hour Siddhartha stops doing battle with his fate, and in his eyes glows the "serenity of knowledge." When Vasudeva sees this, he says, "I have been waiting for this hour, my friend." He "goes into the forest, into the oneness" (721), and Siddhartha is left alone as the ferryman.

One last episode concludes the book—the return of the follower Govinda, who has heard of an old ferryman who people say is a wise man. When Govinda seeks him out and asks him for advice, again not recognizing his old friend, Siddhartha smilingly tells him he is searching too hard, that he is possessed by his goal, and then calls him by name. Govinda is as amazed now as he was beside the river years earlier, when he had also failed to recognize Siddhartha. The monk stays the night in the ferryman's hut, and the latter's advice to his childhood friend is a summary of his wisdom, which, however, he warns Govinda cannot be taught—knowledge, yes; wisdom, no (724). Siddhartha points out that when we attempt to teach, as did the Buddha, then we must divide or categorize the world into *Samsara* and *Nirvana,* into disappointment and truth, into sorrow and salvation, but Siddhartha has learned that, for every truth, there is also an opposite truth. No one is ever wholly saintly or wholly sinful. It only appears this way when we are deceived into thinking that "time is real" (725). The world is never "incomplete" or on its path to "completeness." It is complete at every moment, grace carries every sin, all babies carry death, all the dying carry eternal life (726). Siddhartha's only concern is to be able to love the world as it has been, as it is, as it will be—to consider all creatures with love, admiration, and reverence (729). Hesse finishes the novel with a touch of magic by having Govinda kiss Siddhartha on the forehead,[7] which permits him to see the timeless flow of forces and images pass before his eyes, just as Siddhartha had envisioned them in the flowing river. With tears streaming from his eyes, Govinda bows down to his friend, whose smiling face is no different from that of the enlightened Buddha.

When the book ends, we are left to assume that Siddhartha will carry on as the ferryman. Vasudeva did not leave him until he felt assured that Siddhartha had learned the wisdom of the river—a motif of mentor-tutor relationships which appeared in less obvious form in *Peter Camenzind* and *Beneath the Wheel* but clearly in *Demian.* Siddhartha's son bears his father's name, implying that he, too, may ultimately follow in his footsteps. As ferryman, Siddhartha will pass back and forth between the two worlds that the river symbolically divides and unites, indicating the never-ending relationship between the polarities of life.[8] As was Vasudeva before him, he will be of service to those who cross over the water and will give his passengers the opportunity to listen to its message, though few will hear it. Thus the theme of service becomes a part of the thematic continuum.

We see in the smoothly flowing symbolism of this work that Siddhartha has reached beyond Hesse's previous protagonists. The conclusion of the novel does imply that Siddhartha lives happily ever after: "I know that I am one with Gotama" (729). Consequently, we would expect that Hesse's own life could now remain in balance. We are pleased to find that such an affirming and all-encompassing perspective of life is possible; we may even envy the author of such a book, who, if his protagonist is any indication, seems able to stand both within and without human existence and, evil and all, find it beautiful and serene.[9] It is a glorious vision, but also a grand illusion, for Hesse's worldly involvements will surface again and again, and not until *Journey to the East* will we find that he has regained his *Siddhartha* perspective.

CHAPTER NINE

Der Steppenwolf

Immortal Reminders

Some five years lay between the completion of *Siddhartha* and the publication of *Der Steppenwolf,* and there is no better proof than Hesse's own depression and despair[1] to bring home his *Siddhartha* message: the path of paths is not an escape; it leads not into *Nirvana* but through life with all of its suffering. In this next novel, Hesse must remind himself as well as the reader of the difference between perceiving universal harmony and living daily life. Mileck calls *Der Steppenwolf* "in terms of *Siddhartha* . . . a distinct relapse" (*Life and Art* 187).

Hesse had drifted into a second marriage with a much younger woman after his divorce from Mia. He felt he "owed it to [Ruth Wenger] and her family" (*GB II* 65). In a letter he wrote, "I'm not pleased to be getting married and have a thousand reservations, even though I love my bride very much, but I'm not doing it out of any real inner conviction, but rather fulfilling my fate" (*GB II* 74). Evidence that signs played a role in his life as well as in the life of his mentor and friend, Dr. Lang, appears in a letter written on July 1, 1923: "Dr. Lang, who is somewhat of an astrologer, has written me that the signs pointing to marriage are so strong for me this year that I can hardly escape this fate" (*GB II* 63).

Ruth Wenger's parents owned a home near the Casa Camuzzi where Hesse lived in Tessin, and the lonely man had gradually become involved with the family, the acquaintance with the daughter eventually turning into a romance. The marriage took place on January 11, 1924,[2] and in the same month Hesse would write to his friend and biographer Hugo Ball that "I, the friend of loneliness and the cloister, old fellow that I am, have taken another wife, who will gladly give up a few ideals for a pair of pretty shoes and a handsome dog" (*GB II* 80). Ruth was a voice student when they married, and although Hesse was genuinely fond of her, they soon proved incompatible and took up separate quarters after a few short months in the Hotel Kraft in Basel. Hesse returned to Montagnola in the spring of 1924, staying until mid-November, when he moved back to Basel for the winter, but this time to separate quarters, making the comment to a friend that "now the Basel period is beginning again, which means marriage, and this doesn't always turn out to be full of smiles" (*GB II* 94).

It is easy to see Hesse's emotional despondency reflected in his *Steppenwolf* novel. In October of 1924, still the first year of his new marriage, he had written stoically to a friend: "Our 'assignment' is to carry our problem around with us, and, except in the lonely hours of trial, not to look upon it so tragically, but rather to know that . . . the haplessness of *all* mankind is being expressed, and to find this dangerous life beautiful and to live" (*GB II* 93). Over the next two-year period, however, despair often forced this stoic optimism into the background. Like his Siddhartha leaning over the bank of the river, ready to let his wasted life come to an end, Hesse often thought of suicide. In April of 1926, he wrote to Felix Braun: "For more than a year, I've been in the worst crisis of my life, and even today I hope that it won't pass, but that I'll break my neck instead, because I'm sick of life to the point of throwing up" (*GB II* 140). By the end of the year, things had not improved. To Emmy Ball, wife of his friend Hugo, he wrote on New Year's Eve: "I'm finishing the final draft of my *Steppenwolf* for the publisher, this is holding me together for the moment, and when I'm finished, I hope to find the courage to cut my throat, because life is unbearable for me" (*GB II* 159–60). Despite these outbursts, made in all seriousness, Hesse makes an optimistic statement of life in *Steppenwolf,* though it is rarely understood as such—a problem Hesse tried to rectify in a prologue to the 1942 edition, in which he called it the "work of a believer" (*GS VII* 413).

What could cause this self-styled Cain to languish in such prolonged states of despair? As a starting point we can note that Hesse, as expressed in *Siddhartha,* could envision the harmony of life but found it too elusive. This, in turn, fueled his depressions. As a result, he repeatedly found himself in Jungian confrontation-with-the-self situations, deep moments of despair that force the victim to choose between suicide or acceptance. The fact that Hesse chose to survive tells us that his faith permitted him to hover a cut above the business of life, however precariously.

The Basel-Zurich years from 1924 to 1927 were even worse for Hesse than the war years, because he had no forced activity. All his strength had to come from within, for the outside world was not a suitable companion. In January of 1925, Ruth was diagnosed with tuberculosis and "condemned" to a one-year bed rest—no singing, no activity of any kind (*GB II* 111). She, too, was suffering from depression. His first wife, Mia, had been running a *Pension* and, in June of the same year, suffered another serious, even violent, breakdown. As a result, Hesse had to take responsibility for his youngest son, Martin, who was fourteen. He was also having publisher troubles and, in addition to these personal problems, was deeply concerned for the bourgeois world around him, viewing postwar Germany as a "collapsing, hopeless, seriously ill country . . . nobody knows if it will still exist tomorrow" (*GB II* 74). He told Helene Welti, "The whole world is sailing full tilt into the next war with crashing music and under full sail" (*GB II* 145)—it is worthy of note that he was right.

True to his artistic calling, Hesse had to express in writing all of these burdens, which had caused him to hover on the brink of suicide for the past two years. They slowly took form in one of his most fascinating novels, *Der Steppenwolf,* which he called "a major work, the most difficult and unrewarding that I have ever taken on." He noted that "[it was] infinitely complicated and newer perhaps than *Demian* was, but this work, which I have been plodding away at for two years at long intervals, doesn't give me any pleasure." Elsewhere he says that "[*Der Steppenwolf*] didn't originate out of a sense of pride, but out of bitter suffering" (*GB II* 169). In still another letter, he calls it a "daring and fantastic book in which something new is being attempted," and he adds that it was begun "a good two years ago in Basel" (*GB II* 159), which would mean when his second marriage was barely underway. Ironically, as he was "working like crazy day after day" on the final draft, Ruth informed him that she was filing for divorce (*GB II* 162). The work was published in June of 1927.

What Hesse refers to as "daring and fantastic" in the novel, it would seem, is his attempt to construct a precise literary metaphor for the Jungian concept of individuation, the building of a "whole person."[3] Even though *Demian* was of similar mold, the earlier work was an eclectic maze of other allusions—biblical, literary, historical—as well, whereas *Der Steppenwolf* is a well-defined case study, a prose painting of Jungian theory.[4] Hesse says as much in a letter to his nephew on January 7, 1926:

> . . . I'm living, insofar as I'm living at all, in a pressing and living, romantic and magic dream, and often swim again in the colorful deep waters of completely abnormal fantastic dreams and imaginary worlds. It is for me the only way to bear life under the present circumstances. And since I have a friend here (the Pistorius of *Demian*) with whom I travel these paths, this horrible period (I was and have been for months constantly on the verge of suicide) also has its greatness and its beauty. (*GB II* 128–9)

The "Pistorius" is Dr. Josef Lang, who was a close companion during Hesse's Zurich stay,[5] as he reports: "Evenings I'm almost always with Lang, we eat in a cheap bar . . . and then sit talking and drinking cognac either at his place or mine" (*GB II* 131). And it seems that Hesse learned not only Jungian theory from his friend. He also credits Dr. Lang and several others with introducing him to the art of the foxtrot and Fasching balls. In other words, Hesse did experience much of the wild life that he portrays in *Der Steppenwolf,* and the novel will challenge the reader to interpret this "amazing time" as Hesse presents it in a truly amazing novel.

We are introduced to Harry Haller, the protagonist of *Der Steppenwolf,* in an introduction written by his neighbor and acquaintance in a rooming house where Harry once lived for nine or ten months. When he moved on, he left a manuscript behind—a strange story he had written during his stay. An attached note told his neighbor to do with it as he pleased, which, admittedly, would have been to throw it away, had he not known the author personally.

Why such an introduction? The traditional reasons for including an outside narrator's introduction are present: the author wants to gain distance from his own narrative and to present an outsider's view of his hero. In this case, the narrator gives Hesse the opportunity to analyze his *Steppenwolf* through the very eyes of one of those bourgeois whose world he is attacking—an ironic attempt at fair play. The narrator says he would like to leave his own person in the background as much as possible (*GS IV* 192), but of course he does the opposite, even going so far as to characterize himself in detail. He is a bourgeois with regular living habits, one who abstains from drinking and smoking (196); his life is secure and filled with duties (204). And naturally the unnamed narrator's characterization of Harry Haller offers an ironic contrast of their respective worlds. The narrator finds his neighbor so convinced of his isolation, his uprooted existence, that the bourgeois activities around him—the punctuality with which, for example, the narrator went to his office or the opinion of a servant or a street car conductor—could enthuse him (199). He finds that Harry, from his rarefied space, actually loved and admired the petty bourgeois world as solid and secure, as one distant and unattainable, to which every approach was closed to him (199–200). He sees Haller as ever-so-friendly, an admirer of the clean and neat and orderly life—especially evident in the scene where Harry sits in the stairwell admiring the flawlessly polished entryway with its flourishing araucaria plant, symbol of housewifely dedication to the home. It is part of the irony that Hesse portrays Haller as such a genuinely likeable, captivating person in the words of this man and his aunt and then permits the narrator to say that Harry represents the "sickness of the times, the neurosis of a generation . . . to which by no means only the weak and inferior individuals have succumbed, but rather the strong, the most intellectual, the most gifted" (205). Hugo Ball also draws attention to the neurosis-of-the-times theme: "One can no longer take it as coincidental that spirits like Nietzsche, Strindberg, Van Gogh,

Dostoevsky . . . fell victim to the neurosis. . . . One ultimately has to see that these are misfortunes for which our religious and social factors and our educational system must bear more than a measure of blame" (177).

The poor narrator simply does not understand that he and his ilk are the root of Harry's problem—as far as the external story is concerned. Yes, Harry longs for the "solid and secure," but at his own level of understanding; he cannot join the herd. But at the subjective level, Hesse is really making fun of himself for letting this bourgeois world get him down when Haller tells his neighbor: "Please don't believe that I'm speaking ironically! My dear man, nothing lies further from my mind than to make fun of this orderliness and bourgeois way of life" (198). Few critics have seen much of the humor in *Der Steppenwolf*. Edwin Casebeer is an exception. He comments that, "if Harry hasn't learned to laugh yet, Hesse has . . . [he] not only suffers with Harry, he laughs at him."[6] The *Literary Advisor for German Catholics* found nothing amusing: "Hesse . . . is still hopelessly caught in a web of scepticism and demoralizing irony. His book remains a venomous, dangerous confusion, venomous in its unbridled sensuality, dangerous in it radical and caustic negation of all values of life, a confusion of abstruse, crass and pardoxical ideas. Great stylistic ability is aimlessly and immeasurable wasted" (quoted in *Werkgeschichte,* 115).

Harry Haller begins his own contribution to the manuscript by describing a typical day in his life—several hours of work, two hours of the various pains that plague older people, a bit of medication, a hot bath, three mail deliveries, breathing exercises, and a long walk (207). But poor Harry can endure just so many of these aimless days before he succumbs to a wild desire to surrender to strong feelings and sensations. In just such a mood, he sets out for a late evening walk. After passing through the entrance hall where the araucaria exudes bourgeois tranquility, Harry tries to recall the last time that he had been granted a moment of tranquility in his world. These moments are few, the last at a concert where he was momentarily "carried through heaven and saw God at work" (212). He can recall other rare occasions—when a verse occurred to him which was too beautiful to write down; thinking about passages from Descartes or Pascal; moments when he was with his lady friend. Why are only these "divine moments" satisfying? Why can he not derive the same feeling from bourgeois pleasures as everyone else? As he broods over his Steppenwolf existence, he approaches a familiar old grey stone wall, which connects a small church and an old hospital. It has always had a peaceful effect on him, but now there is a doorway that he had never noticed before, and above it there are dancing neon lights: "Magic Theater—Entrance not for everyone." Harry tries unsuccessfully to open the door, and the lights stop flashing, but when he goes back across the street and turns to look again, several colored letters drip off his coat onto the wet asphalt, forming the words "Only for Madmen." As he stands contemplating how beautiful the flashing letters were, his previous thoughts return—images of those shining golden moments (215–6).

This experience is the first of many mysterious events that will occur in *Der Steppenwolf,* and when they occur, as we learned in *Demian,* we are to look for the metaphorical meaning behind them. Harry labels these magic moments *Gottesspuren* (traces of God)—Jung's "flashes of insight"—and with Harry's vision at the wall, his Jung-inspired crusade begins. The old wall, from the vantage point of the street, had obscured the common courtyard between the hospital and the church, whose presence Egon Schwarz also notes, though he does not comment on the imagery.[7] The hospital symbolizes the suffering Harry feels he undergoes in this bourgeois world, and the church symbolizes the divine world he perceives beyond it. His hallucination is a humorously ironic message that the Kafkaesque door is waiting to be opened.

He walks on, passing through the central area of the city, where other flashing signs are advertising dancing, floor shows, movies, and the like, but these are for everyman, not for the likes of Harry. We should not fail to see the humor, however, in the fact that his longed-for world—hidden away somewhere in a magic theater, where wolf and man can share a common stage—also had to advertise its existence with neon signs to draw his attention.

After his second carafe of wine in an antiquated pub, he can laugh at the nonsense of a newspaper article, and he recalls a forgotten melody that rises like a soap bubble, reflects "the whole world," and then bursts (218). If this little melody can secretly take root in his soul and blossom forth in colorful flowers, can he be completely lost to the world? Even if he is a roaming animal, there is still meaning in his foolish life; something in him can receive calls from distant worlds; a thousand images are stacked in his brain—Giotto's hordes of angels, Hamlet and Ophelia, parables of all the sadness and misunderstanding in the world, and many more. And who is it that can read these omens? It is the Steppenwolf (218–9)—that is, not all are privileged to perceive the "traces of God."

Still basking in this moment of inner satisfaction, Harry sets out for home, stopping for a moment in front of a dance hall where jazz music is blaring, and he has to admit that its wildness and strength have an appeal for him. It is, however, the music of decline; Rome must have had such music under its last emperors. As he passes the old wall, he searches in vain for the door and can only smile to himself and walk on, but suddenly a strange man carrying a placard and a tray of wares appears out of a dark side street. Harry reads the dancing letters on his placard: "Anarchistic Evening Entertainment. Magic Theater! Entrance not for everyone" (223). When Harry tries to get more information, the man hands him a brochure and disappears into an archway. Harry hurries home and takes a look at his acquisition: *Treatise on the Steppenwolf—only for Madmen*. To his surprise, it tells his own story.

The so-called *Tractat vom Steppenwolf* is a part of the book that the reader tends to hurry through to get back to the narrative. If read cursorily, it leaves an impression of redundancy, repeating ad nauseam Harry's problems. It bores and annoys the reader just as Harry's life has bored and annoyed him. But what is the treatise? How can it be his own story? Ziolkowski and Mileck provide psychological explanations for this stylistic mystery, Ziolkowski taking it for a booklet with perhaps such a title as "How Can I Become Twenty Years Younger in One Week" and explains that Harry is an eidetic—one with a vivid imagination who can read his own story into the pamphlet (*Novels* 197). Mileck agrees, saying that "it is Haller's hyperactive and lucid mind that converts a chance pamphlet on whatever theme into a penetrating study of himself and of his age" (*Life and Art* 190). Just as Hesse did not permit readers to understand precisely why Kromer suddenly feared Sinclair, how Demian's message found its way into Sinclair's notebook, so we are to seek the meaning of the treatise at the metaphorical level—it is a message from the "immortals." (The Ghostwriter even mentions "*our* [emphasis provided] magic theaters.") Realistically, if we are in need of the real explanation, the treatise is no more than a part of the manuscript that Harry left behind—his own work, which he composed following his enlightenment. In the little brochure, he is chided—that is, he chides himself unmercifully for his childishness and simplistic attitude. He believes, like Goethe's Faust, that "two souls live within his breast." He can be man or wolf, but the two natures cannot seem to get along. But then he is reminded that, in rare moments (that Harry himself has enumerated for the reader), they have lived in harmony and love, actually strengthening one another (227–8). Harry's crass oversimplification is an attempt to escape having to take a deeper look at these two souls, which, in fact, are not two but thousands, the treatise informs him. Unlike Harry, the good burghers can easily compromise. They can rationalize and let themselves think that they can serve God but also have their creature comforts (247). And if the conventions of bourgeois life change along the way, so be it; they will change. This is why they can burn a heretic today and dedicate monuments to him tomorrow. Harry's desire to be above such compromise has led him to think that he should commit suicide, but in some corner of his soul, he knows that suicide is a shabby and illegitimate emergency exit, that it is more noble and beautiful to succumb to life, itself (233–4).

But the question remains for Harry: How can he participate in compromise? He realizes that only the strongest can cast themselves completely out of the bourgeois atmosphere and into the cosmos, but unless such an Olympus is conquered, the rebels must compromise, and this they can do with humor; this is the conciliatory path. (This is where the great secret of the treatise is imparted to Harry.) Humor makes it possible to live in the world as though it were not the world, to honor the law yet stand above it. To reach such a vantage point, the Steppenwolf must look deeply into the chaos of his own soul and come to full consciousness of his own self. Then he will find out that the man/wolf duality is a fiction—that he is not two beings but thousands. Then wolf and man can join in a marriage of reason (239–40). After mulling over this message, Harry decides to give himself until his fiftieth birthday, and if the change is not forthcoming, he will be permitted to commit suicide. (Hesse himself was forty-eight when he began the novel.)

The solution to Harry's dilemma is presented in Jungian terms of individuation, and we shall now join Harry on this adventure—not forgetting that the flash of insight that caused him to be given the treatise is also Jungian. In fact, we can even determine what prompted the flash of insight, for no sooner does Harry finish reading the treatise then he recalls having written a poem several weeks earlier in which he asked the very question that has now been answered for him: "Am I separated from everything that makes life a little happier?" (252). In other words, Harry's subconscious mind has been working on the problem.

Thus, Harry has been told that he can coexist with his diverse compatriots, that he is of immortal caliber himself and must make the decision to accept the challenge. But Harry fails his first test when he is invited to a professor friend's for dinner. He has no more than arrived before the professor scoffingly reads him an article by a namesake; someone called Haller has written an unpatriotic piece, but it does not occur to the professor that this very man is standing before him. Harry, in turn, insults the professor's wife by finding fault with one of her favorite possessions, a picture of Goethe in a vain and noble and most sentimental pose. He asks how one can dare to present the prince of poets in this manner (269). His hostess is deeply offended. Harry has obviously not taken the message of the treatise seriously and simply smiled quietly to himself regarding her bourgeois taste. He leaves the house in disgust after informing the professor that he, himself, is the "traitor" Haller who wrote the newspaper article, and the country and the world would be a far better place if the few people who were capable of thought—for example, the professor—would join the side of reason and peace rather than sailing blindly forth into a new war.

Harry's sense of humor appears to be nonexistent, and as he leaves the house, he decides on suicide. Tonight it will be the razor, despite his previous decision to wait until his fiftieth birthday. In prayerful language he cries out silently, "Oh father and mother [and we should note the duality], oh distant, holy fires of my youth . . . Nothing has remained" (271). This juncture in the novel is the Jungian meeting with the self. Harry is at his lowest ebb: is it to be suicide or rebirth? He wants it to be death, but the razor frightens him. He is drawn through the streets to wander into an unfamiliar bar, the Black Eagle. Here he sits down next to a girl who takes him in hand. She seems to know exactly what he feels, what he needs, and she even reminds him of someone out of his youth. She, like the treatise, chides him unmercifully for thinking he has tried so hard to live when he confesses that he has never even tried to dance.[8] He marvels at her voice—a good, deep, motherly voice.

Hermine, as the girl is eventually identified, becomes Harry's guide into the "deep chaos of his soul," a Demian-like figure (Mileck calls her "Haller's *Daimon*" [*Life and Art* 191]), but this time the Jungian guise is more explicit. To give the narrative some semblance of reality, however, Hesse has clothed the Jungian *anima*—the male's feminine self, the bridge to the unconscious—in external form and given her a real role to play. Jung explains: "As long as man is unconscious of his anima, she is frequently projected upon a real woman, and the man's fantasy equips her with all the fascinating qualities peculiar to the anima" (52). Hesse leaves little doubt that Hermine plays precisely such a role, for he tells us, even during their first meeting, that her thoughts are Harry's thoughts (346).

Obeying Hermine's order, Harry sleeps while she dances with someone else, and he dreams of interviewing Goethe, accusing the venerable poet of seeing through the facade of life, recognizing its despair and meaninglessness, and yet preaching the opposite—faith and optimism (284). As did the treatise, Goethe chides Harry for taking life too seriously. Reminiscent of a *Siddhartha* theme, Goethe says that seriousness occurs when we overvalue time. Eternity has no time, only the moment exists, and it is just long enough for a bit of fun. So all that Harry has been told about laughing at life—that humor is what makes it bearable—is reinforced by the immortal Goethe in the dream, another Jungian-Freudian messenger from the unconscious. When Harry awakens, Hermine returns to the Goethe story at the professor's, which Harry had told her. She feels the same about depictions of the saints as he had felt about the Goethe likeness. She despises the stupid representations of Mary, St. Stephen, St. Francis, and others, just as Harry despised the sentimentality of the Goethe picture. But she knows that these are just human pictures and do not approach the original. This statement is a subtle reflection of a *Demian* theme, where Hesse accused the church of obscuring the essence of Christianity with its facades.

As Harry lies down to sleep that night—in a room at the tavern rather than at home where the razor awaits him—he feels that "[s]uddenly there was an open door [reminding the reader of the Magic Theater door] through which life was coming in to [him] once more" (290). As he tries to slink unseen into his room the next day, his landlady tells him, "You shouldn't feel like a foreign body in my house. You should live the way you want to" (292–3). Thus, it seems, the bourgeois world has always been holding its doors open to Harry.

From this point on, Harry submits to Hermine's direction. At their next meeting, he insists on knowing her name, and she makes him guess. Does she not sometimes have a boy's face, she asks (296), that "speaks to him" and "reminds him of his own boyhood" and of his friend Hermann? "If you were a boy," he says, "your name would be Hermann." "Who knows, perhaps I am one and simply disguised," she answers. Thus, he correctly guesses Hermine. The unlikely exchange is again meant to draw our attention to Hermine's real role. By reminding Harry of his childhood, she is reminding him of a time when he accepted life without the myriad questions he now wants answered. (Remember that, after leaving the professor's, Harry had cried out to the "distant, holy fires of my youth.") Hesse playfully brings a personal note into the game by using his own name, Hermann, for Harry's boyhood friend, and its relationship to the name Hermine is obvious. Hermine's suggestion that she is a boy in disguise emphasizes her Demian-like, alter-ego role, or, in this case, the Jungian *anima*—speaking to Harry through his inner voice. He even calls her face a "magic mirror" (298). The implication is that she will help Harry to return to a stage of innocence so that he can again live in accord with the world, but this time, obviously, at a higher level of understanding. At this meeting Hermine tells Harry that he will follow her many orders and enjoy doing so, that he will finally fall in love with her, and that she will then give him her last order. Harry suspects what it will be even before she tells him—he will kill her, a strange situation to say the least, and we should be suspicious that the meaning of her death will be cloaked in metaphor.

They buy a phonograph, and Harry learns to dance. When Hermine tells him to ask another woman to dance, Harry is hesitant, and she tells him, "Anyone who approaches a girl risks being laughed at" (312). (This is an utterance we should keep in mind for later novels, for the meaning of the masculine-feminine metaphor, begun in *Demian,* will become even clearer.) The girl turns out to be Maria, a friend and "colleague" of Hermine, and from more intimate moments with her, yet to come, Harry learns that sex is a natural part of life and need not be accompanied by feelings of guilt. The name Maria—that is, Mary—carries the implication of purity, thus expressing Harry's acceptance of the sensual side of feminine life which he could equate earlier only with guilt, temptation, and with his Steppenwolf nature.

Even more important than Maria is another friend of Hermine. He is Pablo, an exotic, handsome young musician who "plays all instruments" and "speaks all languages" (311). Harry does not like him at first. When he tries to draw Pablo into an intellectual conversation about the nature of jazz, the musician just smiles at him (reminiscent of Vasudeva smiling knowingly at Siddhartha), and Harry comes to the conclusion that he has no other purpose in the world than to look handsome and to please the ladies; he has no problems, no thoughts (314)—little different from Siddhartha's first impression of Vasudeva. But Harry will change his mind. In a later conversation, Pablo explains that Harry's lofty thoughts about music are all true, but it does not matter. The only important thing is to "make music"—in other words, to "live life" (323). When Harry argues that there is spiritual as well as sensual music, Pablo does not dispute him. This they can leave to God (324), again an indication that the inner voice will direct everyone according to plan. Pablo is also an expert at mixing drugs and introduces Harry to his products, and at one point while they are relaxing, he suggests a three-way love game for himself, Harry, and Maria, which Harry, somewhat shocked, turns down (not, however, without feeling a twinge of interest). He also discovers that Maria and Hermine are lovers, which does not disturb him now. For 1927, these were sensual and erotic extremes. Why did Hesse use this tone in the novel? There are two answers. Realistically, he is simply emphasizing that such extremes exist. If Harry is to live in the world, to accept it at face value, he must be able to laugh at what goes on. Metaphorically, Pablo's suggestion foreshadows the three-way relationship that he, Harry, and Hermine will eventually have. Just as Pistorius could not fill the shoes of Demian, Maria does have the full complement of "anima" qualities that Hermine possesses. Pablo, with his primitive music that arouses the rawest emotions, with his satchel full of drugs that can dispel any and all inhibitions—at this stage of the narrative—is Hesse's attempt to personify the sensual depth of the Jungian unconscious, where primitive urges and instincts lurk in everyone.[9] With the help of Hermine, who acts as a bridge to this netherworld, Harry must first sample its offerings before learning how it can coexist with his loftier concept of life. To be whole human beings, Hesse discovered in Jung, we must connect with both ends of the spectrum and consciously balance our personalities. Only then will we not break when life "hammers at us." Only then we can we see the humor of this game of life. This is individuation. Will Harry reach such heights?

His final test in the novel occurs at a Fasching ball—what better place to see the bourgeois world in full abandon? Hermine will be waiting for him there but will not tell Harry what her disguise will be, and Maria already has an escort, so Harry must, as should be expected, face the lively scene alone. And, since he is to learn to be himself, he does not go in costume. The ball is to be held at the Globe Hall—what better place to see the world? Hesse's description of his own life during the winter of 1925–1926 personalizes this culminating experience of the novel, in which Harry is to be challenged to accept what he has learned. Hesse, himself, attended a masked ball for the first time in his life and commented that "this whole winter . . . I've been leading a by no means saintly and model life, but after long years of loneliness, I've rubbed myself vigorously against the world again and tasted its colorful outer side, to which, naturally, women and even the simpler of the modern dances belong. It was a marvelous time; while . . . I was running around everywhere among the superficial pleasures of the modern world that I . . . hadn't known before . . . I was constantly occupied with the most difficult problem" (*GB II* 139).

The problem, from all indications, is his suicide-or-life decision, which he had mentioned repeatedly in letters, but it appears that after this wild living, he can, in fact, joke about suicide: "When Fasching is over, I'm going to kill myself out of regret that I was a bigger-than-life idiot and wasted my whole life. I was a real 'Foxtrot fool'[10] for wearing myself out for thirty years over the problems of mankind without knowing what a masked ball was . . . what friends I have that would let me run around that way for decades! But, Hubacher [to whom the letter is addressed], everything will be forgiven if you take me to a ball again soon. . . . Lord God, if I only knew that beautiful girl's name from yesterday. I have to trot another fox with her" (*GB II* 130). It would appear that Hesse, himself, was learning not only to laugh at bourgeois life but even to enjoy it.

Harry's magic day is now tomorrow. During a long conversation, Hermine summarizes the learning experiences he has undergone—his apprenticeship. He has been an artist and a thinker, one of those with a "dimension too many" (344) for whom "this world is not a home" (343). Only death and eternity belong to such rarities as they, and they could not live if there were "not another air to breathe, if not outside of time, eternity did not exist, which is the kingdom of reality. To it belong the music of Mozart and the poems of . . . great poets, to it belong the saints who have performed miracles, who have suffered martyrdom and been great examples to mankind. But to this eternity also belong the images of every great deed, the strength of every genuine feeling, even if no one knows of them" (345). Those who belong to this world are the "Community of Saints [the "Cains" of *Demian*] . . . the genuine people, the younger brothers of the Savior" (345), and, says Hermine, it is "toward them that we strive all of our lives, with every good deed, every brave thought, every love" (*IV* 345–6).

When she has finished her discourse, Harry says, "Perhaps, so it seemed to me, these were not her own thoughts but mine" (346), and again we have Hesse's overt sign that Hermine's voice speaks Harry's thoughts, fulfilling the Jungian role of the bridge to the unconscious, revealing truths that have been surfacing slowly in Harry's own mind. He now has learned what he was supposed to learn from Hermine: "The world of the divine, the timeless, the world of eternal values, of divine substance, had been given back to me today by my friend and dancing teacher" (346). We can now understand that Harry no longer needs Hermine, and we recall what her final command will be.

He spends a last night with Maria. It is the tenderest and most meaningful of their love-making experiences, and it clarifies her symbolic role: "From her I had learned once more . . . to give myself in child-like fashion to the play on the surface [of life], to seek the most fleeting pleasures, to be a child and an animal in the innocence of sex" (350). He returns home to sleep all day and, like Faust after the Gretchen episode, awakens to prepare for his new life. Since it is still early, he goes to a movie, *The Ten Commandments,* watches the Red Sea open up for Moses, and comments, "My God, to guard against this obscenity even the Jews and all the other people should have gone under as well as the Egyptians" (355). Casebeer sees Moses as "another immortal, a hero with whom Harry identifies" (77). In other words, Cecil B. DeMille has cheapened the meaning of the mystery with his film magic, just as Sinclair had felt the pastor was doing with literal biblical interpretation.

When Harry arrives at the ball, festivities are in full swing, and the spectacle is almost too much for the aging man. After a fruitless search for Hermine, the grinning Steppenwolf in Harry starts to make his presence felt, and he decides to leave, even if Hermine may not forgive him, but his coat-check stub appears to be lost. As he fumbles through his pockets, a "little devil" gives him his. Harry finds no number on it but, instead, an inscription:

Tonight beginning at 4, Magic Theater
—only for the mad
Admission costs you your reason
Not for everyone. Hermine is in Hell. (357)

Harry is rejuvenated! But in Hell he looks from one end to the other and cannot find her, finally sitting down beside a handsome young boy who eyes him mockingly. After studying his profile, Harry exclaims "Hermann!" but it is Hermine who answers: "Have you found me?" (359). Harry is surprised: "Is this the costume in which you're going to make me fall in love with you?" They both dance with other women, trying to see who can be most successful in their conquests. Hermine cheers up a sad young girl, disappearing behind an arbor and telling Harry she had used the "Magic of Lesbos" to conquer her, which emphasizes the bisexuality of her role in the novel—that is, an embodiment of Harry's anima, his feminine self. During the Fasching ball, Harry comes to understand fully the secret of the "destruction of the self in the crowd" (361): he understands and accepts that most people have little interest in his divine vision; they actually find meaning in what, to him, is a superficial life.

Harry suddenly realizes that Hermine has disappeared, "not only from sight but even from [his] thoughts" (364), and again Hesse is pointing out that Harry no longer needs her. He is drawn, however, to a new figure, a charming Pierrette in black costume and white-painted face, a death-like figure, even though she is beautiful. As he dances with her, he discovers it is Hermine, no longer Hermann, and her conquest is made; he is in love with her, he belongs to her, and they dance their "nuptial dance" (*Hochzeitstanz*) (365) on and on, until Hermine asks, "Are you ready?" Pablo, whose band has been playing at the ball, appears in the doorway and announces: "Brother Harry, I invite you to a little entertainment. Admission only for the mad, it costs your reason" (367). With Hermine on one arm and Harry on the other, Pablo leads them to a small, round, cavern-like room with blue lighting and a rarefied atmosphere reminiscent—at least for those versed in German literary history—of both the love grotto of Tristan and Isolde and the ice cave of Stifter's *Bergkristall,* where two children, lost in a blizzard, were miraculously saved on Christmas Eve.

Harry wonders why Pablo is talking so much: "Was it perhaps not I that made him speak, I who was speaking out of him? Wasn't it my soul looking at me out of his dark eyes . . . just as out of Hermine's grey eyes?" (367). Now the Jungian trio is drawing together. Both Pablo and Hermine speak Harry's thoughts as personified component parts of Harry's psyche. To make Harry a whole, strong person, all must live in harmony. We shall see shortly how the union is accomplished, but before the final act, we will witness the symbolic psychic enlightenment process that Harry is undergoing. Pablo produces three glasses, fills them with a sweet-tasting liquid, and presents each of his companions with a long, thin, yellow cigarette; Harry's initiation ceremony begins.[11] Pablo invites Harry into a world without time, a variation of Siddhartha's enlightening experience as he listened to the river whisper its secrets. And, as if painting a Jungian picture of the collective unconscious itself, he adds, "You indeed know where this other world lies hidden, that it is the world of your own soul that you are seeking. . . . I can't give you anything that doesn't already exist in you, I can't open any other portrait gallery than the one in your soul" (368–9). He has Harry look into a little round mirror, saying, "This is how you have seen yourself up until now," and Harry sees his own blurred image and within it a sad, hungry, anxious wolf. Now he is to go with Pablo into his little theater to see more.

Thus, the Magic Theater adventure into the self begins. A passageway leads past countless small doors, as many as he wants, a hundred, a thousand, says Pablo. In other words, Harry is now aware of his myriad personalities. But first he must check his own established personality in the cloak room. It is the purpose of this little venture, adds Pablo, to teach Harry to laugh, and all "higher humor" begins when one no longer takes his own person seriously (371). Harry faces a huge, wall-sized mirror where hundreds of Harrys flit before his eyes— young, old, ragged, naked, bald—and finally a sixteen- or seventeen-year-old jumps out, runs down the corridor, and enters a door labeled "All Girls are Yours! Insert One Mark!" The boy himself dives into the slot and disappears. Now Harry, sans the rigidity of his established personality, is alone in the corridor, and he enters a doorway marked "Off to Happy Hunting! High Hunt for Automobiles!"

Behind the door, Harry sees cars running down pedestrians and recognizes immediately the long-expected battle between humans and machines. There are corpses and burning, wrecked automobiles strewn everywhere. People are shooting at cars, even at airplanes, from roofs and windows. Placards tell people to destroy the machines, to let the world of cement become a world of forests and fields again. Others tell humankind that the machines will help them to become gods (374–5)—and we recall the false gods of Hesse's earlier essay, "Dream of the Gods." Harry joins an old school friend, Gustav, in shooting at automobiles and is amazed that he finds it such fun, since he used to be a pacifist. Someday humankind will learn to control the population by rational means, but for now they must react to the unbearable circumstances a bit irrationally— they are "reducing." In the pocket of one of his victims, Harry finds a card that says, "Tat twam asi" ("Thou art this")—that is, Harry, as well as everyone, is both predator and victim.

Eventually, a safety rail breaks, and Harry plunges into emptiness, finding himself back in the corridor facing the hundreds of doors, each with its inscription. He chooses "Instruction for Building the Personality / Success Guaranteed!" Here he finds a man sitting cross-legged before a chessboard. The man takes a few dozen chess men and explains the human psyche: the concept that a person is a constant unity, that there is a unique lifetime order of the many "I's," is wrong. Teachers and educators simplify by professing that there is such an order. Here, in this theater, they show those who have experienced the disintegration of personality how they can put it back together at any time in any kind of scenario (387–8). Harry watches as the man quickly places the figures in one configuration after another, in a tense, active drama. Finally, Harry is given the pieces and told he can play his own games of life any way he wants to in the future. Back in the hallway, he sees another sign—"Miracle of Steppenwolf Training"—and enters. An animal trainer is standing on the stage holding a wolf on a leash. He puts the beast through a series of tricks, showing that he is in complete control. The poor wolf has been taught to deny his own nature completely. Then the roles are reversed. The trainer, who looks like Harry, himself, plays dead, lets his tongue hang out, lets the wolf ride on his back, and lets himself be humiliated in every way. As a grand finale, he devours a live rabbit and a lamb, and Harry rushes away with the taste of blood in his mouth. The Magic Theater is no paradise, he realizes (391).

Now he stands before the door marked "All Girls are Yours" and remembers that his sixteen-year-old personality had thrown itself into the coin slot. He enters and feels himself in the atmosphere of his youth. His head is full of Latin and Greek, of poetry, and fantasies of his dream to become an artist, but stronger than any of these is the smoldering fire of love, sexual hunger, gnawing forebodings of lust (393), which he had obviously suppressed in his "first life." He finds his youthful self walking down a hill and remembers how Rosa Kreisler, his first love, had approached him and how he had tremblingly said hello, how both had blushed and walked on. But this time he has the courage to talk to her, and they spend innocent hours holding hands, walking, sitting in the grass, and picking flowers. Other girls from his past appear, and he loves each as he should have the first time. Had he actually lived these scenes, Maria would not have been necessary.

After all of this he is prepared for Hermine, and he reads the next inscription, "How One Kills through Love" (399). Suddenly he recalls that he was to fall in love with her and then kill her. He is filled with anxiety and reaches into his pocket for some of his figures in order to "rearrange his chessboard," but when he pulls out his hand, he is gripping a knife (400). He hears strains of music from *Don Juan*—the heartless lover—coming from within the theater. He hears "ice-cold" laughter and sees Mozart approaching him. Mozart points out a venerable old man who is passing by followed by ten thousand others in black dress. Mozart explains that the thousands are, according to divine judgment, the singers and players of all of those voices and notes who have participated in Brahms' oppressive attempt to strive for salvation. Wagner follows with the same type of parade. Harry is shocked that they should have to atone personally just because too heavy instrumentation was an "error of their time" (402). But Mozart explains that all must atone for the guilt of their time, and only then will it be determined if there is anything personal left over that calls for atonement. After all, he adds, they cannot do anything about the fact that Adam ate the apple, but they still must atone for it (403).

Harry thinks this terrible, but Mozart tells him that life is always terrible; we are, nevertheless, responsible for it (403). Harry suddenly sees himself trudging through purgatory, loaded down with all the books and essays he has written, followed by all the typesetters and readers who have had to swallow them. Mozart reads his thoughts and begins mocking him in doggerel verse until Harry grabs him by the pigtail and twirls him around until both are flying through the ice-cold world of the immortals. Then he suddenly finds himself confused and exhausted on the floor of the corridor.

He pulls himself together and wanders on until he stands before the final door. Behind it, he finds Pablo and Hermine lying naked and asleep, exhausted from love-making. Without emotion, Harry plunges a knife under her breast and sits watching while she moves only slightly and then is still. After a while Pablo awakens, stretches a bit, then smiles when he sees Hermine's body. He covers her with the carpet and leaves the loge; shortly, Mozart opens the door, but he is without his pigtail and dressed in contemporary clothing. He sits down and starts assembling something, which eventually becomes a radio. When he turns it on, a Handel concerto is barely distinguishable behind all the static distortion of a 1926 radio broadcast. "My God, Mozart, does this have to be?" Harry asks. But there is method to Mozart's madness, and he explains to Harry that this performance is a metaphor for life itself—the primeval struggle between idea and appearance, between eternity and time, between the divine and the human (409). Just as the static of the radio cannot destroy the divine spirit of the music, neither can daily living destroy the divine essence behind life. We should learn to take seriously what is worth taking seriously and laugh at the rest (410). And now he calls upon Harry to pay the consequences of Hermine's murder. Harry cries out that he wants to pay the price, wants to put his head on the block, and Mozart looks at him with scorn. How pathetic he is! He has supposedly just learned to laugh at life—and death. But he will learn; humor is always gallows humor (411).

Suddenly Harry sees another inscription—"Harry's Execution!"—and finds himself in a barren courtyard with barred windows, a guillotine, and a dozen men in frock coats. Mozart presents his case: Harry is guilty of wanton misuse of their Magic Theater. He has not only insulted high art by confusing their beautiful picture gallery with so-called reality, he has not only stabbed the reflection of a girl with the reflection of a knife, but he has also revealed his intention of using their theater humorlessly as a setting for suicide. (We should recall Hesse's own craving for suicide, which helps to reveal the ironical content of this scene.) Without even waiting for a comment from his jurors—apparently the immortals are all of one mind—the prosecutor sentences Harry to eternal life but denies him entrance to their theater for twelve hours, and now he is to be laughed out of court. All the jurors chime in with the "unbearable laughter of the other side" (412). When Harry finally comes to his senses again, Mozart tells him that he will get used to hearing the radio music of life and will revere the spirit behind it. He will learn to laugh (*IV* 413). "And if I refuse?" Harry asks from behind clenched teeth. "Then I would suggest that you smoke another of my cigarettes," Mozart answers, but he is suddenly Pablo, who scolds him a bit for staining his world of images with spots of reality. He hopes it was at least jealousy when Harry saw Pablo and Hermine lying together. Harry did not really understand how to "have intercourse" with Hermine, but this can be corrected, Pablo chides, as he picks up Hermine, who immediately turns into one of the toy figures, and puts her into his vest pocket (414).

Harry grasps everything—he understands Pablo, Mozart; hears their laughter; knows that all 100 thousand figures of the game of life are in his pocket; is ready to begin again to taste life's torments, to wander through his own inner hell again and often (415). As a fitting conclusion to the novel, he might have added: "The Steppenwolf is dead! Long live the Steppenwolf!"

Hesse has painted a metaphorical picture of Jungian integration of personality. Even though he used the same stylistic technique to carry Sinclair into the world of the Cains, Harry Haller's approach to the world of the immortals is more explicit and tightly drawn in terms of narrative structure. Hermine is a textbook example of the anima, and Pablo is the personified spokesman for the collective unconscious, who, via musical metaphors, bears the gospel that a synthesis between Harry's intellectual world and the enemy—the sensual, bourgeois world—does exist. Pablo and Frau Eva are but two sides of the same coin. It need not be confusing that one, at the narrative level, is feminine and the other masculine. Pablo "speaks all languages" (not "many," as Rockwood notes [50]), "plays all instruments," is both the jazz musician Pablo and Mozart, and is bisexual. Frau Eva, in the painting, was both man and woman. Neither need be a particular archetype—a condition that has proven problematic to *Steppenwolf* interpretation.[12] Hesse was interested only in providing Harry Haller access to "the hot line" to his inner self and makes it clear that both Hermine and Pablo are "speaking Harry's thoughts." The fact that Hermine introduces Harry to the musician indicates that the Pablo/Harry connection has need of a go-between. To become a whole person in the Jungian sense, Harry must discover how to reach into his collective unconscious, must be aware when its demands are affecting him, and must continually strive to balance them against other drives, desires, and feelings. Hermine has made this communication possible, and when the story is over, Harry no longer needs her help to bridge the gap; he can kill the imaginary girl. But the death takes place only at the narrative level; at the symbolic level, she and Harry and Pablo are one. In the integration picture, Harry is the ego—the face presented to the world. He is not in costume when he goes to the ball, where he symbolically marries his anima, as the wedding dance implies (365). But Pablo must also be part of this ménage à trois, or, more properly, mariage à trois; hence, he consummates the marriage, and thus the union, the integration, is complete. The two symbolic figures have appeared out of the Jungian world to merge with Harry's consciousness, and he can now play the game of "hammer and anvil" with life, the game of "open conflict and collaboration," and, according to Jung, "the suffering that results shapes the individual into an unbreakable whole" (27).

Horrocks misses the Jungian implication of Hermine's death, finding that it "suggests that [Harry] still has not overcome his sense of disgust, still cannot cope with his sexuality" (142). Had Hesse not meant the denouement of his novel to profess optimism, the immortals would have sentenced Harry to death for the murder, but instead they sentence him to eternal life. He can now live in the bourgeois world, and its gods will not destroy the eternal values behind it. He now knows that Mozart and Pablo are one. By barring Harry's entrance into the Magic Theater for twelve hours, Hesse is simply saying that the grand entrance to the divine world can be made only at death, a concept that will be made still clearer in the conclusion of *The Glass Bead Game*. After all, the immortals need no longer participate in the games of life, but until that final step is taken, the Cains of the world—the immortals in the making—still must cope, to the very end, with the growlings of the Steppenwolf. Horrocks overlooks this nuance here, as well: "Haller's stabbing to death of Hermine . . . and his subsequent desire to do penance by being executed as a murderer both demonstrate his failure to achieve this ideal aesthetic distance" (143).

Harry has accomplished what his inner voice has told him would be possible. He has learned to pick up his bed and walk—no different from Jung's hammer and anvil metaphor. The ending illustrates how aptly Rose entitled his Hesse study, "Faith from the Abyss."[13] Most critics, however, who have tried to take Hesse at his word and find the ending positive usually find themselves expressing reservations.[14] If we cannot easily grasp Hesse's affirmation of faith, it is an indication of how strongly we would all like the Garden of Eden to reopen its doors to this world, but according to Hesse's self-directed irony, life demands that we laugh not only at the distorted music, itself, but also at how seriously we listen to it.

CHAPTER TEN

Narcissus and Goldmund

The Artist Creator

Hesse's inner turmoil seems to have lessened slightly as a result of his cathartic outpourings in *Der Steppenwolf*. His own fiftieth birthday, which he had fictionally portrayed as a to-be-or-not-to-be deadline for Harry Haller, was made much of. One of his closest friends, the historian Hugo Ball, completed the first Hesse biography,[1] but Ball barely survived his effort, succumbing to stomach cancer on September 14, 1927. Hesse felt the loss acutely, even though he had known Ball only since 1920, calling him "the only person who stood spiritually close to me, who understood my language completely, with whom I could speak about spiritual matters" (*GB II* 186).

Hesse was somewhat surprised at the attention being paid him and complained bitterly to his sister, Adele: "If I had suspected what this fiftieth birthday would bring, I would have suppressed everything from the beginning, even Ball's book. Every few days something new comes along, the publishers want to make money from the occasion, composers want to publish songs [set his poems to music], painters want to etch and paint me . . . the mayor of Konstanz wants my . . . presence at a Hesse festival on July 2, etc. It's enough to make you vomit" (*GB II* 163). He refused the mayor's invitation, responding firmly: "I regret that it is absolutely impossible for me to accept any public honors. I live outside of society and have to live . . . in my own way, accommodations to fit the world aren't possible" (*GB II* 181). He even received a letter from an admirer in Japan telling him that he was their "most trusted European writer" (*GBII* 180).

Something new was about to happen, however. Nearly twenty years earlier, a fourteen-year-old girl had written a letter of admiration to the budding author, and over the years they had kept in occasional contact, meeting briefly for the first time in the summer of 1922.[2] Ninon Ausländer was an art historian living in Vienna, married but separated from the painter and caricaturist Fred Dolbin. Hesse mentions her for the first time in his published letters on February 4, 1927, calling her "a friend visiting me from Vienna." By May he was calling her "my sweetheart." From now on, Ninon would be a frequent companion and eventually become Hesse's third wife.

By the end of 1927, Hesse was at work on a new novel, which would be published as *Narcissus and Goldmund* but to which he referred constantly as his "Goldmund." On April 9, 1929, he could finally report that it had been polished and was going to the publisher (*GB II* 212). The setting is medieval Europe. The introductory paragraph is saturated with subtle sensual and sexual metaphors,[3] most of which perish in the loins of English translation. Hesse has crowded the first 198 words into two sentences—a stylistic clue to the duality motif, which will continue throughout the novel. The adjective-rich paragraph describes two objects: the Mariabronn Cloister and a chestnut tree brought from Rome by a pilgrim in times past, which stands in front of the archway entrance. The imagery is overtly masculine-feminine and more than subtly erotic. The masculine cloister name Maulbronn of *Beneath the Wheel* has become Mariabronn. *Bronn* (fountain) is grammatically masculine and, thus combined with Maria, gives a bisexual connotation to the cloister itself.[4] The same is done with the tree, which is once described as *der Kastanienbaum* (the chestnut tree), the word being grammatically masculine and called "a lone son of the south," and then labeled *eine Edelkastanie* (a noble chestnut), now grammatically feminine.[5] It has a *starker Stamm* (sturdy trunk) with a *runde Krone* (a round crown), and it breathes *breitbrüstig* (broad-breastedly) in the wind. In the spring when the nut trees in the cloister still bear their *rötliches Junglaub* (reddish, virginal foliage), the chestnut tree sends whitish-green jets upward out of its leaf clusters. In the fall when the harvests are over, prickly fruits fall from the yellowing crown. In a final biological image of pollination, the beautiful tree lets its crown wave gently and strangely over the entrance to the cloister—a round portal supported by the two slender pillars (*GS V* 9).

Even though the mother/father, masculine/feminine imagery has clearly been a thematic emphasis since *Demian,* Hesse is now expanding its sensual nuances and alluding to a distinctly (bi)sexual kinship between the cloister—with which the masculine qualities of discipline, order, learning, religious dedication, and devotion are immediately associated—and the tree, which symbolizes life, growth, beauty, death, and rebirth—in short, everything we associate with the inner workings of nature, gifts of the primal mother. These are, to Hesse, feminine.[6] The tree's southern origins even add an exotic dimension.

To continue the duality theme, Hesse uses a host of contrasting correlatives to describe the inhabitants and the activities of the cloister: art/science, pious/worldly, dark/light, folk beliefs/mockery thereof, simplicity/craftiness, wisdom of the gospels/wisdom of the Greeks, and white magic/black magic. "There is room for everything," he adds, "all depends upon the current abbot or the dominant signs of the times" (10), reminding us of the treatise's statement in *Der*

Steppenwolf that good citizens can burn a heretic today and build a monument to him tomorrow (*GS IV* 247). In other words, simplistic duality concepts may change as the cloister leadership or *Weltanschauung* changes with the times, an observation to be recalled when we become familiar with Joseph Knecht's role as Magister Ludi of Castalia in *The Glass Bead Game.*

At present there are two opposites in the cloister, the old abbot Daniel and the novitiate Narcissus. The abbot is "full of goodness, full of simplicity, full of humility, but he is not a scholar." Narcissus, on the other hand, is a brilliant young man "with elegant Greek, faultless courtly manners . . . with whom many are in love" (11). Again we sense the homosexual connotation of the language, but by now we should be aware that Hesse often uses such expressions of love to imply allurement, meaning, in this context, that there is something all too enticing about Narcissus's brilliance. And we see immediately what this danger is, for Narcissus feels that he is fated to rule men because he has a special gift to know others, to see into them, and he proves it to the abbot by telling the old man exactly what kind of person he is, what his feelings are, what he is thinking. Hesse is emphasizing that intellect can rule. Narcissus is proud, as the name implies, whether it is a conscious pride or not—the epitome of what humanity always thinks the individual capable, if he is sufficiently intelligent and studious. Since Narcissus is but a predecessor to the more advanced Joseph Knecht of *The Glass Bead Game,* he is less of a visionary. He is afraid of the other side of life: "at the first call, the first fleeting brush with the life of the senses, with the first greeting from femininity, he irresistibly felt that woman was a danger" (*GS V* 34). The abbot warns him that "God demands much more of us than to have visions" (15).

It is into this medieval cloister setting, in early spring, that a new pupil is delivered. Goldmund arrives with his father, a nameless imperial official who is neither seen nor heard of again, but the reader is informed, piecemeal as the novel progresses, that he intends his son to remain in the cloister for life to atone for the sins of his mother, a beautiful dancer of high but pagan birth whom the father had married—so he would have it known—in order to give her a respectable life. But she again succumbed to the call of the wild, abandoned her family when Goldmund was a small child, and is now nothing more than a repressed memory. In accord with the father's wishes, the young boy willingly enters Mariabronn with the dream and intention of devoting himself to an ascetic Christian life.[7]

A close relationship, bordering on dangerous in the eyes of the abbot, soon develops between Narcissus and Goldmund, but the abbot allows it to continue. After the newcomer has been a student for some time, he is invited by several other boys on a forbidden, late-night adventure into the village, where they visit girls. When it comes time to depart, one of the girls kisses Goldmund, and the experience affects him so strongly that he is nearly in a state of collapse the next morning. As he lies recovering in the cloister hospital, Narcissus probes for answers, recognizes that the girl's kiss had frightened his young friend, and provides a "medieval" Freudian interpretation: "You find that a woman, that sex, represents everything that you call 'world' and 'sin'" (39). And in symbolic language reminiscent of *Demian,* he continues to himself: "It was Eve, the original mother, that stood behind it. . . . There must have been a demon at work, a secret enemy, who succeeded in dividing this splendid person, to separate him from his instinctive drives . . . the demon must be found . . . then conquered" (40).

As Goldmund gradually gives up his desire to follow in Narcissus's footsteps (that is, to succumb to the lure of intellectual aloofness), the latter points out that their goals are not to become like each other but to recognize each other, to see and honor in each other the fact that they are opposites, yet complements (49), that they both have the same goal—to return to God (48). Thus, we have a capsule summary of the thematic investigation that Hesse is undertaking: how do intellect and senses work together in the search for God?

In the course of their conversations, Narcissus says to Goldmund: "You have forgotten your childhood," a sentence that "strikes Goldmund like an arrow." That night, in a dream-like state, he sees the image of his mother, which he has suppressed for so long, and in the days that follow, he continues to see her image. She is not only "all that was dear [to him] . . . not only a sweet . . . loving glance . . . a smile promising happiness . . . consoling caresses . . . but also everything that was frightening and dark, all the desire, all the fear, all the sins, all the misery, his birth, the inevitability of death" (65). She is "mother, madonna, and lover" (65)—descriptions little different from those in *Demian,* when Sinclair was puzzling over the dream image he was trying to paint, whose features he finally discovered in Frau Eva. In both novels, Hesse has used the onset of puberty as a time of life when the young male protagonist gradually perceives that the feminine contribution to life is more than motherly love. Behind the warmth and kindness, there is also something mysterious and forbidden. As did Sinclair, so must Goldmund search out this symbolic mother at a higher level of understanding, and we should not forget that it was the mind of Narcissus that perceived the path his friend was born to follow and urged him to take it—the proper interpretive role for the masculine component of life.

Goldmund's decision to leave the cloister is made when he is sent out to gather herbs and is seduced by a peasant girl. He promises to meet her again that night, expecting that they will roam the land together. In a final farewell conversation with Narcissus, the now "experienced lover" explains to the "innocent" Narcissus that "loving a woman, surrendering completely to her . . . is for him the pathway to life and the pathway to the meaning of life" (85). Hesse, of course, is being ironic. Having lost his virginity but hours earlier, Goldmund has excessive faith in his new-found meaning of life, which is portrayed with a touch of immortal humor. However, on the other hand, the underlying meaning of the scene—that Goldmund's search for self will entail responding to the urgings he feels—is serious and no different from Sinclair's inner voice calling out to him, no different from Siddhartha's desire to discover Siddhartha. Narcissus, conversely, is now in the final stages of his probationary period in the monastery. Thus, both are beginning their apparently separate lives, but Narcissus tells his departing friend, just as Demian had told Sinclair, "You will never find me unaccessible, when you call me in earnest and think you need me" (73)—that is, the mind side of life will always be available to interpret and find meaning in the sensual adventures Goldmund is about to embark upon.

Accordingly, for the next six or seven years, Goldmund leads the life of a vagabond. Women are drawn to him wherever he goes, and he momentarily "loves them all." He begins to think that "the meaning of his wanderings is perhaps to drive him from one woman to the next, so that his ability to know and differentiate will become refined, deeper, more complex" (107). The young lover needs to see no purpose for this ability to differentiate among feminine adventures at this point in his life.

After a year or two, he is invited by a knight to stay at his castle to help the latter write an account of a pilgrimage. Since the knight has two daughters, Lydia, eighteen, and Julie, sixteen, Goldmund readily agrees and begins his subtle courtship. Both girls are attracted to the handsome, golden-haired youth but know that they live in a different world; there can be no question of either of them marrying out of their station. (Hesse seems to have forgotten that he had introduced Goldmund's father as "an imperial official," thus implying a rank of some importance.) Only when Goldmund makes Lydia jealous by plying his seductive skills on a visiting female does Lydia gradually and grudgingly give in to the attraction she feels for him and permits the relationship to reach all but the final act. One night as she is lying beside Goldmund in his bed, the door opens and the younger Julie enters and joins them. Goldmund is beside himself with lust, but the older Lydia realizes they have gone too far and convinces her sister to leave with her, much to Goldmund's dismay. Lydia tells her father as much as she deems necessary, and the knight sends his guest packing, just as winter is setting in.

132

Hermann Hesse's birthplace in the Black Forest city of Calw. Photograph by Lewis W. Tusken, summer 1995.

Hesse's beloved Nagold River in Calw. Photograph by Lewis W. Tusken, summer 1995.

Hermann Hesse Platz in Calw. Photograph by Lewis W. Tusken, summer 1995.

The Demian Pub in Calw. Photograph by Lewis W. Tusken, summer 1995.

Hesse at age 4. Reproduced with permission of Suhrkamp Publishers, Frankfurt am Main.

The Heckenhaurer Bookstore (center building) in Tübingen, where Hesse worked from October 1895 to August 1899. Photograph by Lewis W. Tusken, summer 1995.

The "Petite Cénacle," the group comprised of Hesse (front) and his student friends in Tübingen, 1899. Reproduced with permission of Suhrkamp Publishers, Frankfurt am Main.

"The connoisseur"—Hesse, circa 1907. Reproduced with permission of Paul Rathgeber, director of the Hermann Hesse Museum in Calw.

Hesse in 1955, age 78. Reproduced with permission of Suhrkamp Publishers, Frankfurt am Main.

Bronze bust of Hesse by Otto Bänninger. On display in the Hermann Hesse Museum in Calw. Reproduced with permission of Paul Rathgeber, director of the museum.

Items from the desk of Hesse on display in the Hermann Hesse Museum in Calw. The inscription reads, "What one writes lasts forever." Reproduced with the permission of Paul Rathgeber, director of the museum.

The near orgy paints an unpleasing picture of Goldmund, as was often made clear to Hesse by shocked readers. But having followed Hesse's quest thus far, we know that the metaphorical meaning of Goldmund's escapades is what is significant. He must revel in the dark side of sensuality before learning that there is a danger to the feminine side of life, just as succumbing to intellectual pride presents a danger from the masculine side.

Goldmund must take up his wandering as before and finds that he has lost none of his appeal to the fairer sex, but he adds more than sexual experience to his life during the next several years. He watches a woman give birth and surprisingly finds that her grimaces of pain differ little from the expressions of a woman in the ecstasy of love-making. He travels for some time with an older wanderer, Victor, whom he is eventually forced to kill in order to prevent Victor from killing him. He feels that there is little left for him to experience. He knows the desire and pains of the homeless; he knows "loneliness, freedom, the sounds of the forest and its creatures, faithless love, bitter, deadly want . . . the fear of death and the nearness of death, and above all that the strongest, the strangest experience had been to defend oneself against death . . . and . . . in the final desperate battle with death to feel this beautiful terrible strength and tenacity of life" (147)—a phrase that will be repeated with new meaning in the conclusion of *The Glass Bead Game*.

One night Goldmund finds shelter in a cloister and dreams of ridding himself of his past and of changing his life—his one-sided existence is losing its meaning. The next morning he confesses for the first time in many years, and as he is leaving the church, a statue catches his eye. It is the Mother of God, and he stands transfixed before it. He learns from the priest that the sculptor is a Master Niklaus who lives in the bishop's city. Goldmund must find him.

It is easy to overlook precisely what it is in the sculpture that so enraptures Goldmund, but Hesse stresses that "so much pain" and "so much sweetness" blend into each other until "all sorrow has become complete happiness and smiles"—the same symbolic message reflected in *Siddhartha*'s river. In other words, the artwork is a unity of all feminine attributes of life in harmony, but whence the synthesis? The artist must have known all of life, understood its mystery and harmony; he was someone who had the intellect, understanding, will, patience, and skill—masculine attributes—to produce them in a single image. Goldmund's experiences have led him to the same point; his mind will now drive him to express what he feels and has experienced. His cloister training and his love for Narcissus will now come into play.

After seeking out Master Niklaus, Goldmund impresses him with both an emotional and intellectual commentary on the master's Madonna and begs to be accepted as an apprentice. An apprehensive Niklaus tells him to sketch something, which Goldmund does—a likeness of his friend Narcissus, and the master is sufficiently interested to permit him to work with him. He cannot be a regular apprentice, for he is far too old, but Niklaus knows that his protégé is an artist.

The period that follows is the "happiest and least difficult time of Goldmund's life" (165). Here, Hesse is making the point that Goldmund is satisfying his creative desire, he is giving of himself, giving form to the lessons of his vagabond experience with all the love and mind-skill he can command. Thus, at this halfway point in the book, we become fully aware of Goldmund's role in the novel. He is to live life to its fullest and, out of his experiences, produce something that will share life's meaning and beauty with his fellow humans. Eavesdropping (or should it be "Evesdropping"?) on Goldmund's thoughts, we also become privy to Hesse's perception of the necessity humankind feels to leave something of itself behind. He sees that the "root of all art and perhaps everything intellectual is the fear of death. . . . We shudder before transitoriness, we look with sorrow on the wilting flowers and falling leaves and feel in our own hearts the certainty that we too are transitory. . . . If, as an artist, we create images, or, as thinkers, seek laws and formulate ideas, we are doing it to save something from the great dance of death, to produce something that will last longer than ourselves" (162–3). Art he calls a "joining of the father and mother worlds, of mind and blood" (176). "Every genuine and unequivocal work of art has this dangerous, laughing double face, the masculine-feminine, this union of instinct and pure intellect" (177). In puzzling over his endless patience for studying and learning when he had been a pupil at the monastery, Goldmund realizes that it was really his love for his mentor, Narcissus, that had "given him wings" (167), and again we see Hesse's metaphorical message: The will and desire to search for meaning, and especially to express life, derive from the mind. Narcissus inspired Goldmund just as did Niklaus. Goldmund had said to Narcissus, "How do you do it? Again and again you say words to me or ask questions that shine right into me and make me clear to myself" (70)—the same Jungian language found in *Demian* and *Der Steppenwolf.*

Eventually, Goldmund is assigned to carve a statue of a disciple, which is to be a part of a crucifixion scene. The disciple is to be John, and Goldmund carves him in Narcissus's likeness, letting all the love he feels for his friend flow into the carving. While he is working on it, another face takes form in his imagination—the face of the mother. It is not the same face that Narcissus caused him to recall, no longer a personal mother, but the face of Eve, the mother of humankind, the original worldly mother, life itself (169–70). She is the "fountain of happiness and death, she gives birth eternally, kills eternally; in her, love and cruelty are one" (176). We can expect to hear more of this mother image.

The day comes when Goldmund finishes his John sculpture, and he is empty. He has poured all of his years of wandering into the work, and he looks anew at life around him as he strolls through the fish market, where he is struck by the suffering of the dying creatures. "Why were they so dull and crude, inconceivably ignorant and stupid, why did they see nothing, neither the fishermen nor the fishmongers nor the bargaining customers, why didn't they see these mouths, the eyes showing the fish to be frightened to death, the wildly slapping tails . . . as the last tremble ran over the dying skin, and how they then lay dead and expired, stretched out, miserable pieces of flesh for the table of these satisfied gluttons" (183).

This outbreak shows that Goldmund's creator does not miss the opportunity to remind his readers that these unthinking citizens lack sensitivity. In fact, Goldmund's interior monologue on the dying fish can be seen as a step forward along Hesse's thematic continuum: Goldmund's heightened consciousness of the suffering and tragedy of death makes him doubly aware of the beauty of life and, consequently, the need to make life, itself, a contribution—a theme that will evolve into the Law of Service in the next novel, *Journey to the East.*

As he ponders his situation, Goldmund suddenly has another vision of the *Urmutter* (primal mother), "leaning over the abyss of life with a forlorn smile, smiling at the births, at the deaths, at the flowers, at the rustling autumn leaves, smiling at art, smiling at decay. Everything [was] the same for her . . ." (186). This brief insight appears to Goldmund as his fellow mortals begin to depress him, and it can be likened to a reminder from the *Steppenwolf* immortals—that he, too, must smile at all of life as does the mother of life. And to emphasize the message with an additional image, Hesse sends Goldmund to sit on the bank of the river, where he peers into the depths, where, among the rubble and garbage, he can see subtle golden flickerings, as if sunken treasures are lying in the darkness. Goldmund makes an analogy with "soul pictures," which only let themselves be perceived as distant, beautiful possibilities (189). This is what his art can reflect.

Returning to Master Niklaus, Goldmund finds him so impressed with the statue of John that he will present it to the Guild Board and insist that Goldmund be granted his master's certification. He will also offer him a position as his equal in his workshop and give him his daughter Lisbeth in marriage. When Goldmund politely and sensitively refuses, Niklaus can barely suppress his anger. He cannot believe Goldmund's explanation that he has no choice, that he is empty of inspiration and must take up his wandering again to renew himself. The parting is not cordial.

The next vagabond stage of Goldmund's life lasts several more years, and he is again completely engulfed in the "impulsive motherly primal world" (200). Eventually, he gains a traveling companion, a younger boy named Robert, and a good part of this episode in Goldmund's life is taken up with his observations of human suffering and behavior during the Black Plague, which is ravaging Europe. Just as Hesse had jumped from the psychology of the individual to mass psychology in *Der Steppenwolf* by portraying the war, so does he show here humankind's reactions to death and fear of death on a large scale. Goldmund's manly behavior is contrasted with Robert's, who is petrified of any and every contact. Goldmund is strangely drawn to the sight of so much dying and seeks out the horrors of death rather than avoiding them. He entices a young girl, Lene, to come with him and leave the horrors of the city. They find a deserted hut in the forest and live a brief and blissful life, until a lone stranger attempts to rape Lene and is killed by Goldmund. He sees the same strange ecstasy in her hate-filled, vengeful eyes as he chokes her attacker that he had seen in the eyes of the woman giving birth and in the eyes of women in the throes of love—another Hesse effort to express the similarity of deeply felt emotions, that all are the same to the mother. But the stranger has infected Lene with the plague, and Goldmund must watch her die. Hesse again attempts to show that Goldmund is learning the whispered lessons from the mother, that joy and sorrow are the same, by having Goldmund silently formulate the thought that "the world was beautiful on this tragic morning" (223). However hard Hesse tries to impart this visionary, God-like overview of life—even if the ravages of the plague are intended to show that God views the joys and sufferings of his individual creations impartially—few readers will be able to relate to it except from an abstract distance. We may no longer concern ourselves with the cruelties of ancient wars, but how often has it been asked of the twentieth-century Holocaust and other ongoing horrors: "Why does God allow this to happen?" We cannot easily distance ourselves from the present.

Following Lene's death, Goldmund is again alone and feels himself filled with images. The voice in his heart is calling him back to Master Niklaus. On his way, he again stops in a church for confession, but the priests are dead. He falls to his knees and tells God that he is a worthless human being who has wasted his youth, has killed, stolen, whored, taken bread from others. Then, in typical human fashion, he asks God why he has created humankind in such a way and led him along such paths. Are we not his children? Did not his son die for us? Are there no saints and angels to lead us? He accuses God of creating an evil world and keeping it in poor order. Why did God create the world as he did? Goldmund finds the question answered as he rises and looks around the church. There are saints and angels; they stand unmoving all around him, and he is reminded that they have been created by the hand of humans and out of human imagination—an eternal consolation and triumphal victory over death and despair (234–5). This is another example of Hesse's major theme in the novel, that art can unite the two worlds, that the artist, via the mind, can perceive and reify those divine and eternal values that lie behind worldly suffering and dejection.

The plague has run its course, but when Goldmund arrives at Master Niklaus's house, he finds that the master has died and that Lisbeth's once-beautiful face has been horribly disfigured by the plague, and he is refused entrance. He learns that the bishop fled the city when the plague began, that a certain Count Heinrich has been sent to restore order, that he is soon to leave along with his beautiful but devilish concubine, Agnes, and that negotiations are now underway with representatives of the church to prepare for the bishop's return.

Soon after Goldmund's arrival, he sees a woman—blonde with cold, blue eyes and a face filled with desire—and all of his sensuality is awakened. To measure himself against this woman, to conquer her, is a noble goal (245). The woman is Agnes, the count's mistress, and day after day he places himself in her path until she eventually asks why he is following her. Her eyes take up his challenge as he tells her that he is offering himself as a present; she may do with him as she will. She tells him she can love only men who, if necessary, will risk their lives for her, which seems to Goldmund a worthy enough challenge, and a tryst is arranged in the lady's chambers. That night, while the count is in conference with priests, Goldmund experiences his finest hour, and the lady, too, it would seem, for she begs him to return the next night. But the second evening she is uneasy, and suddenly the count's voice is heard. Goldmund flees into her closet with its outside door, but finds it locked. He has been trapped. And Agnes's last words to him were, "Don't betray me" (256–7). Seeking frantically to show evidence of a purpose for being in her closet, he heaps dresses over his arm just as the count opens the door, drawn sword in hand. Apparently believing he has caught a thief, the count has him led to the dungeon with orders to hang him in the morning. Hesse has furnished evidence, by making reference to Agnes's uneasiness and Goldmund's own outburst when he finds his exit locked from the outside—"I've been trapped!"—that somehow his presence had been made known. Agnes's contrasting mood—the fearless abandon on the first night and her suspicious behavior on the second—suggest that Hesse wants the reader to infer her treachery, that he is portraying a woman who illustrates the sameness of emotion that Goldmund discovered in women giving birth, in women making love, and in Lene's eyes as he choked her assailant. It gives Agnes no less satisfaction to cause a man to die than it does to make love to him, as her original warning to Goldmund had made clear.

As the prisoner stands between armed guards before the door leading to the dungeon, two priests approach, and one says he will come before early mass to hear his confession. Then Goldmund finds himself in a dark cell. In the night a cry escapes him: "Oh mother! Oh mother!"(263). He is not ready to die. (Goldmund has not yet lived his life fully; his father insights have not brought him so far). He works out a plan: when the priest comes, Goldmund will kill him and escape in his robes. When the door finally opens, he is ready, but as the priest enters, Goldmund recognizes the robes of the Abbot of Mariabronn. When their eyes meet, Goldmund slowly recognizes his friend Narcissus, who informs him that he is free. Only later does Goldmund realize that Narcissus must have made heavy concessions to Count Heinrich in exchange for his freedom.

As Goldmund and Narcissus journey back to Mariabronn, their conversations are dominated by serious discussions of the duality of life and their own opposing, but nonetheless complementary, natures. Goldmund, driven by his sensual urges, has followed the call of the mother, while Narcissus, driven by his intellect, has followed the call of the father. The question of God's failed creation returns, and when Goldmund gets Narcissus to admit that life is a hell, Narcissus laughingly answers that he has always honored the creator as perfect, never his creation (275).[8] Humankind must place the idea of justice in juxtaposition to original sin and attempt to measure the unfulfilled life according to this yardstick, to seek to correct evil, and constantly to place this life in relationship to God (276). Finally, too, Narcissus points out that what are images in the soul of the artist are no different from the ideas in the soul of the philosopher (279). Thus, Hesse implies that both Goldmund and Narcissus, in pursuit of their respective mother and father worlds, have the same goal. The implication is reinforced when Goldmund is once again walking through Mariabronn, reacquainting himself with its statuary: "What has been built, chiseled, painted, lived, thought and taught here over several centuries, was of one stem, one mind, and fit together like the branches of a tree" (284–5). Thus, we see the validity of the metaphor so subtly portrayed on the first page of the novel—the intercourse of cloister and tree. In another conversation, Narcissus admits that his task to realize himself here in this cloister setting has been far easier than Goldmund's, which again reveals a Hesse feeling sorry for himself; he would have preferred escape into the intellectual realm.

Narcissus supplies Goldmund with a workshop, tools, materials, and an apprentice, and the artist begins his creative work once again. Over a period of time, he produces two major works of art, one for the Mariabronn Cloister and one for a nearby chapel.[9] He begins with a stairway and pulpit for the refectory. From its base depicting the creation story, steps lead to a lectern, from which monks read scripture to their fellow monks during meals. This is an example of the symbiosis Hesse has been professing—that, out of the creation or the Earth Mother, with its images of nature, the monks rise daily to bear witness to the Father's word, the mind-stuff of life. The pulpit, itself, portrays the four evangelists—those who spread the word as best they understood it.

Goldmund's second work for a nearby chapel is a statue of Mary, her facial features patterned after those of the chaste but lusting Lydia, the knight's daughter whom Goldmund had not been able to seduce. To most observers, the figure of Mary will symbolize only her purity, as she is traditionally perceived, but by including in her features the sensual qualities of Lydia, Goldmund produces a Mary who is a synthesis of the Old Testament's Mother of Man and the New Testament's Mother of God, symbolizing but one long continuum of feminine qualities, from the temptress to divine purity; they are not separate entities. Art, Hesse repeatedly tells us in the novel, is the medium that can express their union in symbol and metaphor.

The alliance of the mother world of the senses and the father world of the mind is given yet another dimension through Hesse's choice of names for his dual protagonists. Neuswanger and Milek have both pointed out that Goldmund's name comes by translation from his patron saint, John Chrysostom,[10] a fourth-century patriarch in Constantinople who was called "golden mouthed," or, in German, *Goldmund,* because of his oratorical skills. Narcissus's name, in Hesse's novel, was changed to John when he took his final vows, unbeknownst to Goldmund, who, nevertheless, as if unconsciously aware of the change, incorporated Narcissus's features into his sculpture of the disciple John. Thus, the Johns created each other, for it was Narcissus who helped Goldmund discover his own identity.

When Goldmund's work on the two pieces is completed, he is again empty; he must go out into the world again. Narcissus provides him with new clothing and a horse, and he sets off. When he returns several months later in the fall, he looks aged and is close to death. One reason for his leaving the cloister was the rumor that Agnes was in the area. He had found her, but she had rejected him because he was now too old and not handsome enough for her anymore (319). Struck with this revelation, he had ridden on carelessly and despondently, his horse had stumbled in a stream, and he had fallen, breaking ribs and lying the entire night in the cold water. The next morning he had managed to mount his horse again and ride on until the pain was too great, then he had found a hospital and remained there until his return to the cloister. After hearing this story, Narcissus kisses him on the forehead and tells him that he loves him (316), something Goldmund has always longed to hear. Just as Demian had kissed Sinclair and said he would always be with him, in him, so does Narcissus's kiss and confession of love indicate a symbolic union. Goldmund now understands the passage of life and accepts death, no longer fearing the latter, as he did in prison. The mind-side can show us the meaningful relationship of death to life— a message to be repeated in the Joseph Knecht story.

In their final conversations, Goldmund says that he no longer believes in the beyond. The withered tree is dead forever; the frozen bird does not come to life again, nor does the human being. He is curious about death only because it is his belief that he is "on the way to his mother." Instead of a grim reaper coming with his scythe, Goldmund envisions his mother taking him in her arms again, into nothingness and innocence. Death will be a great happiness, as great as the fulfillment of the first love (318). He has not made peace with God and does not want to, because God has made the world poorly, but he has made peace with the pain in his chest. As he lay in the stream, he heard a voice laughing; it was the voice of his mother, the pains in his chest were her fingers. She has been many things in his life—his seductress Lise, the beautiful Madonna of Master Niklaus, life itself, love, passion, fear, hunger, instinct. Now, she is death (321). He tells Narcissus that it has long been his dream to create this mother in a sculpture; this was the most holy of the images he carried in him, and now he could create her if he had the strength in his hands, but she does not want him to "make her secrets visible" (321). (Compare Frau Eva's words to Sinclair: "One never reaches home" [*GS III* 232].) Instead, she wants him to die, and he will gladly die. His last comprehensible words to his friend are, "But how will you ever die, Narcissus, if you have no mother? Without a mother one cannot love. Without a mother one cannot die." The words "burn like fire in his heart" (322).

After all the effort Hesse has expended to show that Narcissus and Goldmund have the same goal and that their respective lives complement one another, such an ending to the novel seems inconsistent. He even stressed the equality of his two protagonists in later letters: "The book and its world become meaningless if you split it into halves: Narcissus is to be taken just as seriously as Goldmund" (*GS VII* 584); and "Goldmund is a whole only together with Narcissus (or in his relationship to Narcissus)" (*GB II* 275).[11]

Field's comment, that "Goldmund lived a full sensual and creative life, yet failed to create the transcendent figure of oneness, presumably because he himself lacked the *summum bonum:* synthesis of *Natur* and *Geist*" ("Polarities" 94–5), again exemplifies the difficulty we have in relating to Hesse's message that transcendence comes only with death. The message, despite its lack of complete clarity, is implicitly evident if we recall that the proud, mythical figure who was Narcissus's namesake fell in love with his reflection, pined away, and died; thus, the name alone reflects Hesse's intention to exemplify intellectual pride with his Narcissus figure. Whereas Goldmund has given form to his feminine experiences via Narcissus's masculine guidance and made meaningful and lasting contributions to the world as a result, Narcissus (his contribution to Goldmund notwithstanding, it would appear) has nought but his intellectual achievements to bring to his final judgment. It seems an unfair condemnation. The reader is left with the impression that Hesse simply liked the final sentences of his novel, intending the situation to mean that Goldmund was now doing for Narcissus what Narcissus had done for him—pointing out that he had forgotten his mother. But Hesse has painted Narcissus much too sympathetically for the analogy to be clear to the reader. This stylistic failing aside, however, just as the disciple John (whom Goldmund created for the crucifixion scene) learned his lesson of death from Christ, so will Narcissus's witnessing of Goldmund's death permit him to ponder as he awaits reincarnation in *The Glass Bead Game,* where both Joseph Knecht and Father Jakobus will inherit offices of responsibility comparable to that of Narcissus. If we now know that death is the final call and consolation of the mother world, the father's role in this most necessary transition is not yet fully clarified.

CHAPTER ELEVEN

Journey to the East

The Law of Service

Hesse had "no plans for anything new" after completion of *Narcissus and Goldmund,* as he noted in July of 1929 (*GB II* 222), but before long *Journey to the East* began to take shape. A friend, Alice Leuchthold, had read a manuscript of the new work by May of 1931 (the first time the title is mentioned in Hesse's published correspondence (*GB II* 282), and the book, the shortest of his major works, appeared in print in March of 1932.

Hesse's life appears to have been moving all too slowly toward a semblance of stoic acceptance of his fate—to follow his own inner-voice dictates despite the weak-spirited world around him. To a friend he wrote: "It is, in fact, true that the world doesn't want to know anything about spirit, and that every ideal demanding more than a polite mask is hateful to the egotism of mankind. . . . What you call progress isn't something that takes place, as is also the case with the spiritual [*geistige*] history of mankind, among the masses, but in a small minority of people of 'of good will'" (*GB II* 229). He brought the lament down to a personal level in two other letters a short time later: "I am so burningly conscious of the uselessness of a poet that I can hardly endure life" (*GB II* 234). And he adds in the second letter: "The hell in which I have constantly lived since my awakening during the war would be unbearable and only answerable with suicide, if my inner voice . . . didn't say: 'There is, despite everything, a purpose, it is an experience that is to be lived out, and a hell that must be crossed'" (*GB II* 267).

His life, it seems, was still a balancing act, a matter of faith that there was reason to endure. Plans were afoot for his third marriage to Ninon Ausländer, and a generous friend and patron, Hans Bodmer, had given Hesse leave to build a house of his own design (*GB II* 251). It was Ninon who did most of the consulting with the architect and builder, and despite a certain anxiety about the "new life," expressed in the early summer of 1931 (*GB II* 284), Hesse could report that he was "very pleased" by the time they were getting settled in September. Marriage with Ninon would prove beneficial to his health and peace of mind for the rest of his life. Hesse would become as bourgeois as it was possible for him to be, and he was undoubtedly well aware of the irony: his own allotment of worldly stability was helping him to tolerate the same, though larger-scale, bourgeois values around him.

Hesse referred to *Journey to the East* as a "fairy tale." We become very aware as we read it, because of a plethora of strange names and allusions, that it was his own fairy tale. Hesse was conscious of this fact, as he noted in the letter to Alice Leuchthold in May of 1931: "I've sometimes wondered if I wasn't a little too personal in this piece of writing and put much too much of my private thought into it." But on the basis of her response to the book, he decided that she had understood it well despite the personal references: "I see that the actual meaning and admonishment has . . . sounded clearly to you anyway" (*GB II* 282). Hesse was right to leave it as it stands. The many tributes or allusions to personal friends, painters, writers, thinkers, which will not be known to most readers, are not a hindrance to understanding the meaning of the book and add considerably to its fairy-tale tone.

The narrative begins with the attempt of a certain H. H. to tell the story of a "journey to the East" in which he was once involved. The so-called League of Journeyers, to which he belonged as a novitiate, has since dissolved, so he believes, and he looks upon himself as the lone survivor. He is hampered in his attempt to tell of the adventure because he had taken an oath not to reveal the League's secrets. Despite the difficulty this is causing him, he is determined to hold to his oath of allegiance, even if the League does not exist anymore: "No enticement and threat in the world can bring me to break my vow" (*GS VI* 10). In reiterating this determination at a later point, the narrator notes that "a happy memory flowed through him like a sunbeam" (36). Thus, we can infer that H.H.'s recollections of the big picture play the same role as did Harry Haller's magic moments—they are *Gottespuren* (traces of God) and remind him that life has meaning. Nonetheless, with such restrictions, H.H. finds himself producing a superficial account of these strange journeyers who "denounced all the common aids . . . [such as] trains, steamships, the telegraph, cars, planes, etc." (10). Despite the apparent limitations this must have imposed, certain contingents of travelers managed to "penetrate into the heroic and the magic" (10).

So what kind of a trip can this be? Even without H.H.'s pledge not to reveal certain secrets, he would have trouble explaining to most readers what the League was about, as he expresses in a poem:

> He who travels far will often see things
> Far removed from what he considers truth.
> And when he tells of it at home,
> He is often taken for a liar.

For the stubborn people will not trust him
If they cannot see it and feel it clearly and distinctly.
Inexperience, so it seems to me,
Will give little credence to my song. (11)

Hesse is again casting aspersions on those poor, disinterested bourgeois, who strive after the comforts of this world, govern themselves by strict, self-imposed and socially imposed statutes of limitations, and, in so doing, make of world history a "most violent and blind longing to forget" (12). "Haven't we just experienced," H.H. adds, "that a monstrous, horrible war that lasted years, has now . . . been forgotten, denied, suppressed and conjured away?"

With this lament expressing that his potential audience of readers will, under the best of circumstances, be a small one, H.H. goes on to explain the League in somewhat more detail. It began in the post-war years when times were desperate, which, in turn, directed minds and souls to higher goals. As times became better, so Hesse implies, the lofty goals were apparently forgotten and the League, accordingly, disbanded. But if the League's goals per se were confidential, this was not the case with individual goals, which each traveler had to have. One was looking for a treasure called "Tao," another a magic snake that he named "Kundalini"; H.H., himself, had the goal of seeing Princess Fatme and, if possible, to win her love (13). Harking back to *Demian* and *Narcissus and Goldmund,* we can easily equate H.H.'s search for Fatme (Fatima)—a name that has become a synonym for feminine curiosity and, more popularly, feminine beauty— with Sinclair's and Goldmund's search for the mother and, hence, an understanding of their relationships to the feminine side of life, especially its positive components of beauty and love.[1] The relevance of the individual goals should also not be overlooked, for it implies that each journeyer was following his own inner voice, making the particular search a sine qua non for belonging to the League.

The journeyers can magically wander through time and space. H.H's company varies from time to time; he may be with favorite characters from his own (i.e., from Hesse's) books—Goldmund, Pablo/Mozart—or he may travel with Parzifal or Sancho Panza (23). The travelers even encounter Noah's Ark. In what appears to be approaching a breach of his secrecy promise, H.H. reveals that "our goal was not only the East, or, rather, our East was not only a land and something geographical, but the home of youth and the soul; it was everywhere and nowhere, it was the union of all time" (24). Needless to say, the journeyers are Hesse's kindred souls: the artists, thinkers, musicians, poets, and his own created personae—the Cains, the immortals, all those who obey or obeyed their inner voices to participate in humankind's spiritual quest.

In one of his conversations with a servant, Leo, H.H. asks him—and we return to a *Narcissus and Goldmund* theme—why the artists themselves sometimes seem to be only half-people, whereas their paintings can look so indisputably alive (27). Leo looks surprised that H.H. would ask such a question and answers with an analogy: "It is the same with mothers. Once they have given birth to children and given them their milk, their beauty and their strength, they themselves become insignificant and no one asks after them anymore." When H.H. finds such a situation sad, Leo agrees but calls it beautiful, as well. It is "the Law of Service" (28).

This is a point where the reader should pause and reflect. There is a calmness in Leo that we have not encountered since the final pages of *Siddhartha*, where the old ferryman could see the union of all of being reflected in the water. Hesse understood this universal harmony full well even at that time, but it was first and foremost a vision. Just as Pistorius had put all of life together symbolically but could not live his vision and had retreated to his father's house, so did Hesse/Siddhartha again fall victim to a world that was "too much with him." But for Leo/Hesse, the harmony is returning. This does not mean that, once and for all, he has found "contentment"; this is "bourgeois yearning," and such is not of Hesse's world. But he has found the key to the Kafkaesque barricades on his pathway to being, as did Goethe's Faust, in the Law of Service. This is what could make him whole, could give him peace of mind in the troublesome world—simply to use his gifts to the best of his ability to serve posterity and to "laugh at the rest," as Harry Haller had been sentenced to do by the immortals.

But we must return to Leo, who has been assigned as servant and guide to H.H.'s basic traveling group of ten, who remain together despite their forays into space and time and their occasional journeys with other assemblages. Unfortunately, Leo, a most efficient and able servant to whom animals and birds readily flock (think of Hesse's idol, St. Francis), disappears one day without a trace. Everything seems to go wrong at this point. Everything anyone needs seems to have disappeared with Leo. And most important, all are sure that he must have taken the League Document with him—that secret statement, so they believe, that set forth the purpose of the League, although none of the group can actually recall having seen it.

Leo left his charges at a place in Italy named *Morbio Inferiore* (72), the "lower gorge," which, in Hessean humor, can be translated as the "birth canal"; the travelers have been "born into the world" and left to their own resources.

(The remark in the introduction to *Demian,* "We all come out of the same gorge [*Schlund*]" [*GS III* 112], is a similar thematic image.) As we later learn, it is a test, a statement that leadership and help from others can take us only so far; then we must journey alone. H.H. calls Leo's disappearance "in no way an accident, but a link in that chain of persecutions through which the arch enemy attempted to destroy our undertaking" (29). The identity of this arch enemy (in German, *Erbfeind,* which has the biblical ring of "Satan" just as it does in English) has not been discussed in criticism. If the travelers are, indeed, being placed into their own hands, the arch enemy is none other than the self, the *daemon* aspect of our inner natures that can easily lead us astray, the seductive side of the mother world. H.H. says he is "left with a bundle of a thousand knotted threads in his hand which would take a hundred hands years to unravel and sort out" (34–5). He likens the situation to that of a historian who is seeking the center of events, one common thread to which the events lead and which binds them together (35). The analogy underscores Hesse's consistent theme that we cannot expect to pull meaning together out of the countless dangling threads of credos, doctrines, isms, and laws. If the historian is seeking to give coherence or causality to an event, he must "*invent unity* [emphasis provided] in the form of a hero, a people, an idea" (35), thus fallaciously creating roadsigns which lead us astray. The topic relates also to the reasons why Sinclair left the institution of the church and to why Siddhartha could not follow the Buddha. Ultimate answers are not found in externalities, but within.

Hesse implies that few, indeed, are able to accept the responsibility of rebirth, for the entire group of ten disperses after Leo's disappearance, with H.H. thinking that he is the only one continuing the journey. And as he is the lone survivor, it is to his credit that he is determined not to abandon his task. But where can he find help? He decides to visit a boyhood friend who served in the war and who has just published a book about his experiences. H.H. wants his advice: how was he able to write it? When he poses the question to his friend, explaining that he wants to write about the Journey to the East, the friend, Lukas, smiles ironically. He has heard of this "children's crusade." When H.H. explains that Zoroaster, Lao Tse, Xenophon, Pythagoras, Albert the Great, Don Quixote, Tristram Shandy, Novalis, and Baudelaire were cofounders of the League (38), Lukas smiles again, but nonetheless gives H.H. his answer: he wrote the book because it was necessary. It was either write or succumb to despair, and the work had rescued him. During the writing, he adds, he could not think for a moment of readers other than himself, at most of a war comrade (40). That is to say that Lukas expressed *his* story, the war that *he* had lived; this could be his only goal. If H.H./Hesse has just castigated the historian for inventiveness, he gives approval to Lukas in this passage because it is a personal story; it is not Lukas's intention to invent unity for others. We might even infer that Hesse is drawing a subtle analogy to the Book of Luke; this was Luke's wondrous story, written to give meaning to his feelings.

Lukas points out to H.H. that Leo seems to have become an *idee fixe* for him, reminding the reader that, Govinda-like, H.H. could not stop searching for guidance from others. "Throw him overboard," says Lukas, and when he asks if Leo was really his name, H.H. breaks into a sweat, a curious reaction to say the least, which, as we should realize from our observation of Hesse's stylistic technique, means that he is drawing our attention to the underlying significance of the episode. Just as Goldmund was thrown into a state of near panic when Narcissus told him to seek out his mother—his real nature—so does H.H. break into a sweat when asked if Leo is this fellow's real name. In other words, does H.H. not know that he is really searching for himself?

Lukas actually finds an Andreas Leo listed in the city directory but still thinks that H.H. should forget about him. H.H., however, does not give up easily. He seeks out the address, and his inquiries indicate that Mr. Leo is a jack of all trades: he is a manicurist, podiatrist, and masseur; he can make healing salves and perform herbal cures; he can even train and shear dogs.[2] In a brief moment of reflection, H.H. considers how he thought his effort to write his history of the League to be a noble undertaking, but now he sees it more and more as an attempt to give his own life meaning again, just as Lukas's war story did for him. But H.H. needs Leo's help and cannot possibly throw him overboard, as Lukas suggested. He even prays (which to Hesse is always a turning inward): "Dear God, help me a little!" (43). So great is his need for Leo that he goes to the *Seilergraben* address twenty times or more and finally hears a beautiful whistling from the house that transfixes him. Just as Siddhartha was reawakened by the sound of "*om*" as he was about to throw himself into the river, H.H. is reminded of his former faith by Leo's whistle. A short time later, the door opens and the long-sought servant emerges. The youthful-appearing man wearing rope sandals—no doubt a Christ-like/St. Francis-like resemblance is intended—passes him, and H.H. follows him, eventually joining him on a park bench. There is no sign of recognition from Leo, and, as they become involved in a friendly chat, Leo mildly chastises H.H. for having sold his violin. King David, after all, was a much better man when he was young and calmed Saul with his music. After he became king, himself, he waged war and committed other evil deeds. H.H. replies that one does not always remain young. Life is not just a game! But Leo begs to differ; it is precisely that (48).

As Leo gets up to leave, H.H. cannot contain himself. Does Leo not recognize him, his League Brother? The former servant saunters amiably away but allows H.H. to walk beside him, saying, "Who knows anyone else or even himself. . . . It doesn't interest me. Dogs, yes, I know them very well, birds too and even cats. But I really don't know you, sir" (49–50). When H.H. pleads, "But you were on the journey!" Leo replies, "I am still on the journey . . . so many come and go, one knows people and doesn't know them" (50). As they walk, Leo stops to pet a huge wolfhound behind a fence, who wags his tail in friendliness but growls at H.H., who is beside himself and must go home. As was the case with Harry Haller after his failed visit with the professor, so is H.H. now in total despair and ready for suicide—the Jungian meeting with the self. The only salvation that seems possible to him is to rejoin the League—which he was not even aware of having left—and he sits down at his desk to fill page after page of a letter to Leo—complaints, remorse, pleas for help. In the middle of the night, H.H. posts the letter, then returns home to collapse into bed and sleep well into the next day.

The letter is a purging, a confession, an admission of despair, a call for help, a clearing of the game board for a new beginning, just as was Lukas's outpouring of his war memories, and when H.H. finally awakens the next day, Leo is sitting beside his bed—a stylistic variation of Demian's initial appearance when Sinclair was desperate and of Harry Haller's convenient first encounter with Hermine when he was on the brink of suicide. Leo tells him that the League authorities have sent him because of the letter. H.H. is expected at League Headquarters before the High Throne. Only now does it strike him that the League really does continue to exist but that he is no longer considered a member! He is ready at once but grows very impatient as Leo strolls nonchalantly through the streets, leaving him for a time while he enters a church to pray, stopping to explain the construction of the city hall, finally leading him into an inconspicuous structure in a suburb, a building that might have been full of state offices or possibly a museum. The first person H.H. sees when he glances into a studio is the artist Klingsor (a medieval artist and a character from one of Hesse's own short stories). There are many others in the building, all silently occupied (56)—that is, they are pursuing their own goals[3] but are all present in the League Headquarters, where personal goals merge into a universal goal. Finally, H.H. and Leo come to the upper story, which is an archive. When Leo begins to sing one of the League songs, the workers disappear, and the room is transformed into a huge hall full of chairs. Officials come out of myriad doors to fill them, and H.H. recognizes Albert the Great, the ferryman Vasudeva, Klingsor, and others. The chairs rise to a podium where an empty throne stands.

A speaker steps forth to label H.H. a "self accuser" who deserted the league shortly after *Morbio Inferiore,* but despite H.H.'s desertion, the speaker recognizes his desire to write a history of the Journey to the East and gives him permission to break his oath of secrecy. He may make public any League document or secret; the entire archive is at his disposal. The hall empties, and H.H. suddenly discovers his own manuscript before him. He reads it through, but it seems to have no context whatsoever—the letters appear to dissolve into playful forms.[4] He decides he must start over. He is surrounded by card catalogs and begins by searching out the League Document, which sends him to look for "Chrysostomos" (the medieval saint whose name gave a common bond to Goldmund and Narcissus). He finally has the great document in his hand, but, alas, he can make out practically nothing of what he takes to be ancient Greek or various Greek dialects. He seeks further. Under "Leo" he encounters the Latin word *Cave*!—"Warning!" In Fatme's file, he finds a tiny medallion with a miniature of the beautiful princess, which reminds him of the fairy tales of his childhood, and the reader can compare her to the Beatrice of *Demian,* Hermine of *Steppenwolf,* and even to Hesse's new wife, Ninon (as Hesse, himself, does elsewhere in the book). As he breathes in this magic fragrance of Fatme's presence, he realizes that it had long since disappeared from his life, and as he looks around at the endless archives, he knows what a fool he has been to think he could recount the history of the League.

At this point we should realize why a novitiate had to take an oath not to reveal the League secrets. At such a low level of understanding and at the bare beginning of his journey, any foolish initiate might well think he could tell others the great secret of the search, that they need but follow in his footsteps. The situation might also be interpreted as a metaphor for novitiate isms, religions, and philosophies. Should any of them have the temerity to claim knowledge of the League Secret? When the humbling revelation strikes H.H., he realizes that the authorities have been toying with him. As soon as this becomes a conscious thought, the doors open and the hall fills again. The speaker once more steps to the podium and asks, now that H.H. has recognized how amazing and blasphemous his intentions were, is he ready to recognize the judgment of the authorities and subject himself to this judgment (63)? He is, and it is to be the highest authority, himself, who will pass sentence. From the far reaches of the room, a man enters, his robes sparkling with gold. He walks slowly, humbly, silently, and H.H. recognizes Leo! The lowly servant holds the highest office in the League.

Speaking softly, Leo points out to H.H. that he has been unfaithful to the League, blaming it for his own guilt and foolishness, that he had doubted its continued existence and had the amazing gall to want to become its historian. These, however, are only novitiate stupidities. The authorities can laugh them off (just as the immortals laughed Harry Haller out of their court for taking his life so seriously). But, Leo continues, "the accused is guilty of other, more serious sins" (65). And the worst of it is that he doesn't seem to be aware of them. Leo points out that he sold his violin, that dogs growl at him, that just today he was so "egotistically impatient" when Leo stopped to admire the city hall designed by a League Brother and when he went into a church to pray, thus "slighting religion" (66–7). The latter accusation is interesting, because it shows how Hesse recognizes the church as a symbol, as a place for turning inward, even if he has chastised it elsewhere for thinking it possesses the only path to salvation. Pistorius, too, made a comment to Sinclair that reflects the inner sanctity of the church, but there was also criticism in his statement: "Each and every religion is beautiful; religion is soul . . . [but] is practiced as though it were something else" (*GS III* 204).

Leo now turns to address the authorities, telling them that H.H.'s fall and wayward wanderings were a test. He had been hiding but now had reached the point where he could hide no longer, and as soon as suffering is great enough, there is progress, for despair is the result of every serious attempt to deal with life, with virtue, justice, and reason, and to fulfill its demands. Children live on "this side" of despair, adults on "the other." H.H. is no longer a child, but he is not fully awakened, either. Though he is in the midst of despair, he will survive it and will perform his second novitiate (68). Thus is H.H. welcomed back into the League, and his membership ring is returned to him, which, until now, he did not realize was missing. But even though he has returned to the fold, H.H. must still pass a test: Will he tame a wild dog? Will he burn the archives? To encourage him, Leo digs into a file and burns a handful of documents.[5] H.H. can do neither of these, but when warned that the choices will become progressively harder, he accepts the next challenge—to seek out the League's opinion of him. Nervously, he opens the "H" file and finds his (Hesse's) Latinized name, "Chattorum." As he studies it, the authorities exit the hall, leaving him alone. He looks further and comes to a card marked *"Morbio Inferiore,"* where he is surprised to find two fellow travelers' accounts of their journey to that point; apparently all had failed the test; all had gone astray without Leo's help. H.H. finds a niche of sorts in his file, and opening it finds a figure, actually two figures joined together; one resembles him and the other, Leo. When he holds a candle behind the statuette, he can see thick, viscous fluid slowly flowing from his figure into Leo, until finally, it seems to him, his own will disappear. Now he understands fully what Leo had told him: characters of fiction are more vital and real than the writers, themselves; children are more important than mothers. The journeyer, in other words, has importance only if he becomes a servant. We cannot expect to be led forever; as we grow wiser from experience, it becomes our responsibility to serve.

The *Journey to the East* is a touching fragment of imaginative autobiography as well as a serious statement of purpose, but it is not without its lighter side. As has been mentioned, following the expression of a lofty vision in *Siddhartha,* Hesse allowed himself to be pulled back into a world of which he did not approve but within which he had to learn how to play a positive role. The failure of H.H.'s first novitiate reflects Hesse's *Steppenwolf* period, where Harry Haller had fallen into a Nietzschean depression, perhaps because of his failed egotistical desire to enlighten the world. The much lighter tone of *Journey to the East* indicates that Hesse's quest is coming back into perspective. Leo's calmness permits us to infer that Hesse has stepped back to tell this story, that he can be more objective than he was when playing Harry Haller. It is much easier for the reader to see that Hermann Hesse is smiling ironically at H.H than it was to discover that he was also smiling ironically at Harry Haller.

In his *Journey to the East,* H.H. returns to the League—that is, to the realization that he must decide on his own goals and not let the world distract him. But his victory can be no more than willingness to continue the battle at a higher level, for he is entering a second novitiate when the book ends and is sent off to rest up for the ensuing confrontation with life at this level.

The significant addition of *Journey to the East* to Hesse's thematic continuum is the heavy emphasis on the Law of Service. Ironically enough, we must return to his first novel, *Peter Camenzind,* to find the same devotion, which Peter displayed toward his crippled friend Boppi but which Hesse could not keep in perspective following the war years. Now it seems, by 1931, that Hesse is stable enough to rejuvenate his earlier vision. His character Leo bears more than a slight similarity to St. Francis, the ideal of Hesse's early adult years. This reminder, alone—the return to a youthful dream at a higher level of understanding—lets us conclude once again that Hesse is portraying his own progressive journey through life, and his *Journey to the East* reflects a significant step forward.[6] What we see happening at the end of the novel—H.H. envisioning himself becoming a Leo in the statuette imagery—is presumably the challenge that Hesse is extending to himself as well as to all higher novitiates. Boulby points out that this is also a biblical allusion to the relationship of Christ with John the Baptist (257): "He must increase, but I must decrease" (John 3:30). The same double figurine, we can assume, is waiting to be discovered in every journeyer's file, and the best of these Cains will be perfect servants. The theme of life as service will now carry over into Hesse's magnum opus, *The Glass Bead Game.*

CHAPTER TWELVE

The Glass Bead Game

The Game of Life

In his *Kurzgefasster Lebenslauf (Brief Autobiography)* written in 1925, Hesse expressed his intention of writing in his later years a "kind of opera in which human life in its so-called reality is taken less seriously, even ridiculed, and instead its metaphor is held high because of its eternal value as the fleeting robe of the deity" (*GS IV* 485). He wanted "to ascribe a lofty and charming meaning to human life . . . to praise the innocence and inexhaustibility of nature [*Natur*], and portray its course to a point at which it will be forced because of inexorable suffering to turn to the spirit [*Geist*], the distant counter pole, and the hovering of life between the two poles of nature *and* [emphasis provided] the spirit should be represented as serene, playful, and complete like the arch of a rainbow" (486). The sentence is second to none in importance if we are to understand the duality theme in the final novel, for it again illustrates that Hesse's *Natur* has two poles (the sensual/feminine/mother-world and the cerebral/masculine/father-world) and that beyond them lies the realm of the spirit (*Geist*). In other words, what should be understood as a triadic motif in Hesse's thematic continuum is often confused as simple duality, for the word *Geist* can also mean "mind" and "intellect" (see note 4 to the Introduction), and Hesse often uses it with the latter meaning. (He expressed the concept even more clearly in *Siddhartha,* where he said, "Both thoughts [*Gedanken*] and senses [*Sinne*] were fine things; it was behind both that the last meaning lay hidden" [*GS III* 652]).

Hesse's vision of life turning to the spirit has a religious essence that seems strangely optimistic for a man who constantly talked about suicide at this very time, but it helps us to understand that behind the self-pity and depression spiritual values always dominated. A comment from a letter written in 1938 pulls the paradox into perspective: "I sometimes have the feeling of having waded through blood and muck the whole day and of not being able to bear human life or take it seriously anymore, but nevertheless, my fundamental faith is completely untouched or influenced by these moods and exhaustions" (*GB III* 91).

The Glass Bead Game, when published in 1943,[1] was not an opera and stopped short of being a clear picture (as dozens of critical analyses can attest) of a serene and playful life hovering between two poles. If it was clear to Hesse, it has obviously proven more obscure for readers than he anticipated, though some of the obscurity was intended.

The introduction to the book is formidable reading. We are introduced to the Glass Bead Game, but its precise nature is perplexing. We are informed of a nebulous purpose behind the forthcoming narrative—that "nothing is more necessary than to place before the eyes of mankind certain things, the existence of which is neither demonstrable nor apparent, which, however, are brought one step closer to being and the possibility of being born, precisely because pious and conscientious people treat them, to a certain degree, as existing things" (*GS VI* 79). At this point we can only speculate as to what Hesse is about to bring to our attention, but we should realize that he is going to deal with symbolic meaning and that our task is to search out the all-encompassing metaphor that he will create. We should expect, too, no little irony, for even this most serious literary effort will be but a game, if we can take Hesse's title seriously.

The novel is set in Castalia, an intellectual province of the future, "about 2400" (*Werkgeschichte* 181), in which an unnamed scholar-narrator announces his intention of telling the life story of a long deceased former Magister Ludi (Master of the [Glass Bead] Game), Joseph Knecht, from records, letters, and other archival materials. This goes somewhat against the grain of Castalian tradition, for every attempt is made in the province to "extinguish the individual" and subordinate him completely to the hierarchy (80). But the narrator's effort is, more importantly, a service to the truth, because research has shown that every developmental phase that has taken place in the province can be understood most clearly in terms of the instrument of change, itself, namely of the person who introduced it. Thus, we are reminded that Hesse's emphasis, as always, remains on the individual. Already we can see the irony—that individuals are responsible for developmental changes in a system that attempts to extinguish the individual—and can suspect that the collective intellectual province will prove to have its shortcomings.

The origins of Castalia go back to a period in history which a literary historian, Plinius Ziegenhals, called the Age of the *Feuilleton, feuilleton* being a section of a newspaper containing low-brow serialized literature; and, as Hesse himself characterized the age in 1929, prior to beginning *The Glass Bead Game,* it "knew only money and quantity, but not soul" (*GB II* 223). All energies, it seemed, were funneled into bourgeois life, ruled by the lesser gods. Academics submerged themselves in such topics as "Nietzsche and Women's Fashions around 1870" or "The Role of the Lap Dog in the Lives of Great Courtesans" (90). The period to which Hesse refers, of course, is his own, which turned into the nightmare of National Socialism and World War II as he was writing the novel. His vision in the 1920's—that the world was rushing pell mell into the next war—did not take long to materialize. The era is described in Knecht's writings as one of collapsing morality, of mechanization of life, of loss of faith, of insincerity. One could, in fact, "hear the music of decline" (94).

At the zenith of this Age of the *Feuilleton,* consciences of individual artists, professors, and writers were awakened, and small groups were formed to remain true to the *Geist*[2] and to salvage a core of tradition, of discipline, of methodology and intellectual conscience. These saviors fell into two basic groups, one made up of researchers and teachers of the history of music, the other composed of mathematicians. A more contemplative branch of the music group called itself the League of Journeyers to the East, and they especially strove to preserve the *Geist,* thus enabling the survival and growth of a peaceful society; it was this group that would evolve into Castalia, and a bead game would become its symbol.

Thus, in the early pages of Hesse's novel, we can discern that he is aiming at a synthesis of the mind, or father world (its metaphor the precise science of mathematics), and the senses, or mother world (its metaphor the most abstract of the arts—music). Hesse names the man who eventually reduced music and mathematics to a common denominator "Lusor," or Joculator Basilensis, a Swiss scholar of music and fanatical amateur mathematician (108), the name itself ascribing a playful quality to the process of symbiosis. Whereas Mileck finds the name Basilensis a tribute to Hesse's friend Otto Basler ("Names" 175), Kurt Fickert makes a more interesting association by relating the name to the city of Basel, where Hesse lived for some years, thus identifying himself as the creator—that is, he is the Joker of Basel. Fickert also notes that Basel is the home of Jacob Burkhardt, hence the name foreshadows the appearance of Pater Jakobus.[3] More than likely the name is simply a tribute to Burkhardt, Hesse's favorite historian, who, he felt, had learned Harry Haller's lesson: he understood what is important and could laugh at the rest.

The game grows in complexity and universality until it eventually becomes an *Unio Mystica* of all branches of learning, sometimes characterized by the term Magic Theater (109). Later in the novel, Joseph Knecht, himself, will state that "every symbol and every combination of symbols doesn't lead just here or there, not to single examples, experiments and proofs, but to the center, into the secret and the core of the world, to original knowledge . . . a direct path to the inner sanctum of the world secret, where in the push and pull of inhalation and exhalation, between heaven and earth, between Yin and Yang, the eternal divine is consummated" (197). (And we should not fail to note the subtle sexual connotations of the language!) For the narrow circle of real Bead Game players, the game is the equivalent of a worship service, but it *separates itself from every specific theology* (113) and is a game played by an *individual*—points to be remembered.

All but the most curious readers will find this long introduction tedious and vague, and, therefore, before beginning with the story of Josef Knecht himself, we should pause to take stock. In the prior novels (in *Journey to the East* only by implication), the protagonist has gone out into the dark world to discover for himself the feminine vicissitudes of life. On the surface of *The Glass Bead Game,* we will not fail to notice that this element has disappeared from the scene completely, and critics have often faulted this masculine, or chauvinist, approach, but in so doing they fail to see that this is precisely Hesse's caveat—that the feminine absence has become Castalia's great weakness.[4] He makes this point clearly, tongue in cheek, when he notes how the local girls fulfill the needs of the elite young Castalians; obviously, it is not a dire need, and in the figure of one Fritz Tegularius, whom we shall come to know as the ultimate Castalian, the need does not appear to exist at all. Thus, we see the direction that Castalia is heading, so Joseph Knecht will warn, and only a reawakened interest in the vitality of life—an infusion from the feminine side—will save it from demise. We should also be aware that, just as Hesse gave Goldmund's role far more emphasis than Narcissus's, here he has reversed his procedure. Castalia is a masculine province *non plus ultra.* If Goldmund, the creative artist, came to know the meaning of life by applying masculine/mind principles to his myriad feminine/sensual experiences—but left his masculine counterpart with the burning question, "How can you die if you have no mother?"—we shall now accompany Hesse through some six hundred pages as he pursues this question. And, surprisingly enough, we shall note that the elder Hesse has altered his views somewhat: We need not learn exclusively from personal experience. As will be exemplified in the characters of both Father Jakobus and Joseph Knecht, the masculine mind, via history and dedication, can experience life and thereby join hands with the feminine senses. Hans Küng fails to see the irony with which Hesse portrays the synthesis taking place, commenting that "(unfortunately) only men belong [to the Castalian Order] for the sake of simplicity" (*HHudR* 75). He then takes Hesse's response to this oft-noted sin of omission quite literally, pointing out that "the now old Hesse answered morosely that 'a reader with fantasy would himself create and imagine all clever and spiritually [*geistig*] superior women from Aspasia to the present in Castalia'" (75).

The Call

The first chapter of *The Glass Bead Game* is entitled "The Call" (note the religious connotation), and we are introduced to the young protagonist, Joseph Knecht, whose intelligence and musical genius are noticed by his teachers and drawn to the attention of the Castalian authorities. He is an orphan—information that alerts us immediately to expect no less than a quest to determine the roles that both the mother-and father-aspects of life should play.

The Music Master, himself, comes from the elite province to judge the young Knecht. The boy is nervous when asked to play for the great man, but the master easily puts him at ease by reaching out to him with his own piano playing. Knecht is, in fact, awakened in a way that establishes a frame of reference for the path his life will take: "Behind the rising tonal pattern . . . he perceived the spirit, the elevating harmony of law and freedom, of serving and ruling, he saw himself and his life and saw the entire world being directed, ordered, and explicated" (126). It was an "inviting revelation of the ideal world . . . [which] existed not only somewhere in the distance, in the past or future, no, it was here and active, it radiated, it sent out messengers, apostles and ambassadors" (127). Knecht, in other words, receives a vision of universal oneness through the spirit of the music. He needs no mysterious Demian-Hermine-Pablo-immortal intermediary. With Knecht as pathfinder, Hesse will lead us on a lofty journey, and at journey's end the union of feminine and masculine drives will be consummated, although, paradoxically, we shall realize at the same time that the journey has no end.

Shortly after the Music Master's visit, Knecht is summoned to Eschholz, one of the elite Castalian schools. If students succeed here, then their second stage of learning, comparable to graduate school education, will take place in one of twelve advanced schools, each directed by a master, or in a thirteenth school, where the Glass Bead Game is the focus. This is presided over by the most respected of the masters, the Magister Ludi (not unlike the Christ-disciple relationship, implying that the Magister Ludi is the master among masters). The best of these students are granted free study and may, if they so choose, spend their lives involved in their calling. Hesse, with what is now characteristic irony, subtly draws a parallel to the ivory-tower intellectuals of the Age of the *Feuilleton,* for we will discover as the novel progresses that Castalia is in decline, and Hesse is warning of the inherent danger of intellectual pursuit for its own sake—the province is now ignoring the very reality that had prompted concerned visionaries to create it generations ago. Knecht will perceive this weakness and follow his calling to correct it. In a passage reminiscent of *Be-*

neath the Wheel, he is shown reflecting on those who are expelled from the province: perhaps it was not a fall for them but a leap and a deed; perhaps those who remained in Eschholz as obedient students were the weaklings and cowards (144–5). While awaiting assignment to a higher school when he is seventeen, his thoughts return to the same theme: the former students who have left the school "have dared to take a leap, and it took courage. . . . I hope . . . if the hour comes and it is necessary to cut myself loose, to be able to leap, not backwards into a lower sphere, but forward into a higher one" (150). Years later, Joseph Knecht will fulfill this very wish, and this early foreshadowing should be stressed to show how tightly Hesse has constructed his lengthy novel.

Waldzell

The Music Master has invited Knecht for a visit prior to his reassignment, expressly to introduce him to the art of meditation. He approaches it by playing a theme on the piano and telling Knecht to "seek the music inside yourself, pay attention to its configuration" (153). Thus, the focus again returns to the inner voice—now in the guise of an inner musical harmony—and the art of seeking it out. The Music Master notes that "our goal is to recognize opposites correctly, first as contrasts, but then as poles of a unity" (155). Further, he says, "each of us is only a human being, only an attempt, only en route. We should, however, be on the path to where fulfillment is found, we should be striving toward the center, not toward the periphery" (156). "You should," he adds, "not long for universal perfection, but for perfection of self. The deity is in you, not in concepts and books. Truth is lived, not taught" (157). The Music Master's last statement to him is: "He who climbs higher and receives greater assignments does not become freer, but only more responsible" (159). These few sentences outline the journey that lies ahead. All advanced schools in the province have their particular specialties, such as mathematics, philology, or Aristotelian thought, but Waldzell, because of its emphasis on the Bead Game, the symbol of Castalia, is the school that tends toward universality, that seeks to bring the sciences and the arts closer together. In keeping with the constant Hesse theme that only a select few possess such universal interests and vision, Waldzell is also the smallest of the schools, and the students and faculty have the aura of the elite among the elite. The seventeen-year-old Knecht cannot help but feel a certain pride when he learns of his assignment (161), a warning of the inherent Narcissistic danger in being superior, and the name of the school, itself, *Waldzell,* meaning "Forest Cell," underscores the temptations of intellectual escape. He soon makes two friends, one a Carlo Ferremonte,[5] a brilliant music student who spices Knecht's own interest in music to the point where he neglects his other studies. Attention is drawn to Knecht's immersion in music, because, as the most abstract, universal, and sensual of the arts, it symbolizes his baptism into the feminine side of life. The narrator points out that the year in which Knecht throws himself into his musical studies is the onset of puberty—that is, Knecht's adolescent sexual drives are symbolically sublimated and satisfied in his love affair with music, whereas Sinclair, Siddhartha, Harry Haller, and Goldmund had to immerse themselves in the sensual world to learn the same lesson.

Knecht's second friend brings about a most important experience at Waldzell. Plinio Designori is a *Hospitant,* one of the rare outsiders who is allowed to be educated in the elite schools as a guest student, in this case because he belongs to one of the old, wealthy, and respected patrician families in the Waldzell area. Unlike resident students, he spends holidays at home and will return to the world. He is somewhat older than Joseph and ungratefully outspoken in his criticism of the ivory-tower province. As one of Waldzell's most successful debaters, Plinio begins to notice one student in particular among his listeners who seems to be challenged by his accusations against the elitism of Castalia. Knecht tries to avoid Plinio, but the latter senses a worthy opponent and persists in attempts to befriend him. Knecht brings the problem to the Music Master, admitting that Plinio's charges bother him. He is close to agreement with this Castalian critic, who says that the Glass Bead Game is a step backward toward the Age of the *Feuilleton,* is an "irresponsible playing with letters," and is "unproductive" (171–2). The Music Master challenges Knecht to defend Castalia against Designori and to carry the debate to the highest possible level (173). The assignment compels Knecht to research Castalia's origins, goals, and accomplishments for his defense. Plinio is forced to recognize, through his opponent's brilliant arguments, that he does not have the intimate knowledge of and feeling for Castalia that the younger student already possesses. As the debates progress, he comes to understand and even respect Castalian traditions, while Knecht, for his part, finds a new respect for the outside world that Plinio represents. Knecht's reflections express the thematic thrust of the novel and the goal toward which he will strive:

> No, the Plinio-world was not the better and more perfect world . . . many peoples had never known any other, knew nothing of the elite schools and the pedagogical province, or orders, masters, and the Glass Bead Game. . . . To do justice to [this primitive world], to grant it a certain

homeland status in your own heart, but . . . not to retreat into it, this was the assignment. For beside it and above it was the second world, the Castalian, the world of the mind, an artificial, well-ordered, protected world, but one in constant need of supervision and attention of the hierarchy. To serve it without doing injustice to the other and without despising it, without looking askance at it . . . must be the right way. . . . Why, apparently, were not the two worlds living harmoniously and fraternally beside and within one another . . . ? (175–6)

Knecht's ongoing debates with Designori are strenuous and begin to tell on the young student, a condition that is noticed by his visiting mentor, the Music Master. He notices that Knecht has given up his regular meditation practice and points out to him, "The really great men of world history have all either understood how to meditate or unconsciously known the path where meditation leads us. The others, even the most gifted and powerful, have run aground and been defeated because their goal or their proud dream took possession of them so completely that they lost the ability to distance themselves from the present" (180–1). What the Music Master says is a repetition of the message stated in Harry Haller's sentencing—that the real immortals-in-the-making learn to live with and laugh at the distractions and temptations of daily life. Listening for the inner voice is tantamount to meditation. Our Hesse narrator labels Joseph Knecht's devotion to the defense of Castalia his "second call," which cast him in the mold of the "complete Castalian" (182). At this early point in the narrative, the significance of many such comments is easily overlooked, but Hesse is preparing Knecht for his role as the perfect Castalian, a point to be remembered when he must ultimately leave the province in order to serve it.

When it comes time for Plinio to return to the world, he invites Joseph to spend a vacation with his family, but this is denied him (185)—an indication that Plinio's charges of elitism ring true, that the Castalian authorities keep the province aloof from the world and its contaminated inhabitants.

Knecht's last year in Waldzell is devoted to the Bead Game, and in a notebook he expresses his thoughts on the theory behind it and its application in practice: "The entirety of life, the physical as well as the intellectual, is a dynamic phenomenon, of which the Glass Bead Game concerns itself basically only with the aesthetic side . . . mainly with the image of rhythmic events" (186)—that is, Joseph sees that most play the game for fun, but he also perceives that its symbols can penetrate and reveal the rhythmic patterns of life; the mind can lead the way to synthesis.

Free Study

The next chapter of Knecht's life begins with the end of his formal schooling when he is "about twenty-four" (186) He has been granted several years of free study, a privilege that not all receive. Those who are selected have absorbed the "discipline of the elite school and the spiritual hygiene of meditation" (187), without which the freedom could prove dangerous. The one substantive requirement will be an annual "autobiography"—a fictional account of his life, in which the writer places himself in another age, in different surroundings and a different culture, and creates an existence for himself. To this period of Knecht's life, so the narrator tells us, we owe the three autobiographies that are appended to the Joseph Knecht story (to be discussed later). Knecht's biographer considers himself fortunate to have found a letter from Knecht to his brilliant but hopelessly aesthetic friend, Tegularius, in which the Master explained his major project during his period of free study. He had had a sudden insight while attending upper-level Bead Game classes, that the inner voice of the game was, in fact, a "lingua sacra, a holy and divine language" that led "directly to the inner [working] of the world secret" (197)—the latter phrase perhaps a conscious parallel to Goethe's Faust's quest to discover *was die Welt im Innersten zusammenhält* (what holds the world together at its innermost core). To follow this insight to its source, Knecht has decided to analyze and reconstruct the complete content of a game, to seek out the symbolic synthesis of forces behind a Bead Game— and presumably it could be any game, any personal goal—by tracing it to its universal sources. Hesse takes pains to emphasize that "one can be a virtuoso player without suspecting the secret of the game and its ultimate meaning" (199), again a criticism of intellectuals who may reason to perfection, yet separate themselves from life. When Knecht tells the Music Master that he is "close to discovering the meaning of the game" (199), his elderly mentor replies that he has never said a word to his students about the meaning of music. He teaches them to have reverence for it, but he cannot teach them reverence—that music, like life, is its own meaning.

To penetrate to the source of the particular game he has chosen, one which can be "played in a quarter of an hour" (201), Knecht will spend years in reading rooms, archives, and libraries; he will study mathematics and music, and must even learn Chinese. The narrator notes that the protracted study may have had its subtle ulterior side, as well, for Knecht is beginning to perceive that fate is calling him, his inner voice is telling him that he has been assigned to lead, and a certain fear and reticence manifest themselves; as did Christ, Knecht would like to avoid his fate.

In pursuing his quest, Knecht finds that he must study the *I Ching* (the *Book of Change*), and is tutored by the "Elder Brother," now an older student of the elite schools who lives in his own "bamboo forest." Although European, he has surpassed even the best of his Chinese mentors and established himself as a hermit in his own Chinese idyll, where he is left to himself with a reputation that ranges from saint to eccentric. The episode obviously has its ironic content—a brilliant scholar spending his life in total seclusion studying *The Book of* Change. Perhaps one of the most important discoveries Knecht makes while studying with the Elder Brother is a common theme of ancient Chinese writers: all praise music as one of the origins of order, custom, beauty, and health. The ancient Chinese were aware that the father principle was inherently present in the most abstract mother-world of music.

While he is continuing his period of free study, Knecht returns to Waldzell every year to participate in advanced Bead Game courses and gradually becomes one of the inner circle of elite players. These are despised by some as pretentious, do-nothing geniuses and regarded by others as the cream of the exclusive, aristocratic intelligentsia. Knecht is bothered by neither opinion, only by this question: "Does the Game really represent what is best in Castalia, and is it worth dedicating one's life to it?" (214). He reluctantly acknowledges that this cannot be his path; he feels other forces in him demanding that he serve only the highest master (214). Thus, when the final decisions of Knecht's life are made and his final act carried out, we may justifiably infer that Knecht is answering what he knows to be the highest call. Hesse is paving the way for Knecht's eventual defection and stressing the emotional, spiritual, and intellectual struggle that precedes it. His final actions do not result from hastily made decisions, and we are to understand that Knecht's ultimate call will come from within.

During one of Plinio Designori's annual visits to Castalia, Knecht encounters his erstwhile debating opponent and friend. The latter is now an attorney and official and has come back to Waldzell to take a refresher course in the Bead Game. As they talk that evening, both feel how they have grown apart. When the conversation deals with the Bead Game, Plinio feels himself to be a child beside Knecht. On the other side of the coin, Knecht shows an embarrassing ignorance of the outside world, which only strengthens his perception that Castalia is the ivory tower many purport it to be (217).

Designori is about to become engaged to the daughter of a party leader in the outside world. The word *Führer* is brought into the conversation (217), which reveals Hesse's initial intention to deal more directly and specifically with Germany's rising tide of National Socialism. Siegfried Unseld notes, "From its inception in 1930, the writing of *The Glass Bead Game* was—and this we know only since we have been able to examine the author's posthumous papers—inseparably linked with the course of political developments in the Germany of those times."[6] The novel, in part, was to be an expression of "spiritual resistance against the 'barbaric process'" and a strong statement against the "dictates and the rape of life and spirit" (*Werkgeschichte* 188).[7] Plinio's warning that there may soon be war is also a reflection of the situation in Hesse's contemporary Germany, although the setting for the novel is centuries in the future. Designori cautions that a war may well put the entire Castalian existence in question; it is an expensive luxury, to which Knecht laughingly replies that it costs, they say, about a tenth of what was spent for weapons and munitions during the warring centuries. Thus, at the same time that he is criticizing the cost of war, Hesse is issuing a warning to the intellectual leaders that they must not join the nationalist bandwagon; they must not follow lesser gods, or their freedoms may end. But the warning will come far too late.

The Glass Bead Game Master at this time is Thomas von der Trave, the name a tribute to Hesse's friend, compatriot, and fellow writer, Thomas Mann. Some call him a "cold man of reason who has only a polite relationship to the muses," an apt superficial judgment of Mann, intentionally ironic to be sure, but Knecht sees him, nevertheless, as an expert who possesses a close familiarity with the hidden difficulties of the game world (219). The Master calls Knecht to his office, ostensibly to help analyze various games, and asks him to return daily for two weeks. Knecht wonders why his help is needed for little more than trivial work. He gradually sees that it is really an opportunity for the Master to observe and test him, and when the period is over, Thomas suggests that it is time for him to join the order. Joseph requests that his highly respected friend and mentor, the Music Master, conduct his acceptance ceremony, and the old man gladly obliges, saying that he is stepping into retirement and is most pleased that Knecht is filling the opening. It is as though he has a son (223), a theme to be reiterated in Knecht's fictional autobiographies.

No sooner has he returned to Waldzell from the Music Master's residence than he is again summoned by the Magister Ludi. He is needed. He will be sent to the Benedictine Order at Mariafels, with which Castalia has always enjoyed friendly relations and which has requested a young instructor to teach the monks the art of the Glass Bead Game. Another stage of Knecht's life is about to begin.

Two Orders

The Glass Bead Game remains an all but inexhaustible source for ongoing Hesse research because of its intricacy. Virtually every paragraph offers substance for discussion and interpretation, and the chapter entitled "Two Orders" not only exemplifies the novel's highly integrated framework but also subtly involves Hesse, himself, in his thematic continuum. On the surface, the narrative development appears to do little more than permit Joseph Knecht to absent himself from the felicity of Castalia for a while in order to have access to an outsider's view of the province. Careful study of this chapter reveals, however, that Hesse is playfully presenting the reader with a metaphor of his own awakening and his own call. In a letter located by the narrator, a characterization of Knecht's Castalian colleague Tegularius is no less than a veiled confession of Hesse's own temptation to succumb to the aesthetic life and put the rest of the world out of sight and out of mind. Tegularius is described as having fragile health, depression, periods of sleeplessness, nervous pains, bouts of melancholy, an intense need to be alone, fear of duty and responsibility, and thoughts of suicide (226), all exact descriptive words, phrases, and complaints that appear in Hesse's correspondence time and again during his *Steppenwolf* period. Tegularius is the "most gifted, brilliant Glass Bead Game player" that Knecht knows (226). Thus, if we now realize, as we should, that the Bead Game symbolizes the game of life, Tegularius, as its most discriminating observer and aesthetic manipulator, is a portrait of the younger, immodest Hesse,[8] who had always felt himself of such caliber. He, too, could analyze, play linguistic games with symbols and imagery, and might well have become a Tegularius. The latter's every Bead Game "strove so internally and earnestly for resolution, only to renounce the final resolution with such noble denial, that it was a grand elegy to everything beautiful from the past and to all the exalted spiritual goals of inner doubt"—not a far cry from the Pistorius dreams, actions, and renunciation in *Demian* (228). But after embodying his own emotional fragility and fears in Tegularius, Hesse separates himself from him to continue his journey in the cloak of Joseph Knecht, but not without paying tribute to that "extremely gentle, precious, but endangered property" (228) which, underneath the scars of life, Hesse had always felt himself to be. But he has finally turned from self-pity and made the Faustian decision to become a servant—a Knecht. Thus, we shall now see Joseph Knecht taking his first steps out of the Castalian refuge.

Before his departure for the Benedictine Cloister of Mariafels (and again we should note the masculine/feminine components of the cloister name), Knecht spends three weeks with the "police," as Castalia's Political or Foreign Ministry is called (229). Here he is briefed on the rules of behavior for the Castalian who is to spend a prolonged period of time in the world, though few have an opportunity to present their noble image beyond Castalia's walls. Herr Dubois, one of Castalia's few politicians, is responsible for the province's external relations. When the orientation period comes to an end, Dubois, as if in passing, suggests that Knecht keep his eyes and ears open. Should he hear "political conversations" or sense "political moods," he might inform Dubois (231).

In taking leave of Tegularius, Knecht reflects on this highly intelligent and aesthetic Castalian and reluctantly admits he feels the temptation to exploit the power that he has over his friend who is weaker in strength but not in love. The passage is a reiteration of the danger one faces in possessing the gift to attract and to influence others. If Hesse is professing the idea of service as leadership in the novel as a whole, at this point he is warning that even the natural leader will always be tempted to rule by power rather than by serving. It is the story of Christ's temptations in the wilderness and of Goethe's message in his *Novelle*. A parallel is also drawn in a letter Hesse writes to a young German in April of 1932, when he was working on *The Glass Bead Game*. Luise Rinser, a well-known German writer, pointed out that the letter was, in fact, a public reply to a private letter she had written to Hesse (*HHudR* 19) seeking advice. Hesse answered her as follows:

> You have found in my books a reflection of a way of thought for which you take me to be the teacher. It is, however, the way of thought of all spiritual thinkers, and it is . . . diametrically opposed to the way of thinking of the politicians, of the generals and "leaders." It is beautifully expressed . . . in the gospels, in the sayings of Chinese philosophers, especially Confucius, Lao Tse, and in the fables of Dschuang Dsi, in some of the Indian writings such as the *Bhagavad-Gita*. This stream of thought flows quietly through the literature of every people. You will search in vain for a leader in this type of thinking, for none of us has the ambition or even the possibility to be "Führer." We think little of leading, everything of serving.[9]

The chapter "Two Orders" is the threshold for Knecht's conscious entrance into the world of leadership as Hesse would have us understand it. Knecht is taking outward steps onto the inward path and entering into the feminine world, just as did Sinclair, Siddhartha, Harry Haller, and Goldmund before him, although the similarity is not immediately obvious, for the Benedictine Cloister will hardly resemble Pablo's Magic Theater nor will Knecht find a Kamala or a Kamaswami.

His first impression of life in the monastery is its slow tempo. The fathers seem less intellectual, less active, but calmer, more difficult to influence, older, more reserved. Most importantly, though, the spirit that rules here seems to have "returned to nature and feeling" (239), the very qualities Knecht has found disappearing from Castalia. His ostensible assignment, acquainting the fathers with the Bead Game, is so elemental that Knecht immediately senses that he is serving another purpose. But what? He recalls his instructions from the Magister Ludi himself: "Use your days, learn, seek to make yourself loved and useful . . . don't force yourself on anyone" (239).

A young student, Anton, is attracted to Knecht and appears from time to time in the chapter. On the one hand, the episode emphasizes Knecht's charisma, but Anton performs a second function, as well (and a third to be mentioned later), namely to make Knecht aware of the awe in which the Benedictine historian, Father Jakobus, is held. When Anton looks at him, it is in hero worship, and Knecht muses that scholarship must be so rare in the Order that its one great scholar is looked upon as a *Wundertier* (244). This studious older man (as Mileck points out, the name is Hesse's tribute to Jakob Burckhardt ["Names" 175]) is also aware of the young visitor's presence and one evening invites him to his quarters. Knecht's descriptive reaction to Father Jakobus reveals the historian's purpose in the novel: "The soft voice and the elderly intelligent face gave to his overly polite words that amazing, glistening ambiguity which lies somewhere between earnestness and irony, devotion and gentle mockery, pathos and playfulness . . . this mixture of superiority and mockery, of wisdom and stubborn ceremonial was well known to Knecht from the Chinese and was refreshing for him . . . the Bead Game Master, Thomas, was also a past master of this tone" (245).

We thus recognize Father Jakobus as an enlightened Vasudeva/Siddhartha figure, one who stands both in life and outside it. He is present in the novel as a model for Knecht, to give substance to the latter's own maturing vision of life and to articulate Castalia's weakness, which Knecht only surmises at this point. As we learn from the various discussions of these two spiritually *and* intellectually dedicated men, Roman Catholicism has survived into this future era, whereas the Protestant Church has disappeared from history because it lacked the imagination and involvement that the Benedictine father now exemplifies and imparts to his church. Jakobus accuses the Castalians of totally lacking a sense of history. They have "distilled themselves a world history that consists only of intellectual history and art history . . . without blood and reality" (251). The historian must "retain the most touching child's faith in the ordering power of the intellect . . . but . . . he must have respect for the incomprehensible truth, reality and the uniqueness of events" (252). We can see in Father Jakobus's speech the same idea that Hesse expresses in the Latin foreword to the novel— that to study history is to start from the premise that the historian is striving to do something impossible, yet necessary and highly important. It means to surrender to the chaos but at the same time to believe in order and meaning. A blatant criticism of run-of-the-mill historians is added by Father Jakobus: ". . . there is no lack of historians, biographers, to say nothing of journalists, to whom the guessing about and grasping of an historical moment wants to say: the momentary success appears as a characteristic greatness. The corporal, who between today and tomorrow becomes dictator, [is]. . . a favorite subject of such historians" (252)—another of the few passages in the book that point to Hesse's subtle intentions to relate his novel to the contemporary political situation in Germany. In the end, he remains ironically aloof—which, however, does not obviate his criticism of the Third Reich.

A particular conversation with Father Jakobus, which Knecht reproduced in a letter to a friend, illustrates where the historian and Hesse find their common ground. Jakobus confesses that his love and curiosity belong to phenomena such as the Benedictine Order, in which "the attempt is made to gather men of intellect and soul, to raise them, to mold them through education, not through eugenics, to make them noble through the spirit, not through blood, a nobility that is capable of serving and of ruling," an allusion to National Socialism's racial purity concepts (253). Jakobus sees such phenomena in antiquity in the Pythagorean system, in Plato's Academy, in China's Confucius, and above all in the serving orders of the Christian Church (253). Jakobus adds that he is not speaking of the "sacred church itself . . . it stands for the faithful beyond discussion. Rather it is the congregations such as the Benedictines, the Dominicans, and the later Jesuits who . . . despite all . . . the degenerations . . . the violence, have preserved their voice, their bearing, their individual souls, who are the most remarkable and honorable phenomena of history" (254).

We have little difficulty relating Father Jakobus's description of such congregations to Hesse's collective Cains and Journeyers to the East, or even to the original Castalian dream. All of them recognize a sacred universe. They and their fellow journeyers, like Father Jakobus, struggle and serve within their own individual arenas. The *Unio Mystica* is as sacred and beyond discussion for each as is its equivalent, the sacred church, for Father Jakobus. It is here that Hesse both merges with, and separates himself from, sectarian isms and religions. He can and does recognize a sacred church—that is, a divine spirit—but it must be found within each and every breast. Father Jakobus can believe the same of an entire order, which is where Hesse separates himself from the Catholic father, for the orders have rules and doctrines. For Hesse, the Journeyers to the East, once they have survived their *Morbio Inferiore,* must travel their own paths. That they will occasionally meet, however, is a foregone conclusion.

Thus, we see that our pacesetter, Hesse/Knecht, will take a step beyond the thinking of even the revered Father Jakobus.

The authorities in Castalia read with care the semiannual reports filed by Knecht with details of his Jakobus friendship. The younger Castalian makes just as profound and positive an impression on his Benedictine colleague as the elder man has made on him. Ultimately, Father Jakobus, because of Knecht, recognizes Castalia as an order that, like his own, is an attempt to build spiritual nobility; its Glass Bead Game, he concedes, is not just aesthetic dandyism.

Hesse ends the chapter with Knecht's reflections on a Pietist theologian, Johann Albrecht Bengel, one of the few who had, in his time, "served a tiny, transitory church without failing to serve the eternal. Piety . . . devout service and loyalty, *even unto sacrifice of life, is possible in every denomination and at every step, and is the only really valid test for sincerity* [emphasis provided]"(258). Critics who have been surprised at the abrupt ending of the novel and the meaning of Knecht's death have overlooked this passage. Kenneth Negus, for instance, says that "Hesse is exaggerating when he writes [regarding "Knecht's sacrifice that he bravely and joyfully fulfills" (*GS VII* 640)], 'Nothing in the text indicates such conscious awareness on Knecht's part'"[10]

The Mission

After he has been in Mariafels for two years, Knecht notes the arrival of another visitor, one that he is prevented from meeting, and the stranger is closeted for discussion with Father Jakobus for many hours. Remembering that the police in Castalia had requested that he keep them informed of just such occurrences, he writes to Herr Dubois. As a result, the Magister Ludi writes to the Abbot at Mariafels, requesting that Knecht be given leave to return to Waldzell for a time. As he makes his way to Waldzell, Knecht finds that he can no longer "shout in jubilation to the birds in the trees" (263), which means to him that he is a man, that he has been called upon to live up to the obligations of his oath, that he is no longer free, but responsible. But, he asks, to whom or to what? It has to be the province, itself, he decides, taking his cue from Father Jakobus's praise of the Catholic orders, and the reader can see that Hesse is temporarily leading Knecht to play a principal role in Castalia—to infuse it with vitality as Jakobus does for the Church.

Following numerous visitations with the various elite of the province, Knecht is summoned by the Magister Ludi, and the real purpose of his Mariafels assignment is divulged. Castalia wants to establish a permanent embassy in Rome. The time has come for the two orders to join hands, both of them having the historical assignment, as noted, of preserving and nurturing the spirit and world peace. Knecht had been sent to win over Jakobus, who has the strongest voice in the church. When he returns to Mariafels to continue to nourish these ties, he joins the priest's classes and asks that the student Anton also be allowed. Thus, Anton is closely associated with two of the "purest spirits and original minds" (273), and, inferring a third purpose for Anton's presence in the novel, we see that Hesse is planting a seed for the future; the budding relationship between Castalia and Rome will have its proponents, perhaps one of the reasons that Castalia has survived.

As Knecht wonders how he can confess his mission to Jakobus, the wise old man tells him he realized long ago that his young colleague had a hidden agenda of which he was not aware. But now, since his return, his behavior indicates that he has been told. And Father Jakobus has already guessed its nature; thus, Knecht can tell his story, and the friendship of the two representatives of their respective orders can continue.

From Jakobus Knecht learns what he could not have learned in the province. The father *lives* in history, *creates* history; he lets the "winds of the world blow through his study . . . and the tones and ideas of his epoch come into his heart. He has been involved in and shared the blame and responsibility for the events of his time" (279). Thus, we see Hesse's new optimism for the future, even as he writes in the 1930s: the mind, via history and commitment, can experience and serve life by giving it direction. And we also become aware that Hesse is answering Goldmund's question to Narcissus: "How will you ever die if you have no mother?" Father Jakobus has found her—as will Knecht—without personally wading through life's dark alleys. The priest is so saturated with historical reality that it has "made of him a person of integrity and significant power" (279). He is a servant to life and thus to his church, just as Knecht—per Hesse's plan—will become to his life and his order. We are informed at this point by the narrator that the Castalia-Rome relationship has "lasted to this day" (281), thanks to Knecht and Jakobus.

While at the monastery for his second stay, Knecht also develops a game for the annual Waldzell competition, noting that there are two competing concepts of the Bead Game. One, the formal, strives to create a game that is structurally without blemish, whereas the second, the psychological, of which Knecht is a proponent, involves constructing games that are not harmonious from any external perspective but which lead the player through his precisely prescribed meditations to experience the completeness of the divine (283–4)—in other words, a player in the "game of life" can build his own unity from the inside (284–5).

Despite his preference for the psychological game, Knecht devises a formal one, possibly—so says our narrator—to show that he has not lost his elegance and virtuosity during his sojourn in Mariafels. More likely, however, Hesse has his protagonist win the competition by means of a formal masterpiece to indicate that the judges are more prone to approve the strictly intellectual, the masculine, approach that underlines the Castalian weakness. A footnote to this weakness is the humorous account of Tegularius's three-day visit to Mariafels. This ultimate Castalian can barely survive the "strange impressions, the friendly but simple, healthy and somewhat uncouth people, to none of whom his thoughts, cares and problems would have had the slightest meaning" (285). Thus, Hesse shows the isolation of the province, its departure from its original objectives, for if a Castalian cannot survive in the rarefied air of a Benedictine cloister, what possible connection can he have with the world outside? The point is emphasized in Knecht's subsequent observations to his friend Ferromonte in a letter: "We people from our beloved province are far more spoiled and sensitive than we ourselves are aware" (288).

In the final pages of this chapter, Father Jakobus informs Knecht that his erstwhile friend, Plinio Designori, has become involved in a bitter political debate and has verbally attacked Jakobus, and that even Knecht's name has been mentioned in various accounts because of his previous relationship with Designori. The episode is a subtle foreshadowing of Knecht's future step into the "real world."

Magister Ludi

When Joseph Knecht returns to Castalia, it is spring, the season of rebirth and renewal; Hesse is forecasting rejuvenation of the province. Its positive future is not in evidence during the present annual games, however, for they border on failure, despite their purpose "to awaken the memory of unity" (292). Hesse's further digression on the games is interesting, for he speaks of their religious and moral significance, stating that for believers they have the "sacramental strength of devotion" and for nonbelievers are "a religious substitution" (292). Implicit in this commentary is a reflection on the makeup of the province. Although not further clarified, the word "believers" obviously does not refer to Christians, in particular, but to Hesse's Cains, those who are focused on the spirit behind life, whereas the "nonbelievers" are those who have escaped into their own aesthetic dreams. This is little more than a reiteration of the brotherhood theme in *Demian*—where the collective Cains formed "an island . . . perhaps a model . . . the annunciation of another possibility of living" (*GS III* 236).

The gradual decline of Castalia over the centuries seems to have reached its nadir, as reflected in the present annual games, which border on failure because the Magister Ludi, Thomas von der Trave, has become critically ill. The planning and administration of the festival must, therefore, be turned over to his deputy, Bertram, or the Master's "Shadow," as the holder of this office is traditionally called. This particular Shadow has become unpopular, especially with the youngest stratum of the Elite. In the present predicament, they help Bertram only enough to spare Waldzell the embarrassment of an unsuccessful festival. In a conversation with Tegularius, Knecht chastises them for their treatment of Bertram, saying that "he has sacrificed himself to the games as his last and most ceremonial act of office. You have been hard, no, cruel towards him." From Tegularius's callous reply, we can draw meaning that will later relate to Knecht's final act: "He knows that his sacrifice was necessary" (304).

Following the games, Bertram simply goes into the mountains and disappears. The several pages devoted to the Bertram episode seem superfluous until we realize that Hesse is purposely comparing the person of Knecht, the natural leader, to this Shadow. Through no apparent fault of his own, Bertram is totally lacking in charisma. Nonetheless, he recognizes his responsibilities and fulfills them to the best of his ability, even surrendering his life when he sees that he has outlived his usefulness. Service and sacrifice for the good of the community, for the future, is the core of the message, and we should recall that Hesse had already discussed the necessity to consider life a sacrifice in *Siddhartha* and in *Journey to the East*. This has become for him the meaning of life, the inner-voice message that he spent most of his own life deciphering.

And now the Knecht narrative moves forward. Scarcely forty, he is selected by the Elite to succeed the Magister Ludi. Initially surprised, he soon realizes that he "could have guessed this last and highest of his calls" (308)—a careless, stylistic slip on Hesse's part, because the calls are by no means ended. After receiving the news, Knecht goes to meditate. In his trance-like state, he has a series of visions, first seeing himself as a small boy waiting in the Music Room of his school for the arrival of the Music Master. Then a young boy is following him, then the master, and every time he turns to look at the boy, who is also Joseph Knecht, the master's face is older, more peaceful and venerable, an "ideal of wisdom and dignity" (310), but the boy remains the same. The vision repeats itself interminably until it is no longer clear who is leading and who is following—the old man or the youth. Knecht identifies himself with both figures; he is simultaneously master and pupil, then organizer, originator, director, and spectator of the continuing, result-less, playful race of young and old. And from this vision comes a new concept, more symbol than dream, more knowledge than image: this meaningful/meaningless circular movement of master and pupil, this eternal winged game, was the symbol of Castalia, was the game of life, per se, that streamed endlessly through old and young, through day and night, through Yin and Yang (311). The metaphor expresses Hesse's concept of eternal humanity as a sacred and endless unity. The individual, via his own calling, is to serve it and, whenever necessary and in whatever fashion, sacrifice himself for it.

The final pages of this chapter deal with the politics of jealousy and ego, for Knecht's first task is to prove himself to colleagues, fellow masters, and the defeated competitors for the position of Magister Ludi. Even these Elite, the descendants of those dedicated souls who founded the province in order to prevent just such human foibles from dominating the world, must now be won over. Three times daily, Knecht meditates to retain his perspective and equanimity, and he is finally accepted by the Elite as their Magister Ludi. He can now go about his business as Master of Waldzell and symbolic figurehead of the whole of Castalia. It is still spring, for the office is not allowed to be vacant for more than three weeks.

In Office

The task of gaining the confidence of Castalia's Elite is an enlightening trial for Knecht. He sees the pettiness, the selfishness, the insecurity that subtly govern the province, even among those who should be above such abuses. He feels himself to be its brain, its consciousness, and its conscience, and he feels responsible for it. From his surviving archival lecture notes for a beginning class of Bead Game initiates, we learn of Knecht's attempt to advance his vision of what the province should be. He calls Castalia a Holy Place with the assignment of protecting its unique secret and symbol, the Glass Bead Game. Every one of its institutes and every individual should know but two goals and ideals: in his own area of expertise he should develop himself to the fullest potential and, in so doing, should make his calling and himself vital and flexible, so that he is bound to all disciplines and to all of humankind. The second ideal is the belief in the inner unity of all endeavors of the minds of humans (324). We see here the two goals of the journeyers to the East—the personal and the universal—and we can easily equate such an exemplary Castalia with the League Headquarters in the previous novel. Hesse emphasizes that both goals must be consciously concomitant and continual. This is the ideal father-side of life.

As Glass Bead Game players, Knecht continues, the students must save the discipline from becoming self-serving, and he warns, from all appearances, Castalia does not want to be saved from itself. Returning to his theme of individualism, Hesse/Knecht tells the students that they cannot force universality upon their colleagues but can only keep themselves at the height of their spiritual lives by carefully and constantly adapting every noble, even dangerous, action to the thought of unity; every researcher and ambitious expert must be reminded that he can easily be led astray (325).

In the same lecture notes, we find a pronouncement of Hesse's elitism. He emphasizes that the best and most vital quality of Castalia is its time-honored custom of searching out the elite (326). It is in these few dozen hearts and minds that the developments, the adjustments, the flights of fancy, the analyses of their game vis-à-vis the spirit of the times and the individual fields of knowledge take place (327). If, through meditation and the practice of yoga techniques, they can prevent the animal in them, the *diabolus,* from leading them into self-seeking vanity and misuse of power, their province will serve its purpose. They are not to flee from the *vita activa* into the *vita contemplativa*[11] but be constantly underway between them, at home in either, participating in both (328–9)—a reflection of the Siddhartha metaphor of the enlightened ferryman symbolically moving back and forth across the river, serving his passengers in the process.

Knecht gradually begins to spend more and more time teaching younger students. The older he becomes, the more he becomes interested in the education of the young (331). This focus, too, reflects a common Hesse theme, as long ago expressed in *Roßhalde,* when the painter Veraguth had told his servant Robert that it is "only in youth, up to the age of thirteen or fourteen that a man perceives things in all their sharpness and freshness; all the rest of his life he feeds on that experience" (*GS II* 477). In the two early novels where the theme of childhood plays a significant role, we recall that Hans Giebenrath had been badgered into helplessness as a young child and was not able to recover, while, on the other hand, Peter Camenzind's youthful sense of belonging to the world of nature had provided him with a freedom that enabled him to remain free as, supposedly, did Hermann Heilner. From the standpoint of narrative development, Joseph Knecht's profound interest in and ability to reach out to the young should be recognized as reader preparation for the Master's implied lasting influence on the boy Tito when the novel concludes.

At this point in the story, Knecht is interrupted by the visit of a student of the Music Master and told that he should visit his old mentor who is "no longer completely among us" (346–7). Knecht does not fully understand but leaves as soon as possible. A description of the visit is recorded by Carlo Ferromonte, the music librarian at Monteport. There is a full sense of recognition in the old man's smiling eyes, and a halo-like aura seems to emanate from him. He only smiles at Knecht's attempts at conversation and eventually replies, "You are tiring yourself, Joseph" (351). It is at this moment that Knecht realizes that he is in the presence of a Buddha-like saint. Ferromonte remarks to Knecht that he does not like the word "saint," because of its religious connotation (352), but Knecht argues: piety is not unknown among the Castalians, and piety in any form can lead to enlightenment (355). The Music Master is another Vasudeva and again embodies Hesse's pronouncement that there is a potential Buddha or Christ in everyone.

Two Poles

This chapter explains why Castalia still exists in the narrator's time, many years after Knecht's tenure as Magister Ludi. He did manage to return the province to a semblance of its former glory, nearly comparable to its zenith under Magister Wassermaler. His first annual games festival was an overwhelming success; even emissaries from the outside world praised his name, and "many an initiate was won over to the game forever" (359).

The biographer now feels that it his task to turn to what he calls the dichotomy in Knecht's life. He sees the "constant pulsing polarity in Knecht's soul as the essential characteristic of his being" (359), hence the chapter title "Two Poles." This is, of course, Hesse speaking, letting the reader know that Knecht has reached a stage of enlightenment where the polarities of life are in equilibrium—that is, interacting with each other as life places its demands on them. We shall see, however, that Knecht has yet to determine where these demands are leading him. "With only the exception of the last moments," continues the narrator, "the report of the Magister's years [in office can be characterized] as glorifying accounts of service, fulfilled responsibility and successes" (360). Again, it is Hesse speaking, this time ironically to show that the narrator has missed the point completely, for Knecht's decision to leave Castalia was his greatest step forward.

Most of the chapter focuses on Knecht's thought processes as he slowly determines how he may best serve his office. The biographer will not tell us for some time exactly what the polarities of Knecht's life are, but clarity is best served for the reader if they are explained at this point. Knecht's two basic tendencies, his yin and yang, are described on the one hand as his "tendency to be faithful to, to preserve and be loyal in, selfless service to the hierarchy" and, on the other hand, as his "tendency to awaken, to press forward, to grasp hold of reality" (371). Knecht sees what other Castalians do not—that the grandeur of their province is an endangered and waning greatness (360). He can feel his own person and activity as simply "one of the cells in the stream of becoming and change" (360). This level of consciousness has been awakened in him by historical studies and the influence of Father Jakobus, and the knowledge of transitoriness has long been a part of him. He feels a sense of responsibility to reawaken the conscience of his province. He muses: are those who are capable of seeing the dynamic struggle between survival and decline, between the spirit and the world, really expected to be responsible for those who are ignorant of it, or for those who surrender to the lesser gods for whatever reason? His eventual answer is a qualified yes. They are responsible to "bring certain things to mankind's attention," as was stated in the introduction of *The Glass Bead Game* (79)—what Hesse obviously feels himself to be doing by writing the novel— but they can do little more. The point is also paradoxical, for Hesse's sympathy for the innocents, for those who live quietly in clean houses, for those who surrender to the little world of simple, even sinful pleasures, is always restrained at best. Hesse's own life, as well as the lives of his protagonists, indicate that it is with some reluctance that those who survive the temptations must accept responsibility for others who do not.

A prolonged discussion of Knecht's lasting friendship with Tegularius, the ultimate Castalian, is a principle part of the background information that we are given as to why Knecht recognizes the polarities so strongly. These friends have a mutual admiration for each other. Tegularius was amazed at Knecht's ability to stay in the "worldly" Benedictine cloister for two years, but, more important, it is Knecht's noble character that draws Tegularius to him (365). And we should remember that Knecht does not *seek* to lead; the point is emphasized once again that the Cains of the world, the immortals-to-be, the journeyers to the East, bring the other seekers to follow only by setting examples, only through their legacies, whatever they may be; they do not proselytize. Such leaders do share the masculine intellectual traits and curiosity with the Tegulariuses, but they have the additional dimension of understanding feminine reality. This combination is what gives them vision and a sense of moral responsibility. It is pointed out that Tegularius's failure is his one-sidedness, brought on because of his neglect of meditation (366); he does not listen for his inner voice and, as a result, lacks universal vision. He seeks only intellectual satisfaction. The Elite, like Tegularius, who do not share Knecht's vision are drawn to the Magister because of his. They, too, are influenced by integrity and, as a result, can be led by the Knechts— those who serve.

As he had said of Castalia, in general, Knecht also says of Tegularius, that "he didn't want to be cured, he was not interested in harmony and order, loved nothing but his own freedom and his eternal studies, and he preferred to remain . . . the suffering . . . the abrasive outsider, genial fool and nihilist instead of entering into the hierarchical order and attaining peace" (367). The use of the word "outsider" is interesting, for whenever Hesse uses it in the sense of a Cain, the outsider who does not fit into the conventional law-and-order society, the word is meant to have a positive connotation. Here, however, it is negative, for the outsider does not fit into the Castalian hierarchy—and Hesse obviously means Joseph Knecht's *ideal* hierarchy, not the hierarchy that is decaying precisely because of the Tegulariuses.

This ultimate Castalian, then, is as necessary to Knecht as are Designori and Father Jakobus. He, too, is an "awakening element" (367). Knecht can see in him what Castalia can become if its members are not infused with new impulses to rejuvenate the province. Tegularius is called a "forerunner of things to come" (367), and Castalia will be naught but a palace of dreams. Thus, against the background of his childhood memories of the world, his natural intuitive wisdom, his historical perceptions gained through debate and discussion with Designori and Father Jakobus, and his vision of a Castalia filled with Tegulariuses, Knecht sets out to bring the world back to Castalia and Castalia back to the world.

What are the specific deeds of the Magister Ludi who can see how the world turns and how it should turn? Hesse concisely summarizes several activities to show wisdom and commitment in concert, the *vita activa* and the *vita contemplativa* in balance. First, we see how Knecht deals with the brilliant problem-child, Tegularius. Taking advantage of the influence he has over him, Knecht makes use of Tegularius's tremendous intellect by assigning him to structure technically the annual festive game, which is played by the master, and it is a success. He gives him research projects and takes time to listen to him. Patience is his primary tool in finding positive outlets for the otherwise helpless, directionless intellect (369). His second activity that serves to rekindle the Castalian spirit is his devotion to the youngest pupils, to whom he dedicates more and more of his time. They are "more closely tied to the entire world and to life" (373). They are attracted to him for the same reason as is Tegularius, and the same such attraction and respect of a young boy for this master will play a role in understanding Knecht's final act in the novel.

The narrator interrupts his praise of Knecht to return to his own present, noting that "in recent times there has been a tendency to remove some of the over-cultivated specialties in research in favor of intensification of meditation"

(374), which the Music Master had reminded Knecht was necessary to retain a sense of universal vision. Thus, we are shown that Knecht's influence on Castalia is still in evidence. In this rather disjointed chapter, Hesse includes a Knecht-Tegularius discussion on the merits of the study of history. Tegularius can see it only as an ugly, banal, boring, evil, power struggle, separate from art history, cultural history, and art, itself, by means of which he can escape from the vulgar world (375). Knecht points out that abstractions are enticing but that one must also breathe air and eat bread (377), and we are reminded why he could so appreciate Father Jakobus, who "lived in the blood and reality" of history. The death of the Music Master also occurs in this chapter. It is described as "not so much a death as a fading away of the physical substance and physical function" with an atmosphere of "sunset and the extinguishing of a pure and selfless life" (377). Hesse, in short, is professing that life simply becomes death—they are not separate entities—the same message that he symbolized in Siddhartha's flowing river.

The chapter ends with an interesting commentary on Knecht's administrative handling of the Elite. The greater the differences of opinion and the more important the debated questions, the more courtesy played a role: "The extremely courteous tone of the debates protects not only the debaters from succumbing to their passions and helps to maintain behavior . . . it also protects the dignity of the order and the authorities themselves . . . and this complementary art form, so often belittled by the students, has its good points" (384). This tone is a far cry from the rebellious visions of the Sinclairs, the Siddharthas, Harry Haller, and Goldmund, but it seems an unequivocal admission on the now middle-aged Hesse's part that the discipline and structured practices of the father-world do have their significant roles to play. Only thus, perhaps, does he think that the unenlightened intellectual Elite can survive their petty personal rivalries and work toward some semblance of what should be their common goal: to serve.

A Conversation

Joseph Knecht has mastered his Castalian appointment. In the eyes of the world, he has restored respect to the province but, nonetheless, has not brought the world to Castalia. He cannot administrate a change to this effect; something more is needed. "A Conversation" will continue to focus on the Castalian ills that need healing and on the rumblings of an approaching decision that will carry Knecht into another sphere of life and eventually to his death. The Magister has met the challenges of his office and, as one of the "great natures"—that is, one of Hesse's enlightened—has realized that he must leave the path of tradition and obedience to the existing order and "with trust in the highest unnameable powers . . . seek the new" (386). A degree of lament, probably Hesse's own, is obvious in Knecht's recognition that he must respond to the responsibilities that those "unnameable powers" are forcing on him (385).

The narrator says he will let the question rest as to whether Knecht was a promoter and a brave fighter, in view of his criticism of Castalia, or a deserter and a rebel. The battle over this question had divided Castalia into two camps for some time and still has not entirely disappeared (386). Thus, the reader can see that Knecht's desertion has had a long-lasting influence, which was his intent. The narrator will attempt, he continues, to tell the story of Knecht's demise objectively, but it is not so much a story as a *legend*—a report mixed with genuine information and pure rumor as it has come down to the "younger ones" from both "clear" and "dark" sources (386). Hesse intends the reader to find religious overtones in this sentence. The German word *Jüngere* can also mean "disciple"; thus, a subtle comparison is already being made between Christ's death and Knecht's (approaching) death.

Just as Knecht is beginning to think of taking a different path into the fresh air, his acquaintanceship with Plinio Designori, his one-time debating opponent in Waldzell, is renewed. This is a favorite stylistic device for a transition: Demian stepped in to help Sinclair when he realized he could not obey Kromer's demand; Otto Burkhardt visited Veraguth to move him to a decision in *Roßhalde;* Hermine appeared when Harry Haller's life was in crisis. The old friend Designori, now a high-ranking government official and political writer, is a member of a commission that has arrived to evaluate Castalia. But he is a changed man, "in part destroyed, in part ennobled" (388), the result, so thinks Knecht, of tragic suffering. He has never seen this suffering on the faces of Castalians but only on the faces of people from the outside world.

His former friend is distant, but Knecht persists in renewing the relationship, and they finally sit down for a long conversation. Designori begins by pointing out that he and Knecht speak different languages. Because of his own Waldzell background, he has less difficulty than Knecht, but how can the latter understand "family" and a variety of other worldly expressions? This is a variation of Goldmund's question to Narcissus: "How can you die when you have no mother?" Knecht replies that people of good will can gain considerable understanding from one another (394), thus, once more, pointing out Hesse's maturer attitude toward learning versus personal experience. In reflecting on his earlier Waldzell experience, Designori notes that, just as the Castalians felt themselves to be superior and better than the people in the world outside, when he returned to the world to study at a university, he found that people felt themselves just as superior, no less proud that they were the ones "pleasing to God" (396). They laughed at the half-Castalian, and some hated him with the pure hatred that "common people can have for anything refined" (396). If his dual life had shown the young Designori anything, it was the revelation that Castalia had distanced itself from its motherland (note that Hesse does not say fatherland, again emphasizing that it is the feminine qualities of the world outside Castalia that have been forgotten) but that, on the other side of the coin, their country was unfaithful to its most noble province and its spirit. Body and soul, ideal and reality, were widely separated (396). When Designori had tried to talk about the Bead Game with friends, they could only look upon it as witchcraft, again a point that begs interpretation for its religious implications: if adherents of a particular religion can accept the magic and miracles of their own faith, they may still find the metaphors of others incredible.

When Designori returned to Castalia and met Knecht during the latter's period of free study, his illusions were fully ended. He was not a comrade, not a man of rank, only a burdensome fool, an uneducated foreigner (404). Knecht smiles, even laughs at the long-ago experience, which he remembers no less precisely than does Designori. This hurts Plinio. How can he laugh at something that has had such a profoundly negative effect on him? But Knecht explains that Designori was still trying to be a Castalian, which he was not. This time he has come as himself, and Knecht can accept him; this is genuine. As readers we are also privy by now to what Knecht's laughter really means. In immortal fashion he does not have to join Designori in his sadness and troubles to give credence to them and to take them seriously—the lesson Harry Haller had to be taught. But Designori is unable to grasp the explanation entirely and holds forth with a long litany of accusations against Castalia. Is it not an artificial, sterile, half-world of appearances in which they vegetate like cowards without vice, without passion, without hunger, without family, without mothers and children, almost without women? (And, again, we should note that Designori does not accuse them of lacking a father.) All difficult responsibilities, such as the economy, the judicial system, and politics, have been left to others for generations. It is the people outside, the poor, the pressured, who live in the dirt of the world and lead real lives, who do real work (413). Designori, himself, following his failed attempt at friendship with Knecht on his previous visit, threw himself into the world, determined to wash all traces of Castalia away. He drank and whored and denounced all so-called decent and honorable ideals—a replay of Sinclair's last attempt to join the herd—and we realize that Hesse is letting Designori play a part of Knecht's role. His misadventures remind us that Knecht does not have to participate in decadence to understand it. Like Father Jakobus, he is able to understand blood and reality—in this case Designori's experiences—without wallowing in them, himself.

As the conversation continues, a word introduced to the reader in *Der Steppenwolf* takes on considerable significance. *Heiterkeit,* which can mean both "cheerfulness" and "serenity," was displayed by Goethe and the immortals to characterize their attitude toward the trials and tribulations of the world which enabled them to perceive the divine essence of life despite its absurdities. The word appears several times in rapid succession (417–20), a clue that Hesse does not want it to escape our attention. Knecht's expression of *Heiterkeit* is not, as Designori thinks, because he has managed to escape from the fears and perils of reality into a clear, well-ordered world. The masculine Castalian setting need not destroy the spiritual essence behind it any more than the essence of divine music is destroyed by a rasping radio.

To attain to this *Heiterkeit,* we are told, has always been Knecht's highest goal; it is the affirmation of all reality; it is alertness on the brink of the abyss; it is indestructible and only increases as one ages and gets closer to death. It is the secret of beauty and the substance of art (419). As far as Castalian *Heiterkeit* is concerned, says Knecht, the Glass Bead Game unites three principles: science, respect for the beautiful, and respect for meditation. Thus, a Bead Game player should be infused with *Heiterkeit.* He should, above all, be filled with music, which is none other than the courage to dance through the horrors and flames of the world as a solemn offering of sacrifice (420)—the latter word again a subtle foreshadowing of Knecht's final act. When the chapter ends, there should be no doubt that Hesse is portraying Joseph Knecht as the most superior and last in line of his immortals-to-be. Designori will soon open the door to the world for him, and he will leave Castalia to see what awaits him outside.

Preparations

Knecht and Designori are close friends once more, and the renewed acquaintance eventually reveals Designori's story. His father had been a pillar of support for the ruling conservative faction, a friend of the church, though not out of any religious convictions—a typical Hesse representative of the father-world. Plinio, on the other hand, disappointed in the university, had become a member of a new, left-oriented wing of an old liberal party, led by a publisher and popular orator named Veraguth. Designori senior had railed in anger against his son, calling him a conspirator and traitor against his father, his family, and traditions of their lineage (422–3). Plinio had refused to leave his party, which he saw as striving for absolute justice and humanity. Before Designori had finished the university, he had become Veraguth's assistant and, a few years later, his son-in-law (424). Although he had found an ersatz father in Veraguth, the battle with his own father had caused his mother considerable pain, and she had died shortly after Plinio's marriage. When his father died, Plinio sold the family estate.

As Designori had become older, he had no longer been so sure of his ideals, no longer so sure that it was truth and justice that had drawn him to Veraguth or whether the latter's powers of speech and his beautiful daughter might also have been part of the attraction. Maybe his own father's viewpoint had been no less noble. Designori had begun to doubt if, in fact, there was a right and a wrong, a good and a bad; maybe the voice of one's own conscience was ultimately the only valid judge (426)—the Hessean conclusion that all are supposed to reach. And Designori has a son, Tito, who has become an object of dispute between father and mother, and the boy is drawn more and more to his mother. Thus, we see that the boy, as did Goldmund after his sojourns in the mother-world, needs the vision and discipline of the father-side. The narrator of the Knecht story speculates, somewhat incongruously, as to why the Magister took it upon himself to teach his melancholy friend to smile and laugh again, noting that Designori later saw it as *Zauberei*—witchcraft, sorcery, magic, and roguery. Knecht was a much greater rogue than people suspected, full of playfulness, humor, a sense of fun in playing games. We might ask why Knecht is described in such a way that we never actually see him act in the novel, and the obvious answer is that, at this point of his development, whatever he does is done in a spirit of playfulness, or *Heiterkeit*. Knecht finds all of life a divine game, and he is its master, another recollection we should make when we are suddenly faced with an apparent enigma at the end of the book. That Hesse intends this emphasis is further supported by Designori's reflection: "I believe people of his kind do most things unconsciously, as reflex actions, find themselves given an assignment, hear themselves called out for in need, and surrender to the call with no further ado" (428). He could so "little resist the urge to educate, to influence, to heal, help, to reveal that the means were next to irrelevant" (429). Hesse is describing, very precisely, the circumstances and motivation of Knecht's final act in the novel.

Knecht is in his eighth year of office when he receives permission from the Board of Directors to visit Designori at his home, his only excursion into the world since he was brought into the order as a child, save for the Benedictine Cloister experience. It is now that the *Bead Game*'s only feminine character is introduced. Despite keeping herself at a distance, Frau Designori is at least in part won over by Knecht, and when he jokingly says it is too bad that they did not send their son to be educated in Castalia, his mother says she would not have agreed; her son is the only thing that makes her life worth living (433). This gives Knecht considerable food for thought—her beautiful house, her husband, her politics and party, the inheritance of a once-devoted father all have little to do with meaning; only her son can give her this. Knecht's repetition of the topic when he reflects on it enhances the Hesse message that the child is more important than the mother.

Knecht must also inform Tegularius of his intention to leave Castalia. To his surprise, the latter finds this exciting and amusing, since he has always been a loner and outsider within the order and has always stood against the authorities. It will be Tegularius's assignment to help Knecht compose a letter to the hierarchy explaining the reasons for his decision. Knecht promises himself little success from such an effort, believing that the authorities will never accept his resignation (439), but he is determined to leave. He asks Designori's help in finding a temporary position, and when Designori offers to place Tito in his hands, Knecht accepts, under the condition that Tito's mother agree and that the boy be placed strictly under his supervision. Tito comes of good stock and has gifts from both parents. What is missing is the harmony of his strengths. To awaken a desire for the harmony will be Knecht's task (442).

Ultimately, Frau Designori agrees, and Knecht begins his attempts to win over the boy. On a walk, Tito stops before the old family estate and complains bitterly that his father has sold it. Knecht suggests that it may very well have been a father-son conflict that prompted it. In selling the house, Tito's father was rejecting the traditions of the family, his father, and his entire past, and slapping his dependence in the face. Such a conflict is often present in animated and gifted personalities. A future Designori might make it a goal to regain the property, but if that is his only goal, then he is nothing more than someone possessed. Sons should serve higher goals than those of the family (445). And with such a beginning to their relationship, the stage is set for Knecht to step into Tito's life, and even now, the boy fears that this man represents a force that could be dangerous to his freedom, even if he appears to be someone who could be loved and honored very much (446).

The Circular Letter

The narrator of Knecht's story is pleased to have the original document that explains to the Castalian hierarchy their Magister Ludi's reasons for resigning his office and leaving the province. Their knowledge of the end of his life, itself, according to the narrator, is somewhat lacking, although the reader will find a detailed account. Thus, if the story of Knecht's death supposedly bears "more characteristics of saga than of an historical report" (449), it is because Hesse wants the reader to realize that the significance of history may well lie in its metaphor.

The two-page preface to "The Circular Letter," which Knecht submits to the authorities, based on Tegularius's draft, is curious. Knecht's simple announcement of resignation and decision to leave the Order stresses his lack of faith in the hierarchy to understand his reasoning and accept his departure. His amicable lack of confidence in most of his other colleagues to perceive any significant truth in what he is saying about their intellectual province simply points out the obvious: the vast majority of these intellectuals are too self-centered, do not see beyond their immediate spheres of interest, and have forgotten Castalia's *raison d'être*. Knecht looks upon his petition almost as a "comedy" (450). We can easily expand the letter's audience: Hesse is standing on his Olympus, in the guise of his Magister Ludi, with his own sense of *Heiterkeit,* presenting his own confessional views to his readers. He does not expect them to pay any more heed to his message than will Knecht's colleagues to his, but we recall his words on the first page of the novel: "Nothing is more important than placing before the eyes of man certain things, the existence of which is neither demonstrable nor apparent, so that pious and conscientious people will treat them to a certain extent as existing things and be led a step nearer to the possibility of their being born, may feel a twinge of conscience that will awaken them to action in the future" (79). Thus Hesse and Knecht are both carrying out their respective responsibilities, and the Circular Letter will tell us what some of these "things" are.

It is the duty of a Magister Ludi to point out to the authorities that the province and the Glass Bead Game, itself, are in danger (451). He explains the threat by means of a parable: A scholar sitting in his dormer study, engulfed in his subtle scholarly work, becomes aware that fires have broken out in the house below. He will not consider whether it is his responsibility to stay here and finish his work; he will run down and attempt to save the house (452). Knecht's instincts tell him that there is a fire in the depths of Castalia. He must hurry to the source of the smoke.

Any nobility, any privileged class, may fall victim to hubris, the characteristic disease of the aristocracy, and this should give the Castalians food for thought. Even if the Castalian has been obedient to the rules of his order, is not lacking in ambition, and cultivates his intellectual pursuits, he does not feel responsible for what happens in the world outside. The teachers who work outside the province are the only ones among them who are really fulfilling the purpose of Castalia (454–6). Their highest and most sacred assignment is to preserve the spiritual foundation of their country and the world; their function has a moral side, a sense of truth upon which justice is based, but the resident Castalians are satisfied to let their teachers, alone, atone for their negligence and justify their privileges (456).

Knecht now returns to the Castalians' dislike for history, intellectual and cultural history excepted. They perceive it only as brutal battles for power, goods, lands, raw materials, and money, because Castalia was founded following the warring centuries or Age of the *Feuilleton*—a period in which history was falsified, a period in spiritual abyss and engrossed in political battles of the greatest proportions—thus causing the founding fathers to see history in the same light as the ascetics and hermits of early Christianity looked upon the world (458).[12] But Knecht reminds the hierarchy that the Castalians, themselves, belong to history and are responsible for the world. Their founding fathers had built their union because there was no solid moral order to oppose the chaos. Sadly, though, Castalia has evolved into a "palace," and its comfortable inhabitants no longer have the desire to hear about painful experiences and world history (462). The province has passed its zenith and is in decline. The collapse may not come today or tomorrow, but it will come (463). If the people are placed in a position of choosing between Castalia and making war to protect themselves against the danger of war and defeat, war ideology will win, and youth especially will be conquered with campaign slogans (464). But the choice of action is still open. What must they do? They are not suited to rule, but one does not have to be stupid and brutal to rule, as vain intellectuals sometimes profess. There must, however, be a constant joy in outwardly directed activity. Castalia's role must be to preserve the sources of knowledge in a state of purity. They must never succumb to demands to militarize or politicize the spirit, to let church bells be turned into cannons, to let schoolboys replace decimated military units (as was happening in Germany at this time). They must never permit the spirit to be confiscated as war materiel (466). The greater the education, the greater the privileges that one has enjoyed, the greater is the sacrifice demanded in times of need.

The Glass Bead Game, their specialty and plaything, the expression of the Castalian spirit, will be the first entity to go if the need for Castalia's survival comes into question (468). Practical disciplines will remain, but no one will believe that the disappearance of the Bead Game will prove harmful. Perhaps this is the reason that the Magister Ludi, the protector of their discipline furthest removed from the world, is the first to feel the coming earthquake (469).

The passage explains the symbolism of the Bead Game in simple terms: it is a fragile metaphor for the game of life, for the tenuous search for meaning, for the veiled world of the spirit; all actions are connected to this common center. As Hesse pointed out in the introduction, Castalian origins of the game are traced to two poles, one symbolized by the precise science of mathematics, the other by music. Every serious act of life belongs to both and should reach out to the spirit, should concern itself with the balance of mind and senses. We can attempt to ignore the metaphor, but we are conscious of it, and the higher the consciousness, the more obligated the player is to the search, to listen for the game's inner voice.

The answer to Knecht's Circular Letter comes quickly. The Elite have taken it seriously and respect his efforts, but there was not majority agreement on any of his prophecies. Culture, mind, and soul have their own history—a secret, bloodless, and sacred history that runs beside so-called world history. Their order is concerned only with this history, not with the real, the brutal world history. It could never be a Castalian responsibility to keep watch over political history or to help make it (475). From the basic tone and substance of the letter, Knecht deduces that it was penned by the Director of Administration, himself, Magister Alexander.

The narrator has now reached the end of his official documentary account; what is left for him to tell is "The Legend," but we should note before proceeding that Hesse undoubtedly intends the word "legend" to be understood in its basic meaning as "the life of a saint"—that is, he is canonizing his final creation.

The Legend

The biographer's information regarding Knecht's departure from Castalia, as we learn later, comes from notes that Plinio Designori had made following conversations with the Magister. Again readers are called upon to overlook stylistic liberties, to accept the explanation that this has all "come to our ears" (480), even though they are privy to interior monologues and an omniscient narrator's viewpoints.

After reading the board's answer to his circular letter, the reply quite according to his expectations, Knecht feels a slight tremble, knowing that the hour has come—language suggestive of Christ's reaction in the Garden of Gethsemane as he awaited arrest and crucifixion. Knecht has experienced this feeling at other decisive moments and calls it an awakening. He will leave the next morning as if for a trip. All arrangements have been made for his deputy to carry on, but a main concern is Tegularius. Knecht had not told him that he would leave Castalia even if his request were denied, and the Magister feels he must pay him a final visit without revealing his departure. Tegularius will, he thinks, recover from the fait accompli much easier than from forehand knowledge of his exit.

With the ostensible reason of asking him if he knows the source of the poem that has been running through his mind—whose theme, incidentally, will also relate to Tegularius's own new beginning when Knecht has gone—he calls on his friend. Tegularius recognizes the poem immediately as Knecht's own, gets it from his bookshelf, and reads several lines:

> A magic dwells in every new beginning,
> That protects us and helps us go on living,
> We are meant to stride serenely, room through room,
> And stay in none as if we felt at home.
> The spirit of this world does not set limits, will not chain us down,
> It wants to lift us, step by step, expanding our horizons. (480–3)

> [Und jedem Anfang wohnt ein Zauber inne,
> Der uns beschützt und der uns hilft zu leben.
> Wir sollen heiter Raum um Raum durchschreiten,
> An keinem wie an einer Heimat hängen.
> Der Weltgeist will nicht fesseln uns und engen,
> Er will uns Stuf' um Stufe heben, weiten.]

Tegularius points out that Knecht had first entitled the poem "Transcendence" but later changed it to "Stages." He criticizes it as too moralizing, pedantic, and imperative. Knecht should have called it "Music" or "Essence of Music," because it expresses the constant present of music, its serenity, its decisiveness, its movement, its readiness to leave the realm just entered. However, it places music and life at the same level, which is questionable and debatable. It makes the driving force of music, its "amoral motor," a life that wants to educate and develop us through calls, commands, and good-teaching (484). Knecht is pleased with the analysis, meaning that Hesse wants the reader to see life in precisely such perspective.

Knecht leaves Waldzell the next morning. There is an early autumn fog—giving his new stage of life an inauspicious beginning—as he has himself driven to Hirsland, the Administrative Headquarters of Castalia for an unannounced visit with Magister Alexander. While waiting to see him, Knecht recalls once again the sentence (this is the third time Hesse has repeated it; thus, we know it is important) he had chosen for meditation when he had taken vows of the order: "If the High Commission calls you to an office, you should know that every step to higher office is not a step into freedom, but into commitment. The greater the power of the office, the stricter and more demanding the service.

The stronger the personality, the more limited the free will" (487). He thinks how perfect these words would be if Castalia were the whole world instead of a little world (that is, the masculine world) within the world. He had once been able to see it as such, and the non-Castalian part as a kind of children's world. Now the same path that had led him along an apparently straight line to Waldzell, to Mariafels, into the order, to the office of Magister Ludi, is leading him away (487–8).

The conversation with Magister Alexander runs its course as Knecht expected, and his comments during the interview reveal Hesse's Olympian viewpoint of life and why he knows that he writes for a small elite. It is not that Hesse is arrogantly professing his own (Knecht's) superior intellect in comparison to these most learned among the learned; he is simply stating the obvious in warning that narrow fields of specialization and expertise, if not considered in historical perspective, worldly reality, and universal concern, will limit vision. It is the mission of the Knechts, the Cains, the immortals, to plant the seeds. Even if the Castalian Elite did not agree with him, they did read his words of warning and took them in.

As Alexander slowly grasps the purpose of Knecht's visit—to announce his resignation from office and departure from the province—he cannot believe that Knecht will not accept the decision of the board. Alexander offers him an indefinite leave of absence but can do no more. Knecht cannot convince Alexander that he does not have simple yearnings for the pleasures available outside Castalia. He wants the opposite: risk, difficulties, danger.[13] He is hungry for reality and its problems, for deeds, even for deprivation and suffering (503–4). He recalls for Alexander the story of St. Christopher, who had to serve the highest master and would leave one as soon as service to a more powerful master was possible (509).

At Magister Alexander's request, Knecht attempts to explain his moments of awakening (and we should recall Harry Haller's *Gottesspuren,* the moments when "traces of God" gave meaning to his life). They are a step beyond, they are a call, inner experiences of truth, and it is their reality, as real as physical pain, that gives them credence. He compares them to catastrophes or disorders in the world. Something positive, beautiful, and bright can result (as with the meaning of the Frau Eva metaphor in the *Demian* battle scene) *or* something dark and evil (507–8). Alexander has never heard of such an awakening in Castalia, and this reply underscores the warnings that Knecht has made: the province has lost contact with the feelings and emotions that really govern the world, or, in Father Jakobus's words, with the "blood and reality" of history. It was from the latter that Knecht learned that he was not only a Castalian but a human being, that the whole world was his concern and had a claim on him. It was then that he understood his assignment to attempt to instill Castalian life and thought with new blood from the world, to warn it against isolation (514). And recently he has found someone from the world with the same ideas of bringing it and Castalia closer together—Designori.

Alexander can see only that Knecht's explanations lead him back to the same conclusion: that under certain circumstances, the will of an individual should involve the right to break laws in which he, Alexander, believes and must represent. The interview is ended. Alexander has always loved this man, for even in Castalia such individuals are gifts of good fortune.

Such a closing scene again emphasizes Knecht's natural gift of influence over others and indicates to the reader that, as intended, seeds have been sown. The very fact that Knecht's story has been dug out to be told these many years later, despite the naiveté of the narrator, indicates that his legend is still alive. Perhaps the narrator's generation of Castalians, as a result of his efforts, will understand the warning better than Knecht's own—we should not forget that "Castalia" was originally the name of a spring.

The following morning, leave-taking over, Knecht departs Hirsland on foot, his destination the capital city and his Designori commitment. When he arrives the next day, Tito's parents are worried. The boy has disappeared, but Knecht correctly surmises that the boy wanted a last day of freedom and also wanted to do something to spite the world, the adults, and his new teacher. Words to this effect are eventually found in a note that Tito has left behind, indicating that he has gone on to Belpunt, the Designori mountain retreat where he and Knecht are to begin their tutor-pupil sessions.

The country house is built on a mountain lake amidst grey boulders, and Tito is awaiting him with a smile at the door. That evening Knecht feels unusually tired and light-headed and has an irregular heartbeat, all of which he attributes to the sudden and dramatic change in elevation. Despite this, he spends the evening with Tito, and they arrange a walk for the next morning to acquaint Knecht with the area. That night Tito ponders his feelings for his new tutor. What is it that impresses him so much? It is his nobility, dignity, masterliness, he decides: "It occurs to this fiery and proud boy, that to belong to this kind of nobility and to serve could perhaps become an honor and a duty for him, that perhaps here, in the person of this leader, through and through a gentleman, who, despite all his gentleness and friendliness, might be bringing him closer to the meaning of his life; he has been sent to set goals for him" (535). These are words to be kept in mind when, just hours later, the boy will find himself standing alone on the shores of the icy mountain lake.

In a parallel passage, Knecht, as he lies in bed, also ponders his situation and relationship to Tito. He wants to bring the boy to a realization of his gifts and strengths, to nourish his noble curiosity, his noble insatiety that gives strength to his love for science and the intellect. He will be a future *Herr,* a molder of social and political influence of land and people, one destined to be an example and a leader (536).

Knecht does not sleep well and, when he awakens early, dons a robe and steps out onto a walk that leads him to the bathhouse and the lake. Tito appears in his bathing suit, and when the sun begins to rise over the cliffs on the far side of the lake, he breaks out into a wild, spontaneous sun dance, his arms pulling the mountain, the lake, and the sky to his heart. Kneeling down, he stretches his hands toward the lake; he seems to offer its waters to the Earth mother and to make a festive offering of his youth, his freedom, his inwardly burning feeling for life to the forces of nature (538–9). Just as Knecht has always lived in the masculine sphere of life in Castalia but gradually come to know the feminine sphere of the world outside, Tito's sensual and emotional display places him at the opposite pole. He is fully alive to the world of nature, but he must now learn how to incorporate discipline and responsibility—the world of the mind—into it, much as Goldmund learned from Narcissus.

When the boy realizes what a strange impression his unintended ceremony must have made on his tutor, he is embarrassed and blurts out the first thing that comes to his mind: "If we swim quickly . . . we can be on the other shore just before the sun" (541). With that, he plunges into the lake. As we have been told several times in the course of the novel, Knecht acts by instinct when the occasion calls for it. He had not come down to the lake to swim, for the morning is far too cool, and he is ill. But more important than his health is what this first morning spent with Tito promises for their continuing relationship. He feels a warning of uncertainty and weakness, but the instinctive feminine call is stronger than the masculine warning. He plunges into the icy water, and the battle with death—which he recognizes immediately—is at the same time a battle for the soul of the boy (542). Tito had seen Knecht plunge into the lake, but when he glances back again, the tutor is no longer visible. He swims back, dives to find him as long as he can endure the freezing water, but then returns to the shore. "I am responsible for his death," he thinks. "He has no more pride to protect and no more resistance to offer, and feels in his frightened heart how much he had loved this man already." He is "overcome with a premonition of sacred apprehension, that this debt will change him and his life, and demand much more from him than he had ever demanded of himself" (543). Thus ends the book, its last sentence expressing Tito's profound awakening, as he picks up the Magister Ludi's robe and begins mechanically to dry himself with it.

This long-contested, much-disputed ending of *The Glass Bead Game* should not be the confusion of critical interpretations that it has been.[14] Having followed Hesse's internal quest through his major works, the reader should have no doubt that Knecht's final act is intended to portray the synthesis that Hesse has so long been pursuing and to embody his final wisdom. He even tells us as much. In a letter to Peter Suhrkamp on November 5, 1936, he states: "If it becomes what I planned, it will be my last major work and will bring to final expression the last phase of my inner existence" (*GB III* 37). Knecht's act of dying—just as the sun is rising—is an act of living. Hesse has affixed numerous labels to these dualities of life throughout his writings. As he noted in a letter to a Japanese professor who had commented on the two souls in Hesse's *Lauscher:* "The two souls have appeared to me in the course of my life under various names and images . . . later I became accustomed to seeing and interpreting them as two poles, between which the back and forth movements and tensions can cause struggle and suffering, but they always signify life" (*Hermann Hesse Briefe* 124). We have seen the polarities as light/darkness, good/evil, wolf/man, freedom/authority, world/Castalia, *vita activa/vita contemplativa, Geist/Natur,* father/mother, and masculine/feminine. It is a subtle sexual connotation of the latter pairing which unites all the collective symbolic implications to express Hesse's ultimate message in Joseph Knecht's final act. The Latin *ludo* does not simply mean "to play" but has a variety of connotations,[15] including "to have intercourse" or even "to sport amorously." Thus, the Magister Ludi's plunge into the lake is a playful act of intercourse in keeping with the game theme of the book, despite its serious consequences.[16] We learned from Goldmund that death is the final feminine act. Now we are to understand that Knecht's willing acceptance of death as a sacrifice to ongoing life is the ultimate application of the masculine principles that he has learned to perfection in Castalia. Knecht could not unite the polarities of his life more clearly. That Hesse had precisely this metaphor in mind is supported by the imagery: both transitions—Knecht's death and Tito's implied rebirth— take place at sunrise at a mountain retreat called *Belpunt* (beautiful bridge).[17] (It is even tempting to believe that Hesse is alluding to Christ's transfiguration [Matthew 17], which took place on a mountaintop bathed in sunlight, thus completing the final stage of the Hesse/protagonist's journey, which began with Sinclair's rebirth on a bed of straw in a stable, and expressing his message that there is a Christ in everyone.) Tito, we are to understand, will now go on living according to the awakening that Knecht's death has provided him, but not without problems, collapse, and renewal, for he, too, like every other human being, must continually struggle between the polarities of life "until death do them join."

Hesse's final work is a statement of faith that all of humanity is one and must be kept on a noble path. The tenacity of life expressed by Goldmund is, for Joseph Knecht, no longer an individual desire to live but a desire to preserve one eternal humanity. It is to this end, so Hesse feels, that we are supposed to live as individuals, as temporary, fragmentary masks of a single, universal spirit. Our task is to serve whatever distant goal lies ahead, which is far more important than our ego-centered lives. This point will be further developed in the conclusion of this study, following a brief analysis of Knecht's own writings appended to the narrator's account of the Magister Ludi and the Glass Bead Game, which has come to an end.

Joseph Knecht's Surviving Writings

During the course of his research, the narrator of Knecht's story discovered several pieces of original writing and appended them without comment to his biography of the former Magister Ludi. They consist of thirteen poems and three "Autobiographies," or "Lives." The poems differ from the lives in that the latter were, as noted, writing assignments done during Knecht's period of free study, whereas the poems were apparently written whenever his creative muse inspired him.

From the standpoint of narrative structure, the poems appear to reveal Hesse's practice of ruminating on dominant themes, first expressing them in verse form and then incorporating them into the prose. The poems, as addenda, provide much the same complement to the narrative action of *The Glass Bead Game* as do the Greek chorus and Brechtian songs for the stage action of their respective dramas. Hesse's poems, however, are not read until the prose narrative, itself, has ended; thus, they do not stop the action but, instead, engender reflection on the whole. Whereas all thirteen poems help to illuminate thematic content, three of them provide additional clues to the meaning behind Knecht's unexpected death, the enigma that has always plagued attempts to interpret the ending. These three, in both the German original and in English translation (my own), are given below, followed by a brief analysis and commentary.

Zu einer Toccata von Bach

Urschweigen starrt . . . Es waltet Finsternis . . .
Da bricht ein Strahl aus zackigem Wolkenriß,
Greift Weltentiefen aus dem blinden Nichtsein,

Baut Räume auf, durchwühlt mit Licht die Nacht,
Läßt Grat und Gipfel ahnen, Hang und Schacht,
Läßt Lüfte locker blau, läßt Erde dicht sein.

Es spaltet schöpferisch zu Tat und Krieg
Der Strahl entzwei das keimend Trächtige:
Aufglänzt entzündet die erschrockne Welt.
Es wandelt sich, wohin die Lichtsaat fällt,
Es ordnet sich und tönt die Prächtige
Dem Leben Lob, dem Schöpfer Lichte Sieg.

Und weiter schwingt sich, gottwärts rückbezogen
Und drängt durch aller Kreatur Getriebe
Dem Vater Geiste zu der große Drang.
Er wird zu Lust und Not, zu Sprache, Bild, Gesang,
Wölbt Welt um Welt zu Domes Siegesbogen,
Ist Trieb, ist Geist, ist Kampf und Glück, ist Liebe. (548–49)

[On a Toccata by Bach

Primeval silence reigns . . . darkness seethes . . .
Suddenly a shaft of light breaks out of jagged clouds,
Out of the blind nothingness, reaches into worldly depths,

Builds spaces, kindles light in the darkness,
Suggesting ridges and peaks, cliffs and gorges,
Leaves breezes misty blue, gives substance to the earth.

The shaft of light creatively divides
the sprouting pregnant earth into deed and war.
The frightened world ignites in brilliance,
Transforms itself wherever light-seed falls,
The majesty arrays itself, sounds tones of
Praise to life and victory to the creator's radiance.

And the mighty impulse, turning God-ward, penetrates
Through every creature's movement to the father's spirit.
It becomes lust, distress, language, symbol, song,
Shelters world after world with domes of victory arches,
It is instinct, it is mind, it is battle, happiness and love.]

This poem is most revealing of the essence of Hesse's new mythology and the masculine-feminine symbolism reflected in the ending of *The Glass Bead Game*. There are subtle sexual connotations in the poem just as in Knecht's death scene. It portrays a Genesis-like creation based on the musical image that Hesse perceives in the Bach toccata—a "shaft" of light "creatively divides" the "sprouting pregnant earth." This metaphor expresses the clashing dualities of life, the dynamic that Hesse symbolizes with his Glass Bead Game instrument, which can grasp in infinite images the intercourse between the feminine and masculine polarities and reach into the spirit behind them. If the "craving" (*Drang*) turns God-ward after letting its "light-seeds fall upon the earth," Hesse is implying that the Divine Spirit, itself, begat earth life in lust, creating a humankind of like desires, but also has imbued it with the longing to return to the father; only a synthesis of all the ambivalent urges is a praise of victory to the creator—what the Abraxas symbol expressed to Sinclair. And the same sexual symbolism evident in the poem is found in Hesse's description of the Bead Game in the introductory chapter—the eternal divine is "consummated" by the "push and pull" between heaven and earth. The poem justifies and approves of the duality of life and at the same time mandates our assignment to return to the father, as Knecht does at death, this last act expressing the same message as the last line of the poem: it is instinct, mind, battle, happiness, and love.

Stufen
Wie jede Blüte welkt und jede Jugend
Dem Alter weicht, blüht jede Lebensstufe,
Blüht jede Weisheit auch und jede Tugend
Zu ihrer Zeit und darf nicht ewig dauern.
Es muß das Herz bei jedem Lebensrufe
Bereit zum Abschied sein und Neubeginne,
Um sich in Tapferkeit und ohne Trauern
In andre, neue Bindungen zu geben.
Und jedem Anfang wohnt ein Zauber inne,
Der uns beschützt und der uns hilft, zu leben.
Wir sollen heiter Raum um Raum durchschreiten,
An keinem wie an einer Heimat hängen,
Der Weltgeist will nicht fesseln uns und engen,
Er will uns Stuf' um Stufe heben, weiten.
Kaum sind wir heimisch einem Lebenskreise
Und traulich eingewohnt, so droht Erschlaffen,
Nur wer bereit zu Aufbruch ist und Reise,

Mag lähmender Gewöhnung sich entraffen.

Es wird vielleicht auch noch die Todesstunde
Uns neuen Räumen jung entgegensenden,
Des Lebens Ruf an uns wird niemals enden . . .
Wohlan denn, Herz, nimm Abschied und gesunde! (555–6)

[Stages

As every blossom fades and every youth
Gives way to age, so too blooms every stage of life,
In its own time, every wisdom too
And every virtue, but they may not last forever.
At every call to life the heart
Must be ready to depart, ready for new beginnings,
To give itself bravely and without mourning
To other, new commitments.
A magic dwells in every new beginning,
that protects us and helps us go on living.
We are meant to stride serenely,
Room through room, and stay in none as if we felt at home.
The spirit of this world does not chain us down,
It wants to lift us, step by step, expanding our horizons.
We scarcely set our foot in one life-cycle,
No more than safely settle in, than apathy will threaten,
Only those prepared to leave, prepared to travel,
Can escape from crippling impassivity.

And maybe it will be the hour of death
That sends new space for us to conquer,
Life's call to us will never end,
So then, heart, take leave and come alive.]

Several lines of "Stages" have already been discussed in "The Legend" chapter of the text, but the ending, with its focus on death as another stage of life, calls for reiteration to emphasize Hesse's vision of a common humanity— past, present, and future as one, with but one soul. If we can grasp this image, we can see that Knecht's death is not final; his life does not end before he brings the polarities together, as critics often contend.

Das Glasperlenspiel

Musik des Weltalls und Musik der Meister
Sind wir bereit in Ehrfurcht anzuhören,
Zu reiner Feier die verehrten Geister
Begnadeter Zeiten zu beschwören.

Wir lassen vom Geheimnis uns erheben
Der magischen Formelschrift, in deren Bann
Das Uferlose, Stürmende, das Leben,
Zu klaren Gleichnissen gerann.

Sternbildern gleich ertönen sie kristallen,
In ihrem Dienst ward unserm Leben Sinn,
Und keiner kann aus ihren Kreisen fallen,
als nach der heiligen Mitte hin. (556)

[The Glass Bead Game

We are prepared to listen reverently
To the music of the spheres and of the masters,
To conjure up in pure celebration
The honored spirits of blessed times.

We let ourselves be lifted by the secret
Of the magic formula, in whose spell
Endless, storming life,
Dissolved into the purity of parables.

Like crystal constellations they resound.
In their service life becomes a cause,
And no one can fall from their circle,
Save toward the divine center.]

This final poem helps us to understand the metaphor of the Glass Bead
Game. Like life, itself, it expresses meaning through the "purity of its parables."
By listening reverently, the player perceives the music of the spheres, the music, in whatever form, of past masters who, themselves, discovered it. The game
can conjure up revered spirits of blessed times in pure celebration of the past.

So, too, can players be lifted by the secret of the magic formulae, which show us how life flows on in parables. It is in service to these parables, to the spirit visible in them, that lives are given meaning. Thus, the poem elaborates on the Bead Game as a symbolic mirror of the spirit behind life. Every life of service moves toward the divine center and, by implication, away from lesser gods. The words "service to life" are the thrust of Hesse's last novel and are intended to be understood in the broadest possible sense as dedication to a single humanity, to its spirit of becoming. Joseph Knecht's transfiguration, in the act of dying, is service and sacrifice to this spirit and at the same time a return to it.

The chronology of the three incarnations appended to *The Glass Bead Game* as "posthumous writings" of Joseph Knecht can be quite accurately documented,[18] but even if it were not known, judging from their respective contents, "The Rainmaker" was obviously intended to be the first of the lives that collectively were to make up the episodic series that was to be Hesse's magnum opus. It is also obvious that the Castalian tale was to be the last and the Bead Game, itself, the unifying symbol of the entire work. The incarnation-fictions, as noted earlier, were ostensibly writing assignments to be accomplished during the students' years of free study. Hesse wanted to show that his hero could feel his way into different ages and cultures, thus (like Father Jakobus) learning via history. The assignment also stresses the theme that, at any given point in time, the individual is no more than a fragmentary and temporary manifestation of the spirit behind the persona. (Hesse is again guilty of thematic inconsistency, forgetting that Castalian authorities had long since decided that actual history was a topic to be ignored, so the task is not really in keeping with the province's ivory tower image.)

Of the three incarnations,[19] "The Rainmaker" is more easily compared to *The Glass Bead Game* in narrative structure than the other two. The setting is the primeval past, some 20,000 years ago (*Materialien* 87), in an age when women ruled. Hesse's choice of words for this phrase—"*Frauen* waren an der *Herr*schaft" (emphasis added)—reveals his conscious intention to emphasize the masculine/feminine wordplay, which is lost in English translation. The only male of importance in the tribe is the Rainmaker; thus, our attention is immediately drawn to the masculine/feminine frame of reference. Because of the apparent lack of a feminine content in *The Glass Bead Game,* itself, we should be curious as to why Hesse has placed the first of the Knecht incarnations in a setting that is, theoretically at least, the polar opposite of the male-dominated Castalia. The word "theoretically" is necessary because the narrative is, in fact, the Rainmaker's story, not the tribal mother's, though she is honored as the queen (*Ahnfrau*). And since it was Hesse's intention to show us a series of masks of *one* personality, we must excuse this stylistic equivocation. The tribal mother is, however, of great symbolic importance, for she is "revered and obeyed" as the mother of seven daughters—possibly an allusion to the seven pillars of wisdom in the Book of Revelations—and bears the features of "the wisdom, tradition, laws, customs and honor of the village" (557). In other words, she is the embodiment of the values that have naturally evolved into tribal lore and been practiced through the ages. The description of the primal mother also helps to clarify one of the ambiguities that have plagued Hesse criticism. Namely, a characteristic that Hesse normally implies to be masculine—obedience to traditions and laws—is shown here to be part and parcel of a matriarchal culture. What Hesse means, as soon becomes clear in the context of the story, is that these ancient peoples lived in accord with the natural world before the masculine quest lost sight of its purpose and became an end in itself. A simple variation on this theme was found in the description of Sinclair's home, which contained "both father and mother," and was "love, discipline, standard and schooling." Sinclair's was a child's world, not yet a house divided (see also Pierre's world in *Roßhalde*), and so is the primitive society portrayed. Hesse's point is that early humankind, childlike, did not question its place in nature but tried to understand its laws in order to live in harmony with it, not in order to oppose, conquer, and control it—not the same as idealizing nature into an Edenic garden or romantic world, as Hesse has occasionally been charged with doing. Hesse/Knecht makes this clear in one of his many digressions on the office of the Rainmakers: they did not "separate themselves from nature and did not attempt to solve its mysteries with force, they were never opposed and antagonistic towards it, but always a part of it, reverently devoted to it"[20] (575). Hesse contrasts their efforts with the science and technology of later cultures, which are on a "completely different path" (574–5).

The question arises in the reader's mind: why did the primal, natural world polarize itself? An explanation of sorts for the origins of the dichotomy is given in the myth of the Witches' Village in "The Rainmaker." The daughter of the now-ancient tribal mother tells the story to the village children who sit at her feet. There were women who were simply evil by nature, usually childless, and they had to be driven out of the villages, eventually to find their way to others of their kind who banded together and lived in the Witches' Village. Here they carried on their evil ways, practiced magic, and, since they had no children of their own, attempted to lure children from the proper villages into their witches' domain. The narrator tells of a young girl who fell asleep in the forest, was left behind by the other children, and was discovered by a witch who led her to her village. There the witch showed her a pot in which plants were growing. The one, said the witch, was the life of her mother, the second the life of her father, the third that of the girl, herself. As long as the plants were green and growing, the girl would be alive and well. The witch then began to pull out the father-plant, which emitted a deep sigh, and at this point the story-within-a-story breaks off (559–61).

Thus, we see, in metaphor, that certain women, evil by nature, attract children into their world—that is, certain feminine enticements are dangerous. And the aberrant wandering takes place when the masculine counterpoint is uprooted and the balance destroyed. It is our continuing task to keep both plants, both mother and father principles, green and growing.

The first of Hesse's Knechts makes just such an effort, ultimately becoming an ideal Rainmaker, attempting, as mentioned, to discover nature's laws in order to help his people live in harmony with the world—a parallel to the intended role of Castalia. Thus, the first Knecht is the primitive embodiment of the ever-curious mind force that seeks to penetrate the mysteries of life,[21] but he is one who still realizes his place in nature. As a young boy, Knecht—an orphan, as will be his final incarnation—is drawn to Turu the Rainmaker. He follows him, watches him closely, and loiters near his hut, but Turu does not make the approach an easy one. Knecht must earn his acceptance through persistence and honesty—another example of Hesse's sanctioning of an elite; only those journeyers who persist in their search for the right reasons are worthy of acceptance.[22] Their reward will lie only in their devotion to a vision that others will not grasp until they, too, "are able to swim."

The primary god of the tribe is the moon. Its waxing and waning are closely related to death and birth. Spirits of the dead travel to the moon and return to be born again in later generations. Fear of death is the tribe's greatest fear, but through his moon worship, the Rainmaker attains a "consecrated relationship to death" (576)—analogous to Joseph Knecht's acceptance of death in *The Glass Bead Game*.[23]

As Knecht trains his own son, Turu, whom he recognizes as the returned spirit of his predecessor, he also trains another apprentice named Maro but is gradually betrayed by the latter, who wants the esoteric knowledge only for his own benefit, to impress and influence others for the sake of personal power—leading for the wrong reasons, a common Hesse theme. (The concept is reflected in more subtle form in the desertion by the Castalian Elite of their principles. Pettiness, personal goals, and ambitions within the hierarchy have turned the province from its real purpose. These are dangers inherent in the masculine search.)

When the Rainmaker Knecht stands at the height of his powers, the existing order is suddenly threatened by demons of unusual strength. The
tribe is horrified by a meteorite shower that continues for hours. The tribal
mother—to be noted—calmly accepts it as a sign of the end of the world,
but Knecht, with his masculine insight, can see that, behind the falling
flames, the old stars remain solidly in place, a metaphor with the same
meaning as the Mozart/radio imagery. Knecht sees his village collapsing
in panic but wisely intones the familiar prayers and ceremonies, and the
chaos is gradually brought under control. Earlier he had reflected on tribal
rituals, calling them "the official, the public part of [his] activity . . . and
priestly spectacle" (581), but in the end, these are not enough; the two-year
drought that follows the meteorite catastrophe will eventually force Knecht's
sacrifice, to which he willingly submits, passing on his office to his son. In
addition to the spectacle of rituals, however, Knecht has his own higher-
level observances. He watches the signs of nature and surrenders himself
to them until the "weather is concentrated in him . . . which completely
removed the difference between him and the world, between inside and
outside" (581). At times he is so much at one with nature that he can actually make rain or stop the wind, but there are also times when the connection is broken (582)—ever-changing life demands constant reinterpretation of
signs to regain the connection. The religious connotations of the passage are
significant. Like the tribal rites, familiar religious rituals are intended to connect humankind to the spirit behind their symbols, but time will overtake them.
Thus, it is the eternal task of the rainmakers, the Cains, the journeyers, constantly to seek to renew the spirit of life, even if others are not interested in
peering into the depths at the time.

In what is probably a veiled reference to the catastrophe of National Socialism, bringing hosts of lesser gods into positions of power and influence in
Germany, Hesse/Knecht follows the meteorite calamity with a political-histori-
cal analogy: "We know periods in the history of some peoples in which, at
times of a deep spiritual crisis, people with talent only [i.e., with no moral or
ethical values] stormed into the offices of the communities, the schools, the
academies, the states, when highly talented people occupied all the offices, but
who only wanted to rule without being able to serve" (588). In other words, just
as the old, stable stars stay in the heavens, so is the real goal of governing
always visible behind aberrational and temporary tyrants and dictators, or even
the greed and power struggles of elected officials. As if in accusation, not only
of himself but of other intellectuals, Hesse/Knecht, through the voice of the
Rainmaker, asks, "Why had he not known in advance this time, and why had he

made no preparations? Why had he not said a word to anyone of the dark, warning premonition which he had had?" (593).

Interesting, too, is that long after the event of the falling stars, the catastrophe becomes an exciting memory. Something had happened (597). Only the Rainmaker recalls it as a warning. This analogy may be compared to the glorification of war that Hesse battled against and which is a theme in both *Demian* and *Der Steppenwolf*. Until its realities set in, war is something romantic and exciting, and not long after one war, we hunger for the next.

Of most interest in "The Rainmaker" is his quest, per se. Despite the fact that the story is told in an age when women ruled, Hesse/Knecht says little about them, other than to make it clear that they are more important than men, that girl babies are more highly prized than boys. Women are the earth mothers, the givers of life, and we are again reminded that Hesse's own quest was concerned with uniting life with the spirit behind it. Were it left to the feminine component, alone, according to his metaphor, we would be ruled by instinct and emotion, discounting the masculine drive to understand, question, organize, and order. The emphasis of the Rainmaker story is on the portrayal of this masculine quest to understand the world that the primal mother has brought us into, the quest for knowledge that can bring us back into balance when fears and allurements lead us astray. Hesse/Knecht's conception of this masculine search is the same thought expressed by Goethe in his poem "Edel sei der Mensch" ("Let Man be Noble"),[24] for it is the masculine ability to distinguish what is noble in life that separates him from all other creatures. In the flights of fancy of his young rainmaker, Hesse stresses first of all that he possesses a "perception of the whole" (*Ahnung des Ganzen*)—what Joseph Knecht perceived in music—a feeling that there are relationships, connections, and order; a feeling that there must be a center from which all emanating spirit can be read and understood (570–1), that everything concerns us and that we should know as much about everything as it is possible to know (569). But just as the feminine pole has its dangers, so does the masculine. We note the hubris lurking behind the young Knecht's continuing thoughts that "with the power of his intellect, he would have to unite all of these amazing gifts and abilities within himself and give them free rein: this would be the perfect, the wise, the unsurpassable man! To become like him, to approach him, to be underway toward him: This was the path of paths, this was the goal that made life sacred and gave it meaning" (571). Although this is the boy, Knecht, speaking as he dreams of becoming the Rainmaker, we note the potential danger of his thoughts. It is not only the feminine enticements that lie in wait.

However, none of Hesse's Knechts, in final analysis, will succumb to intellectual pride. The world of nature is as awe-inspiring to Knecht the Rainmaker as is the Bead Game to Knecht the Magister Ludi—a world of symbols "full of wonders, but also order," a world where everything can be grasped by the spirit, where everything forms a whole, where there is "an answer in your heart for all the images and phenomena of the world" (569). Joseph Knecht is grasped by this spirit when he sacrifices himself for Tito, the Turu of *The Glass Bead Game,* who has already revealed his oneness with nature in his early morning sun dance. As the older Turu taught the apprentice Knecht more by showing than by words and instruction (574), so does Joseph Knecht's death show Tito the spirit behind the man. The Magister's death is a fearful experience for Tito, but, as Hesse/Knecht said of fear in "The Rainmaker": "Those who ennobled a part of their fear into awe had accomplished much. People of this kind, those whose fear had become piety, were the good people, the avant-garde of that age" (575). Both the first Knecht and the last end their respective lives in pious sacrifice to the future—an outward expression of the inwardly perceived Law of Service, the one sacrament at the core of Hesse's religious vision, of his new mythology.

The life entitled "The Father Confessor," as Hesse tells it, is a tale of the growing pains of early Christianity, set in fourth-century Gaza. Josephus Famulus (the Latinized form of Joseph Knecht) is a hermit-penitent in the desert, but until he was thirty, he had led a worldly life and studied pagan doctrines. Eventually, a woman he had been pursuing had introduced him to Christianity. He was baptized, renounced his sins, gave away his worldly goods, and at the age of thirty-six, following the examples of other pious hermits, began a penitent life in the wilderness. Such hermits, author Knecht tells us, were adept at the art of dying—of dying to the world, of effacing the ego, and passing on to Him, to the Savior (606). Recalling that these were the Pietist demands that a younger Hesse had rebelled against, we are forewarned that the hermit's path will be seen as too straight and narrow, and we see this thesis expressed immediately: Some of the hermits are still familiar with ancient pagan purification practices and yoga, but these are no longer spoken of; they have been banned by Christianity, as has everything pagan.

Over the passing years, Josephus becomes known as a confessor. He has a gift of listening (as did Vasudeva), seems to absorb the sins of the penitents into himself, and treats all recalcitrants the same. When the sinners have finished their declarations, Josephus says the Lord's Prayer with them and kisses them on the brow (609). Josephus looks upon his work with the penitent visitors as a sign of grace; he is an "instrument of God" who can "draw souls unto themselves" (610). Word of another Father Confessor reaches him, of a hermit called

Dion Pugil whose special gift is reading souls (Narcissus had this same gift) and who metes out penances of a much different kind than Josephus, sometimes even beating the sinners, as his name suggests. He enjoys a great reputation and the authority of a bishop.

As the years pass, however, Josephus's sense of inner peace dissolves; he feels too pleased with himself for what he is doing, experiences pride and vanity because of his popularity, and begins to feel contempt for these penitents, as did Harry Haller for the bourgeois and Siddhartha for the *Kindermenschen.* Sidney Johnson says the situation represents "the pitfall of intellectual smugness" (163), and we note the similarity to Castalian pride. Although he has the reputation of a holy man who has found peace in God, Josephus finally realizes that peace is also something living that will wax and wane, and eventually he feels a complete absence of joy (612) because of these foolish, anxious, childishly credulous people. Self-hatred wells up in him; he has a craving for death, and life seems unbearable. Like Sinclair, Siddhartha, and Harry Haller, he has fallen into Jungian despair and must make his choice between suicide or a return to life at a higher level of understanding. Josephus chooses flight, aimless at first, but nonetheless the change permits him to see the problem more objectively. His thoughts approve of the flight, for voluntary death is the thought of the devil and could arise only in a soul mastered by evil demons. But Josephus is fleeing from a post for which he is no longer fit, and his action is sincere (614–5). (Recall Joseph Knecht's decision to leave Castalia.) He puts himself into God's hands and cries like a child, afterward feeling like a child—that is, he is ready to be called anew (616).

While spending the night at an oasis, Josephus overhears two men, fellow travelers who are talking about the penitent-confessors—an event that Johnson calls intervention of a Divine Providence (164). Of Josephus, one says he is so pious that if a woman appears among the travelers to his hermitage he will not look at her but turns his back and hurries into his cave (618). Of Dion Pugil, one says he does battle with the devils and "beats the rust" out of penitents. This is the Father Confessor for him (619)! But his comrade prefers the kinder, gentler Josephus.

After listening quietly, Josephus thinks long and hard about what the men have said and makes a decision: he will go to Dion Pugil, confess to him, and accept whatever penance is given him (621). The next evening he finds himself in another oasis and sits down near an old, dignified man, who has snow-white hair and a stern, rigid face. Josephus asks the man if he can show him the way to Ascalon, to Father Dion Pugil. The elderly man has heard of Josephus but inquires why he wants to find Pugil. Josephus explains that he wants to confess to him, that he feels as though "a voice from above" is sending him to Pugil (624). The next morning the old man tells Josephus that he will lead him to Pugil. When his guide stops early, Josephus shows his impatience, but the old man tells him, "As soon as you are certain of your desire to confess and know you are prepared to make the confession, you will be able to" (627). Josephus immediately realizes that his traveling companion is Pugil, himself, and the reader is reminded of the meetings of Sinclair and Demian, Harry Haller and Hermine, Leo and H.H., where much the same situation occurs—when the despairing hero is finally ready to pour out his heart, the savior is there. Josephus confesses all that has been building up in him, ending with his present confusion and despair. When he has finished, Dion says nothing, but gets up, kisses Josephus on the forehead, and makes the sign of the cross over him (628). The kiss—as we know from Giebenrath/Heilner, Sinclair/Demian, and Narcissus/Goldmund predecessors—is a sign of acceptance, a sharing of feelings, a passing on of qualities, a recognition of fellowship. This instance is no different, with the kiss expressing the recognition of brotherhood, a new and reflective beginning for both.

They continue on to Pugil's hermitage in the desert, and Josephus fulfills the role of servant for the older man, whom he holds in reverence. Only occasionally does he attend the confession of the penitents. One visitor, however, is a scholar-aesthete who spends an hour or two with Dion, and the real essence of the Father Confessor story is rooted in this conversation and subsequent discussion between Josephus and Pugil. The learned man is very eloquent and tells Pugil that it is the duty of all men to make the journey, together with the gods, from the beginning to the end of time, through all the stations of the zodiac. Adam is the same as the crucified Christ, he says, and calls salvation the wandering of Adam from the tree of knowledge to the tree of life. The serpent is the guardian of the sacred fountain, of the depths of darkness, out of whose black waters all forms, all men, and all gods arise (630). After the man has left, Josephus asks, almost as a rebuke, why Dion had listened to these false doctrines and this unbelieving heathen. Pugil answers that he did not dispute him because it would have been useless. The man was superior to Dion in his knowledge of mythology and astrology, and, more importantly, it is neither his place nor Josephus's to tell any man that his beliefs are based on lies and errors. The two of them do not need the man's parables and ideas of religion, because they have acquired faith in Christ, the only redeemer. But for those who have not yet found this faith, the faith that has come down to them from their fathers deserves respect. Christianity, he continues, is entirely different. It does not need the doctrines of astrology, primeval waters, earth mothers, and all such parables, but that does not mean that these doctrines are lies and deceptions (631). The man, says Pugil, is not oppressed by suffering; he is content, and things are going well for him. They have nothing to say to such men; people must suffer, the water must be up to their necks, before they feel the need of salvation and redemptive faith. Only then will they make the leap of faith to the miracle of redemption. Perhaps this man will return someday and ask, "Why didn't you tell me this . . . ten years ago?" (632), and Pugil will say that things were not going badly enough for him at that time.

When we delve into this discussion, we discover that Hesse/Knecht has fashioned it badly. The thoughts of the visitor and Pugil run together, and as a result, the ultimate message that the reader is supposed to receive is not entirely clear, although knowing Hesse, we can see his intentions behind the conversations. The scholar-aesthete is enjoying the sin of pride in his knowledge—the same sin that has subtly befallen the Castalians—but Hesse would agree with his ideas, behind their patina of pride and superstition—he, too, sees humankind as having to move through all the stations of the zodiac (recall *Journey to the East*); he, too, believes that Adam, having eaten from the tree of knowledge (recall the poem "A Dream," *GS VI* 549–52) can be saved only by finding his way back to the tree of life; he, too, sees the "frightening serpent" obstructing the entrance to the "holy founts of the dark depths" (630) (refer back to Franz Kromer's role as well as the Abraxas commentary in *Demian*); he, too, feels that there must be suffering before the need for faith is felt (recall Harry Haller's many digressions). And Pugil's words, too, are Hesse's, when he calls the "heathens' ideas in no way erroneous" or "lies and deception," but rather "images and parables of faith" and "things out of mythology" (631). But Hesse and Father Pugil part company when the latter continues with, "we don't need them [the philosophers' ideas] any more because we have achieved faith in Jesus, the only savior" (631). Pugil's statement implies that Christianity's creeds are carved in stone (to which Hesse does not agree); he overlooks the fact that both he and Josephus have had to seek renewal and reinterpretation of their faith.

A dream that Pugil recounts also helps to clarify Hesse's intentions vis-à-vis the expression of fourth-century, Christian-hermit beliefs. While he was fighting his battle for faith in Christian doctrine, Pugil dreamed that he had to "kill his own mother" in order to extinguish his "birth of the flesh" (634), which is contrary to Hesse's belief that earthly life and spiritual life are one. Yet, at the end of Pugil's discourse, author and character merge again. Pugil says that "it was all over with my cleverness" and "since then I have belonged to the simple people" (634)—meaning, however, that he had lost faith in intellectual debate, not that he is one of the *Kindermenschen*. Also like Hesse, Pugil recognizes his responsibility to life as one of those who have eaten from the tree of knowledge, one of those who know. They are not like the children; they cannot be brought to order with punishments. Their only support must come from each other through brotherly love; that is why Pugil kissed Josephus instead of punishing him. And finally, Hesse, like Pugil, must live with the "unsolved riddle" that "creation and salvation are inseparably one [*Ineinander und Zugleichsein*]" (635).

It is only after this long discussion that Pugil informs Josephus why he was at the oasis where they met. He, too, had been in despair and was coming to Josephus for confession and penance, as if Christian humility and residual, Old Testament authority were being instinctively drawn together. When Josephus made himself and his problems known to Pugil, the latter took it as a miracle, a sign from God, an opportunity to cure them both. He could be of real service instead of just spanking children. Josephus had had faith in Pugil, which the latter dared not betray, and by curing Josephus, he would cure himself. When death approaches him, Pugil accepts it with a Vasudeva-like smile. He is leaving a son behind in Josephus, who will carry on in his stead, as Turu carried on for the Rainmaker and as Tito can be expected to model his life on the example set by Knecht.

The message of this Josephus Famulus incarnation is somewhat ambiguous. On the one hand, Hesse/Knecht draws a picture of early Christianity becoming ever narrower by more and more sternly imposed bans on everything pagan, with which Father Pugil and Josephus seem to concur, while in the same breath, Pugil says that the one true faith has no right to dispute the beliefs of others. It appears that Hesse intended to show narrowness and intolerance as a weakness of Christianity, an inference that can be supported by recalling Knecht's charge in his Circular Letter, that Castalia had separated itself from history, considering it "in the same light as the hermits and ascetics of early Christianity—as 'world-theater'" (*GS VI* 458). But, at the same time, Hesse seems to portray the merging of a gentler Christianity (Josephus) with the authoritative, Old Testament Father (Pugil) as a forward step that could eventually result in future growth and change—as Father Jakobus's church exemplifies it many centuries into the future.

We should also note that Famulus was sated with worldly experience before realizing that this was not a meaningful existence. He was introduced to Christianity by a woman, meaning—similar to the Beatrice-Sinclair episode— that he was drawn to the gentle, nurturing, feminine side of Christianity; later he became frightened of women and hid from them, indicating the return of temptation from the dark feminine side. And from Father Pugil he learned the role of masculine discipline and (by analogy to the parallel apprentice/disciple motifs in *The Glass Bead Game* and the other "lives") will presumably grasp the need for synthesis and eventually carry on in an enlightened spirit. We do recall that he had fantasy (*GS VI* 606) and that the "gift of listening slumbered within him" (*GS VI* 607).

The final image of "The Father Confessor" supports the above interpretation, at least in outline, for Josephus plants a tree over the grave of his revered master and lives until it bears its first fruit (642), the image symbolizing the potential growth and maturation of the budding religion.

The meaning of this "life" is obviously not as clear as it should be. Professor Johnson's somewhat vague summary analysis indicates that he finds no clear message either. He sees the story as "the inner struggle of a man who lives almost completely in the realm of the spirit" (omitting any mention of Famulus's preceding trek through the sensual world) and "an examination of the spiritual-intellectual life, conducted in Christian terms" (163). Boulby also has difficulty relating "The Father Confessor" to *The Glass Bead Game,* itself, saying that it "separates the sphere of teacher and pupil sharply off from the world of the 'child-people' and shows a preoccupation with sin, which is uncharacteristic of the parent novel" (308). All in all, it appears that Hesse, in the guise of the student, Knecht, was stylistically careless when writing "The Father Confessor."

Joseph Knecht's third incarnation, "An Indian Life," has a timeless setting in ancient India.[25] Dasa (meaning "servant," thus another Knecht) is born to a war-like prince, Ravana, a "demon-prince" incarnation of Vishnu (the major Hindu deity), and to a mother who bears no name in the text but who passes on a "sense of piety and justice" to her son (642). The mother dies soon after the boy's birth, and the rajah remarries. The second mother, also unnamed, gives birth to Nala, and it becomes obvious to one of the court Brahmins, Vasudeva, that Dasa's life is in danger as Nala's mother maneuvers to make her son heir to his father's kingdom in place of the first-born. Vasudeva arranges with a herdsman to raise Dasa as a cowherd, and the boy grows up in the world of nature with only a vague recollection of his royal birth and palace life.

As a youth, Dasa is one day following a flock of tiny birds and comes upon a hut in the forest, where the light penetrates the thick branches "like golden snakes" and the noises of the forest weave themselves "snake-like" together (643–4). Hesse's double imagery in the same sentence is again a stylistic device to draw the reader's attention, and we can infer a subtle sign of danger. Before the hut a yoga master sits in deep meditation, and Dasa's thoughts describe his impression that "nothing that eyes [can] see, ears [can] hear, what was beautiful or ugly, loving or fearful stood in any relationship to this man" (645). Recalling *Siddhartha,* we remember that Hesse rejected just such an escape from the world, and although the content of "An Indian Life" will appear to idealize the yoga principle, we must remember that the incarnation stories are to be seen not only as individual works but as a thematic continuum in their relationship to one another, including *The Glass Bead Game* story.

Dasa is in awe of the yogi's complete devotion to his service (*Dienst*). His state of meditation is so deep that "the entire world around him had become superfluous and meaningless" (646)—another comment to recall when Hesse's attitude toward this theme is summarized at the end of the chapter. Dasa brings offerings of food to the master as long as the cowherds stay in the area, but eventually they move on, and the memory of the experience fades. Only a vague presentiment remains (recall the vague recollection of "*om*" that lived on in Siddhartha) that the kingdom lost to him could sometime be replaced by the dignity and power of yoga. By juxtaposing the two realms in the boy's mind, Hesse again sets the stage for the ongoing struggle between worldly life and the world of the mind, here synonymous with yogic discipline.

When he is on the verge of manhood, Dasa goes to the city to see Ravana pass on his title and his kingdom, which rightfully belong to Dasa, to his second son, Nala. The cowherd is too taken up with the festival sights and sounds to give much thought to this vague memory; he also "becomes a man" (650) at the festival. We are reminded of Goldmund's experience with the peasant girl in the field and can expect, as happened to Goldmund, that Dasa will seek meaning in that feminine side of life which is dangerous and alluring. It is not long, in fact, until he is blinded by the beauty and sensuality of Pravati, a tenant farmer's daughter, wins her hand, and stays behind in the village when his fellow herdsmen move on. He can scarcely control the lust he feels for her, but life in his garden of delights is short-lived. The new rajah comes to the village with his hunting party, spies the beautiful Pravati, and takes her for himself, apparently with little resistance.

Dasa lurks near the Rajah's tent, where he can see Pravati greet her new lord, and he kills his half-brother with his sling at the first opportunity, feeling that he has extinguished his own life, as well, though not immediately caring. But, as happened with Goldmund when he had so cavalierly decided that making love to Agnes was worth death, the will to live returns to Dasa as well and "orders him to flee" (654), a repetition of the oft-heard Hesse theme that the will to live is the strongest emotion and, by implication, the reason we must attempt to understand life's meaning. As Dasa flees and sleeps fitfully in hiding, he dreams he is carrying a burden wrapped in material of the same pattern as Pravati's festival dress, and when he finally unwraps it, he finds his own head—a warning that Pravati and what she means to him can signify only danger, a warning that he will fail to heed. In flight, Dasa's feet seem to "find their own way" back to the yoga master's hut (656), where he stays and serves the silent man. The yogi, however, does not appear to notice him, just as Turu, the old rainmaker, ignored the boy, Knecht, making it as difficult as possible for him to approach until such time as his complete commitment was apparent.

Dasa decides he must convince the yogi to be his teacher and tries to imitate his lotus position for meditation, but he makes little progress because he is still haunted by visions of Pravati. Finally, he musters the courage to speak to the master, blurting out his story that he was born to become a rajah but became a cowherd, that his eyes were opened to women and he placed his life in the service of the most beautiful of them, that she was taken away by the rajah, whom he killed. Dasa cannot bear this terrible life anymore (659–60). The yogi smiles, and the smile becomes silent laughter, as he answers only "Maya! Maya!" ("Illusion! Illusion!"). Dasa's outpouring can be likened to Siddhartha's nadir of despair, to H.H.'s letter of lament and confession to Leo, and to the desperation of Josephus and Pugil—the point when life must come to an end or be accepted and a different direction taken. And the yogi's laughter reminds us of the laughter of Goethe and the immortals at Harry Haller's "serious" problems in *Der Steppenwolf.* Dasa, too, takes his life far too seriously, but he cannot fathom the yogi's answer and puzzles deep into the night. Finally, he decides that the master meant that Dasa's entire life—his happiness, his misery, the beautiful Pravati, his love and desire for her—were all "Maya." Dasa wishes he could accept this, but he cannot. His memories have become alive again. He can never learn the art of meditation anyway, he thinks, and perhaps the search for the murderer is over. He decides he must leave the next day but has one more request of the yogi—he must tell him more about Maya. The old man hands him a gourd to fill with water from the spring, and as Dasa is about to return to the hut, he hears a voice—Pravati's—enticing, childish, and sweet. She stands before him in all her finery, looking at him with her large doe-eyes, and he runs to take her in his arms. The forest, meditation, and the yogi are gone and forgotten as Pravati tells him that he has been acclaimed rightful heir to the kingdom following old Vasudeva's story. Without even a last farewell to the yogi, Dasa surrenders to the feminine allurement and leaves with Pravati, and there is rejoicing throughout the land.

Pravati bears him a son, whom they name Ravana, and they live year after year in happiness. Ravana becomes the most important thing in his life (as was Pierre to Veraguth). Nala's mother has fled to a rival rajah's court, and the long-time enemy carries out a border raid, stealing cattle and taking captives. Dasa must retaliate because it is expected, but he realizes that he is retaliating mostly out of fear for his son. If his enemy is not stopped, he could capture Dasa's kingdom, perhaps torture his son, and put him to death. The raiding continues on both sides, and as conditions worsen, Dasa thinks back on his life in the forest and longs to seek out the yoga master again. He feels that meditation and wisdom are good and noble things, but he who lives in the stream of life and does battle with its waves, he whose deeds and suffering have nothing to do with wisdom, must suffer fate that has to be fulfilled (674). But, thinks Dasa, even if life is without purpose, it still has a core and a center, and the center of his life is his son. The cleft between Dasa and Pravati becomes a "world-abyss" (675). He realizes how this enchanting beauty has toyed with him, how easily she had been lured away by Nala, how she had sought him out again only after he had been proclaimed rajah. Pravati sees the situation differently. She alone provided him with the good fortune of becoming rajah, and she has given him a son (677). Dasa realizes that he is trying to place all the blame on Pravati but must face his own failing. He was the cowardly one and, as a result, has a beautiful, gentle son, whose existence gives his life meaning and value. But "fate was coming nearer and had to be suffered" (678–9).

Dasa's war becomes more intense, and his capital is captured in a surprise attack while Dasa is leading his army elsewhere. As he fights his way toward his palace, fearing for his son's life, he is wounded, captured, and led into his fine study with its carved images of the gods, which have obviously failed him. He sees Pravati sitting under guard with their dead son on her lap. Dasa is thrown into a cell, and when he awakens the next morning, he is just rising from the stream with his master's gourd of water in his hands. There is no Pravati, no son, no war! Thus, he has been taught the meaning of Maya, and the memories remain; he still sees Pravati, her hair turned white overnight, with their dead son on her knees. They are images on a palace wall to be admired (682–3). It would seem that Hesse is making an analogy to history with this particular metaphor. History's images should be in humankind's memory, for were we to heed them, they could obviate the apparent necessity to repeat the same sufferings in generation after generation. This is why Joseph Knecht could admire Father Jakobus who lived in history and, because of it, could help his church to survive and serve. He understood the creative metaphors of history, worldly and spiritual.

As Dasa stands in amazement by the spring, his thoughts expand. Is this, too, standing here with the water, not also illusion? Is it all play and appearance, foam and dream, Maya, the whole beautiful and terrible, enticing and desperate game of the images of life with its burning joys, its burning pains (683)? What should he do? Take the pitcher back to the yogi and be laughed at? He drops it in the moss and sits down to think. He has had enough of everything, and he wants nothing but to stop this eternally revolving wheel, but there is no end, no extinguishing, so he may as well fill the water jug and bring it to the old man. It is a service, better than sitting and thinking up ways of self-destruction; obeying and serving are far better and easier (683–5). And so he takes the pitcher back to the yoga master, who receives him with a somewhat quizzical look of understanding—half sympathetic, half humorous. Dasa has experienced a moment on the rolling wheel. Presumably, this young man had been awakened several times earlier (in previous incarnations) and had experienced a taste of reality; otherwise, he would not have come here and stayed so long. But now he seems to have been properly awakened and ready to set out on the long pathway (685). It is with this glance that the yoga master accepts Dasa as his pupil, and, adds the storyteller, Knecht, there is nothing more of Dasa's life to tell; he never leaves the forest again. The pejorative tone of the ending reflects the *Siddhartha* conclusion: escape from the world is not the answer.

Each of the autobiographies can be read as a separate entity, but we must also read them as a narrative series in order to understand that Hesse has connected them as stages of human development. The primeval rainmaker embodied the masculine drive to understand and interpret the natural and feminine world around him in order to live in harmony with it. This is life as it should be, and even if Hesse finds creation imperfect and fraught with dangers and suffering, behind this facade the firmament is stable, beautiful, and serene. For whatever reason, we are assigned to live at one level of being and reverently seek its higher order.

It is obviously by design that Hesse respectively places the two autobiographies following "The Rainmaker" in early Christian and in East Indian settings, both major influences on his life. In each he shows the protagonist-journeyers searching for and finding the goals to which they will devote their lives. Each follows his inner voice, and no more can be asked. But unlike the Rainmaker, who opens himself to all phenomena encountered, the early Christian has found the one true answer and, by implication, is no longer free to explore, even though (showing Hesse's stylistic inconsistency) Josephus Famulus supposedly has learned that freedom is alive and must constantly wax and wane. The yoga master, at another stage, has found the solution to be flight from the natural world. The common denominator of the autobiographies is devotion and service to the goal perceived.

An unfinished fourth autobiography, as noted, was to portray a theologian who deserted his church doctrines for music, where endless possibilities of tones can be ordered and reordered at will, ad infinitum; this story would have been a transition to the final incarnation, for this is precisely what the Bead Game's endless combinations of symbols can do. Thus, with the last of the Knechts, the Hesse journeyer is again within a frame of reference where the symbolic search for meaning can be carried out in a man-made world that is comparable in its unpredictability to the natural world of the primeval Rainmaker. In other words, Hesse has come full circle, which was his obvious intention. Like the Rainmaker, Joseph Knecht is attempting to discover how humankind can live in peace and accord with the world as it exists around him. As is implicit in all the autobiographies, those who learn by serving will eventually rule by serving—not the multitudes through political power but the few by example, the few who also care enough to sacrifice and serve. Joseph Knecht's death, like the Rainmaker's, reflects his reverence for life and the spirit behind it, and embodies both service and sacrifice, both instinct and mind.

Conclusion

The Artist's Legacy

Hermann Hesse was sixty-six years old when *The Glass Bead Game* was published in 1943. He would live nearly another twenty years, quietly passing away in his sleep on August 9, 1962. The last two decades of his life in the beautiful Tessin setting in southern Switzerland would seem, to the outsider, at least, quiet years,[1] but even here there was little emotional tranquility for this man who supposedly could take "temporary exits from life" and "leave his body" for other-worldly journeys. He had by no means escaped the tribulations of the Hitler era and its aftermath. The Hesses had harbored many refugees, mostly Jewish or other blacklisted artists, helping them to find safe havens elsewhere, and the persecutions, deaths, and disappearances of his Jewish wife's family members had caused them both to experience suffering "to the dregs."

During the early occupation of Germany, he became embroiled in a petty dispute with American authorities over the publication of one of his poems, for which they had not asked his permission. He blew the incident out of all proportion at a time when the occupied and the occupiers had other things to think about and was chastised both publicly and privately. The affair is another of those which show that even this visionary and creator of an ideal man could not internalize the lessons of life that he had caused his Harry Haller personality to learn some twenty years earlier. He was not always a model of Jungian individuation and could still take life far too personally and seriously. But such incidents actually underscore an integral part of the message in his writings—that we remain human to the end, that the struggle of polarities can end only with death.

Petty grievances, emotions, and wounded ego aside, significant honors and awards made their way to his door: the Goethe Prize, the Peace Prize, and the coveted Nobel Prize for Literature, along with other minor recognitions. Poor health—especially his painful eyes and troubled vision, sciatica, and arthritis—plagued him. He wrote no more major prose works, although he published two volumes of new poetry. He worked as well on various editions of his previous writings and continued his always-voluminous letter writing when eyesight permitted.

Perhaps the final questions to be asked in a study of this lonely outsider, who felt himself not only guided but driven by an inner voice, should be: What was his own artist-legacy that he wanted to leave behind? What were the "cer-

211

tain things, whose existence is neither demonstrable nor apparent," which he wanted to "place before the eyes of mankind"? And we should also ask—since he felt his mission so important—why did he sometimes take pains to obscure his message?

The latter question is easily answered, for just as his inner voice was reluctant to speak to him in a childish tongue, so did Hesse feel that his deepest thoughts could be shared only with those who cared about life as he did[2]—a trickle-down approach to his epiphany, perhaps, but enough to keep his new mythology alive. Harry Haller had said, via Novalis, "Most people will not swim until they are ready" (*GS IV* 199).

Despite his lack of faith in the spiritual perceptions and genuine dedication of most of his fellow humans, Hesse did not condemn any attempt to find God or the meaning of life. He could call all religions equal in their intent, but he found that doctrines tend to develop into confining pathways instead of open doorways to the East. He knew that only time, contemplation, and goodwill might someday permit all seekers to recognize the common goal of their searches—that all teachings meet in the concept of eternal humanity. But such simple spirituality, Hesse felt, becomes layered over with dogma, pushed aside by pride, greed, and desire or, more subtly, by spiritual insecurity, because most of humankind wants rules to live by which promise personal immortality or, in Buddhist terms, rules that permit our particular karma to rise above a world that is too much with us. Hesse could believe, however, that only a universal soul lives on, but we have never been wont to accept such ego finality. Thus, we may find Hesse's thinking (to use once more Thomas Mann's characterization) "dangerously advanced intellectuality" or, perhaps more accurately, "dangerously advanced spirituality."

The theologian Martin Buber must have grasped to some extent what Hesse saw, for in his eulogy he said (as quoted in Freedman 388), "Hesse has served the spirit by telling of the conflict between spirit and life and of the struggle of the spirit against itself." It is the latter phrase that is of interest, although it must be taken to a higher level than Buber intended it to be understood. We recall in the "Toccata by Bach" that Hesse described the creation of the world in subtle, erotic language, showing the divine spirit "penetrating" into the chaos, the creator of life in the "pregnant earth" before "returning God-ward." Thus, he saw humankind's earthly nature as one with its divine nature—a joint inheritance from both the Heavenly Father and the Earth Mother, but this sire also left him with an imperative to "return home"—that is, when our minute persona rises like the wave of a river out of the wholeness as a "temporary mask," we are intended to perceive the importance of our struggle to rejoin and, with our lives,

212

strengthen the whole. But Hesse finds us falling in love, Narcissus-like, with our momentary place in the sun; we disregard the universal soul and want our tiny fragments of being to remain distinct entities.

Hesse came to believe, slowly and reluctantly, that the individual is important for one reason only: to serve all of being, not to rise above it and not to be personally saved. When our wave is again submerged into the river, our thespian mask is removed. And more often than not, he believed, we misuse our mask while we wear it, brazenly ignoring the inner blueprint for living, preferring to be ruled by traditions, customs, and the urges and desires that roam between the earthly poles of the senses and the mind.

Hesse's new mythology, despite its sacrifice of the individual ego into a universal melting pot at death, is an optimistic statement that being, itself, is affirmation and that a single humanity is moving toward a distant goal—so distant, however, that we, its component parts, are easily distracted by lesser games and lesser gods. But when, as we were shown in *Siddhartha,* all the creaking and groaning wheels are heard at once, they are in harmony; whatever static we may produce as individuals, try as we might, we cannot harm the divine essence of being. Whether we can agree with, or even understand, Hesse's metaphor of oneness, where all of being is a single miracle, where all is to be reverenced as a whole, where there is no need to break the one miracle into many, his Olympic vantage point could scarcely be higher. The Hesse legacy, accordingly, is his vision of a human spirit tied neither to ego nor to time, a vision drawn from both East and West—from the West, the Christian ethic of love and service, and from the East, the recognition of a single, universal soul-force.[3] When the dualities merge, every life becomes an opportunity to participate in the progressive resurrection and rejuvenation of the whole. And with the vision comes a mandate that all are responsible to determine their own right path, regardless of the race, culture, creed, or denomination into which the accident of birth or circumstances of life have placed them. Hesse's final paradigm of spiritual progress projects a call for individual faith in being, itself, for he finds that few, if any, collective efforts in our brief and Homocentric history have overcome the self-centeredness inherent in their own particular myths to focus on our universal journey to the East. It would seem a challenge whose time has come.

Notes

Introduction

1. Ralph Freedman, *Hermann Hesse: Pilgrim of Crisis* (New York: Pantheon, 1978), 13.

2. George W. Field, "Hermann Hesse: Polarities and Symbols of Synthesis," *Queen's Quarterly* 81 (1974): 100.

3. Joseph Mileck, *Hesse and His Critics* (New York: AMS Press, 1966), 120.

4. Thomas Mann, in his introduction to Michael Roloff and Michael Lebeck's English translation of *Demian* (New York: Harper & Row, 1965), viii. The word "intellectuality" derives from the German word *Geist,* which can mean "spirit" as well as "intellect" or "mind." The same phrase was rendered as "dangerously advanced spirituality" in *The Hesse-Mann Letters,* ed. Anni Carlsson and Volker Michels, trans. Ralph Mannheim (New York: Harper and Row, 1975), 114. The obvious ambiguity supports an important contention—that the simple word *Geist* is the root of considerable confusion in Hesse criticism.

5. Ball, Hugo. *Hermann Hesse: Sein Leben und sein Werk* (Berlin: Fischer, 1927; reprint, Frankfurt am Main: Suhrkamp, 1977), 21.

6. Mark Boulby, *Hermann Hesse: His Mind and Art* (New York: Cornell University Press, 1967), v.

7. The casual reader may not see a clear thematic continuum, but it is a conscious part of Hesse's writing, as he indicates in a letter to Helene Welti in 1928: "The book [his *Betrachtungen (Observations)*] only has meaning for me because, by placing my works of the last 25 years in order, you can see that there has been turbulence and development in my being and thought, but never a break. The upheavals of the war certainly affected me violently, but the basic ideas of my thinking and faith in life [*Lebensglauben*] remained the same, afterwards as before." *Hermann Hesse: Gesammelte Briefe* (Frankfurt am Main: Suhrkamp, 1979), 2:201.

8. Joseph Mileck, *Hermann Hesse: Life and Art* (Berkeley: University of California Press, 1978), x.

9. Eugene Stelzig, *Hermann Hesse's Fictions of the Self* (Princeton, N.J.: Princeton University Press, 1988).

10. In 1931 he wrote, "Once, a little more than ten years ago, I attempted to express my faith in a book. The book is called *Siddhartha,* and the nature of this faith has often been tested and discussed by Indian students and Japanese priests, but never by their Christian colleagues" (*GS VII* 370).

11. Hans Küng, from a lecture, "Hermann Hesse als ökumenische Herausforderung," given at the Sixth International Hermann Hesse Colloquium in Calw, May 24–26, 1990. Published in Martin Pfeifer, ed., *Hermann Hesse und die Religion* (Bad Liebenzell: Verlag B. Gengenbach, 1990), 57–86.

Chapter 1: Biography

1. Ralph Freedman attributes Hesse's early enthusiasm for art to an episode in the life of Hesse's half brother, Theodor Isenberg, when Hesse was only seven. Isenberg, who was apprenticed to a pharmacist, demanded that he be allowed to study music instead. He was given the opportunity, and Freedman feels that the younger brother began to associate art with rebellion. Hesse started to write poems and take music lessons at that very time (*Hermann Hesse: Pilgrim of Crisis* [New York: Pantheon, 1978], 31).

2. For numerous observations that Hesse made in his letters and writings regarding Heimat, see Friedrich Bran's *Hermann Hesses Gedanken über Heimat* (Bad Liebenzell/Calw: Gengenbach, 1982). The monograph is an expanded version of a lecture given by Bran in 1980.

3. Bernard Zeller, "Hermann Hesse und die Welt der Väter," in *Hermann Hesse und die Religion,* ed. Martin Pfeifer (Bad Liebenzell: Verlag B. Gengenbach, 1990), 35–55.

4. *Hermann Hesse: Kindheit und Jugend vor 1900,* eds. Ninon Hesse, Gerhard Kirchhoff (Frankfurt am Main: Suhrkamp, 1984), 1:523–7. This is a two-volume series, the first containing correspondence from 1877 to 1895, the second from 1895 to 1900.

5. In order to qualify for the examination, Hesse had to change his citizenship from Swiss to German. The fact that he had German citizenship during the First World War caused him considerable difficulty. Because he was living in Switzerland, his critics found it justifiable to label him a traitor and coward. His citizenship would be changed back to Swiss in 1924.

6. This is the only comment on sermon content repeated by Hesse in his published letters, but Freedman (possibly with information from a different, though unspecified, source) calls the sermons "violent and disturbing and painful" (46), adding, "The language of [Blumhardt's] hell-fire sermons intruded into his judgment of the boy, whom he no longer regarded as being ill but as being possessed by evil spirits" (47).

7. The house where Hesse lived during the Tübingen years still stands at 28 Herrenberger Straße and is now a small music academy. A plaque identifies it as the "Hesse Haus."

8. Jakob Burckhardt was the great Renaissance historian, and Arnold Böcklin was a painter.

9. See footnote 1 to *KuJ II* 248.

10. A reference to the young, innocent girl whom Goethe's Faust had seduced.

Chapter 2: *Peter Camenzind*

1. The variations of masculine-feminine metaphors in the Hesse thematic continuum and other duality motifs—although masculine-feminine relationships have by no means gone unnoticed in Hesse criticism—are examined throughout, particularly at the metaphorical level, which has been a confusing issue.

2. There is no direct evidence in the novel, itself, or in letters relating to the move to Gaienhofen following his marriage to suggest that Hesse felt any differently than his protagonist, Peter. He appears to be speaking with hindsight in a 1951 statement to

French students who had written asking him about Camenzind, that "he is not breathing satisfaction and satiety, for this is the work and confession of a young person, and satisfaction and satiety do not belong to the characteristics of youth" (*Neue Züricher Zeitung*, August 4, 1951), as quoted in *Hermann Hesse: Eine Werkgeschichte*, ed. Siegfried Unseld (Frankfurt am Main: Suhrkamp, 1973), 18. Ball also calls the idyllic ending "a paradise of bright-eyed boyhood years," but he qualifies the remark by adding—apparently in defense of the rebel in Hesse—"Camenzind is an affront to modern culture and society" (*Hermann Hesse: Sein Leben und sein Werk* [Berlin: Fischer, 1927; reprint, Frankfurt am Main: Suhrkamp, 1977], 24). And yet another comment suggests that he, too, has the advantage of hindsight regarding Hesse's idyllic dream: "[Hesse] is far less self-satisfied than one might assume. But he keeps his conflicts and reservations to himself" (25). Boulby downplays the Hesse dream at the time, though he eventually proves right— "the initial impulse which led to [the Gaienhofen years], in the attempt to create a vigorous figure behind the thrall of decadence, [was] rooted in nature and its myths"—in *Hermann Hesse: His Mind and Art* (New York: Cornell University Press, 1967), 12. Hans Jürgen Lüthi sees the return to nature for what it is in the book but perceives that the conditions of Hesse's own life would not permit him the dream. He calls it a "return at a higher level" but adds that "the condition of this God and nature-filled unity in no way corresponds to the actual state of being and state of life of [Hesse's]," in *Hermann Hesse: Natur und Geist* (Stuttgart: Kohlhammer, 1970), 16.

3. Hesse, himself, becomes more aware of this as time goes on. In a letter of April 7, 1924, to Lisa Wenger, the mother of his second wife, he writes, after looking through a number of his essays and newspaper articles, that "to me they mean that you will see quite clearly that, despite all the emotions, artistic, and political changes in my life, I have always followed the same goals and had the same convictions [*Gesinnungen*]" (*GB II* 85).

4. Hermann Hesse, *Franz von Assisi* (Berlin: Fischer, [1904]), 9.

5. Hesse is likely not yet consciously portraying Freudian/Jungian implications in *Peter Camenzind*. The relationships are not "deviant," and their primary function is to indicate that the characters now share qualities or understanding, or "pass a torch." Patrick J. Gignac has published the first article to deal exclusively with the theme of homosexuality in Hesse, limiting his remarks, however, to *Demian*. His thesis would be more appropriate if applied to *Peter Camenzind* and *Beneath the Wheel*. By the time he was writing *Demian*, Hesse was deeply involved with the Jungian concept of *anima* in expressing interpersonal relationships. Homoerotic inferences can be drawn, but they are not as dominant as Grignac maintains. His article is flawed with run-on quotations and has Pistorius appearing as "Pretorius" ("Homosexual Identity [Mis]information in Hesse's *Demian*," in *The German Mosaic*, Contributions in Ethnic Studies, vol. 33, ed. Carol Aisha Blackshire-Belay [Westport, Conn.: Greenwood Press, 1994], 295–300).

6. Hesse will use death and departure motifs time and again, viz. Heilner's departure in *Beneath the Wheel*, Pierre's death in *Roßhalde*, Demian's disappearance, the "murder" of Hermine in *Der Steppenwolf*, Leo's disappearance in *Journey to the East*, and Knecht's death in *The Glass Bead Game*.

Chapter 3: *Beneath the Wheel*

1. Boulby agrees that *Beneath the Wheel* is artistically inferior: "As a work of art the novel might even be adjudged a serious disappointment after *Camenzind,* having all the distinguishing marks of a minor talent" (*Hermann Hesse: His Mind and Art* [New York: Cornell University Press, 1967], 63), although he says earlier that "it must compete for the best example of its class" (i.e., the school novel) (41). Boulby's analysis is one of the most thorough studies of *Beneath the Wheel.* Freedman, on the other hand, feels that the work is a "balance of critique and attractive lyricism that ensured [Hesse's] success" (*Hermann Hesse: Pilgrim of Crisis* [New York: Pantheon, 1978], 131).

2. Hesse's *Beneath the Wheel* is not an isolated criticism. Boulby emphasizes in his discussion of the novel that "the German school system stands [at that time] condemned by all and sundry as a kind of civilian recruit training which warps the child's soul, nationalizes it, and then loads down the victim with useless knowledge and a false moral outlook" (41).

3. Ball says that *Beneath the Wheel* was written "about 1905, during the Lake Constance period" (*Hermann Hesse: Sein Leben und sein Werk* [Berlin: Fischer, 1927; reprint, Frankfurt am Main: Suhrkamp, 1977], 44). Hesse says, in the sketch "On Moving into a New House," that he "sat at home in Calw with his father and sisters and wrote *Beneath the Wheel,*" while Mia was "discovering Gaienhofen" (*GS IV* 618). The final revisions were done in Gaienhofen.

4. A suggestion made by student reader Sheri Bodoh.

5. Translated by Boulby from *Freund Hain,* 9th ed. (Berlin, 1905), 123.

6. In "Names and the Creative Process: A Study of Names in Hermann Hesse's *Lauscher, Demian, Steppenwolf,* and *Glasperlenspiel,*" *Monatshefte* 3 (1961): 167–80.

7. Ball, for example, points out that "Heilner" (*heilen,* to heal) indicates a desire for "health" on Hesse's part (44).

Chapter 4: Gaienhofen and Bern

1. See Freedman, *Hermann Hesse: Pilgrim of Crisis* (New York: Pantheon, 1978), 134–5, for a short discussion of the leader of this group, a certain Guso or Gustav Gräser, and his sanatorium in Ascona. Gräser promoted a natural life and vegetarian diet, and he was apparently surrounded by a certain amount of controversy.

2. This was Hesse's first work to receive negative reviews (and rightly so), which upset him. Here, as in *Beneath the Wheel,* the protagonist is really two personalities, the characters Kuhn and Muth. Kuhn is the "outsider-artist," as symbolized by his crippled leg. The Gertrude of the title is a precursor of Frau Eva in *Demian.*

Chapter 5: *Roßhalde*

1. *Roßhalde* is at least as autobiographical as *Beneath the Wheel,* and almost every critic who deals with the work stresses the autobiographical content. For example, see Theodor Heuss, "*Roßhalde,*" *März* 8 (Stuttgart, 1914): 503; Freedman, *Hermann Hesse:*

Pilgrim of Crisis (New York: Pantheon, 1978), 162–3; Fritz Böttger, *Hermann Hesse* (Berlin: Verlag der Nationen, 1974), 186; Ball, *Hermann Hesse: Sein Leben und sein Werk* (Berlin: Fischer, 1927; reprint, Frankfurt am Main: Suhrkamp, 1977), 99; Erwin Ackerknecht, "Neue Erzählkunst," *Ein deutsches Literaturblatt* 8 (1913–1914): 584–5.

2. For a more detailed commentary on this artist-child-world relationship, see Tusken, "Hermann Hesse's *Roßhalde:* The Story in the Paintings," *Monatshefte* 77 (Spring 1981): 60–6. Adaptation of the discussion is reprinted by permission of the University of Wisconsin Press.

3. Others can agree that the ending is flawed. See Oswald Brüll, "Hermann Hesse und sein neues Buch: *Roßhalde,*" *Nord und Süd, eine deutsche Monatsschrift* 38 (1914): 202; Hermann Herz, "Hermann Hesses Roman *Roßhalde.* Ein Typus," *Die Bücherwelt* 11 (Bonn, 1913/14): 283; Ernst Rose, *Faith from the Abyss: Hermann Hesse's Way from Romanticism to Modernity* (New York: New York University Press, 1965), 40.

Chapter 6: World War I

1. For good, precise summaries of Hesse's political essays written between 1914 and 1919, see Mileck, *Hermann Hesse and His Critics: The Criticism and Bibliography of Half a Century,* University of North Carolina Studies in Germanic Languages and Literatures, vol. 21 (Chapel Hill: University of North Carolina Press, 1958; reprint, New York: AMS Press, 1966), 39–45; and his *Hermann Hesse: Life and Art* (Berkeley: University of California Press, 1978), 68–81.

2. As noted, Eugene Stelzig entitled his study of Hesse *Hermann Hesse's Fictions of the Self* and calls his *Eigensinn,* somewhat tongue in cheek, the "beloved voice within a secularized version of the Protestant stress on individual conscience" (New Jersey: Princeton University Press, 1988), 43. He also calls it "Hesse's favorite virtue . . . a transcendental or theologically based version of individualism" (44–45). Stelzig's observation makes clear how deeply the moralizing of Hesse's parents impressed the young boy and carried over into the man. Had his parents not demanded such complete "surrender," Hesse perhaps would not have found the demands of his "own God" so unrelenting.

3. Freedman notes that Hesse was "amazed by the vehemence of the attacks against him" as a result of the Zarathustra publication (*Hermann Hesse: Pilgrim of Crisis* [New York: Pantheon, 1978], 198). Most of the criticism can be traced to a Danish journalist, Sven Lang, who quoted a Hesse comment out of context in September of 1915. Subsequently, "patriotic" critics were lying in wait for any and every word they could construe as disloyal to the German cause.

4. This is the concept that has been continually overlooked in attempts to interpret the meaning of Knecht's death in *The Glass Bead Game.* Virtually all critics want "fulfillment" to mean a fait accompli in *this* life, with the enlightened one leading a Buddha-like existence from that point on, but this is not Hesse's ultimate message.

5. Mileck stresses this point, as well, noting that "all had to begin with the individual and Hesse had faith in the intrinsic [I would add "potential"] goodness of man"

(*Hermann Hesse: Life and Art,* 81). Stelzig says that "[Hesse's] advocacy of the sanctity of the individual remained his highest good as a writer and a moralist" (44).

Chapter 7: *Demian*

1. Oskar Seidlin, in "Hermann Hesse: The Exorcism of the Demon," *Symposium* 4 (1950): 325–48, interprets the apple-stealing incident as Hesse's own daring to take the forbidden fruit: "Protestant to the core, haunted by the consciousness of original sin, Hesse has circled again and again around man's tasting of the forbidden fruit of the tree of knowledge, his awakening amidst fear and trembling" (328). Seidlin's remark supports the idea that Hesse intends *Demian* to be a challenge to Christianity.

2. Seidlin simply calls him "Sinclair's double" (332). Joseph Mileck says, "One could immediately argue that Demian is an anagram for *jemand*. However . . . Demian is indeed an exceptional *somebody*—it is far more likely that Hesse had the Greek *daimon* . . . in mind . . . Sinclair's *daimon*—his admonishing inner voice, his guiding spirit" in his article "Names and the Creative Process: A Study of Names in Hesse's *Lauscher, Demian, Steppenwolf,* and *Glasperlenspiel,*" *Monatshefte* 3 (1961): 171. Rene Breugelmann, in "Hermann Hesse and Depth Psychology," *Canadian Review of Comparative Literature* (Winter 1981): 10–47, calls Sinclair "the growing self" and Demian "the achieved self" (29). Ziolkowski calls him a "Christ figure" (*Fictional Transfigurations of Jesus* [Princeton: Princeton University Press, 1972], 140). Gilles Quispel, in *Gnostic Studies* (N.p.: Netherlands Historisch-Archaelogisch Instituut te Istanbul, 1975), implies that the name Demian is taken from *Demiurg,* which is identified with Abraxas (225). Mark Boulby says that "Demian is so rich in implications that it is difficult to exhaust him" (*Hermann Hesse: His Mind and Art* [New York: Cornell University Press, 1967], 101). He goes on to call him a "Messiah," a "symbol of the Middle Way," an "alter ego," a "synthesis of good and evil" and more (102). Ball writes, "Someone who was closely associated with the origin of *Demian* confided to me that this name came from the studies of the demonic that the author was involved in at the time, and that Dämon-Demian had their common roots in the word daemoniacus" (*Hermann Hesse: Sein Leben und sein Werk* [Berlin: Fischer, 1927; reprint, Frankfurt am Main: Suhrkamp, 1977], 55).

3. See William Reese, *Dictionary of Philosophy and Religion* (New Jersey: Humanities Press, 1980), 193.

4. Carl Gustav Jung, *The Integration of the Personality,* trans. Stanley Dell (London: K. Paul, Trench, Trubner, and Co., 1940), 53.

5. As quoted by G. K. Chesterton in *St. Francis of Assisi* (New York: Image Books, 1957), 54. Chesterton gives no source for his quotation, but Lawrence Cunningham in *St. Francis of Assisi,* Twayne's World Author Series (Boston: Twayne, 1976), 82–84, also mentions the speaking crucifix at St. Damiano. Hesse, tongue in cheek, noted that "Demian was not invented by me, or chosen, rather I met him in a dream, and he spoke so strongly to me that I made him the title of my book," as translated by Mileck from *Hermann Hesse. Briefe* (Frankfurt am Main: Suhrkamp, 1959), 482. Mileck calls this "a

veiled comment . . . [that] tantalizes more than it satisfies" ("Names" 171). Hesse's dream reference might well indicate that he had St. Francis's dream message in mind as well as the other allusions. Still another possibility should be brought up. "Daimonion," a variation of "daimon" and what Socrates called his "personal daimon"—the fact that he felt he had such a personal relationship with the gods was a major cause of his condemnation—fits well with the role into which Hesse places Sinclair, indicating the danger of such a personal relationship to his "secret voice" and the ostracism that it brings.

6. Johanna Neuer, "Jungian Archetypes in Hermann Hesse's *Demian," Germanic Review* 57 (Winter 1982): 11.

7. Walther Sokel, "The Problem of Dualism in Hesse's *Demian* and Musil's *Törless," Modern Austrian Literature* 9, no. 3/4 (1976): 36.

8. In broad terms Abraxas is the god of Gnosticism, an early sect that attempted to bring Christian doctrine and philosophy together by incorporating evil as well as good in the God-figure. For a fuller discussion of the origins and nature of Abraxas, see Gilles Quispel, *Gnostic Studies* (N.p.: Netherlands Historisch-Archaelogisch Instituut te Istanbul, 1975) and Uwe Wolff, *Hermann Hesse: Demian—Die Botschaft vom Selbst* (Bonn: Bouvier, 1979), 20–22. Both writers agree that Hesse's knowledge of Gnosticism came principally from Jung's *Septem Sermones ad Mortua.* In a review of the Wolff monograph, Mileck rightly takes Wolff to task for finding *Demian* little more than the story of a circle of Gnostics. Review in *The German Quarterly* 55 (March 1982): 274–5.

9. Frau Eva is even more symbolically complex than Demian. A sampling of attempts to characterize her and describe her function in the novel follow. Dorothy Cox Ward: "Hesse has created in Frau Eva a most effective symbol of unity of all the possibilities within the notion and reality of 'woman'" ("Two Marys: A Study of the Women in Hermann Hesse's Fiction." [Ph.D. diss., Columbia University, 1976], 108); "She is Sinclair's destiny as Demian and Beatrice had been before her" (109); and "Frau Eva is a projection of Sinclair's persona at a given time in his life, represents his growing ability to unify a dualistic world, to worship Abraxas . . . to combine spirituality and sensuality in his love of a woman" (110). Malte Dahrendorf, in "Hermann Hesses *Demian* und C. G. Jung," *Germanische-Romanische Zeitschrift* 39 (1958), says she is to be understood as a religious symbol, and the world of the religious symbols is "the path upon which Sinclair can find himself; she makes possible Sinclair's self-recognition and finally the mastery of the primal powers that live within him" (96). Seidlin states that "her very name, Mrs. Eve, identifies her as the mythical All-Mother, the great womb in which all life rests" (332). Ziolkowski calls her the "universal archetype of the Magna Mater in Jung's sense" (*The Novels of Hermann Hesse* [Princeton, N.J.: Princeton University Press, 1965], 133). In *Hermann Hesse: Sein Leben und sein Werk* (Berlin: Fischer, 1927; reprinted Frankfurt am Main: Suhrkamp, 1977), Hugo Ball says, "The image of the mother pulls all of the symbolic power, all of the signs that can be attributed to the meaning of mother, unto herself" (154). As can be noted from the above attempts to characterize her and describe her function in the novel, Frau Eva's role is broad, though not overly controversial, however difficult it may be to express.

10. Joseph Campbell made a similar statement regarding conservative Christianity

vis-à-vis other faiths when he related an incident at an International Congress for the History of Religion. The Dalai Lama had said, "We are all intending the same goal— these [the various faiths] are different methods." The American Cardinal Cook stood up and replied: "Oh, no. This is quite different. This is not the same religion, ours as these others" ("Joseph Campbell: Myths to Live By," *Bill Moyers' Journal* [PBS, 1981], 9). Luise Rinser, in "Hermann Hesse und die fernöstliche Philosophie," *Hermann Hesse und die Religion,* ed. Martin Pfeifer (Bad Liebenzell: Verlag B. Gengenbach, 1990), comments on this very aspect of Christianity by interpreting Christ's statement "I am the way." She points out that he did not say, "I am the goal," but only speaks of the way. She then asks, "Is he speaking of himself as a person?" She answers her own question by saying, "he is speaking of what he is in all reality: the manifestation of the divine spirit" (28).

Chapter 8: *Siddhartha*

1. Joseph Mileck, "Hermann Hesse und der Osten: Ziel oder Zweck? Bekehrung oder Aesthetik," in *Hermann Hesse und die Religion,* ed. Martin Pfeifer (Bad Liebenzell: Verlag B. Gengenbach, 1990), 99.

2. See Hesse's "Eine Bibliothek der Welt Literatur" ("A Library of World Litera- ture") for recommended religious readings (*GS VII* 307–43). See also his essay "Aus Indien" (Frankfurt am Main: Suhrkamp, 1968).

3. Siddhartha's refreshing sleep can be compared with Faust's sleep of renewal after Gretchen's death at the the end of *Faust,* part 1. Boulby compares the "*om*" with the ringing church bells that Faust hears on Easter morning (*Hermann Hesse: His Mind and Art* [New York: Cornell University Press, 1967], 146). The "*om*" may also be com- pared with the *Gottespuren* ("traces of God") that awaken Harry Haller occasionally in *Der Steppenwolf.*

4. Boulby gives an interesting interpretation of Kamala's death, saying that "she pays the penalty in the end for her way of life, dies of the poison of that for which she has lived. Hesse thus unconsciously judges Kamala" (149). Boulby's symbolism fits the picture, but it is difficult to feel that Hesse is in any way condemning Kamala.

5. Understanding this concept—that Siddhartha can "inhale" the worst suffering he has had to endure and feel it become "just another part of being within him"—leads to better understanding Joseph Knecht's death In *The Glass Bead Game.* He, too, is "ready at any time" to "feel the oneness of life," and his death provides this symbiosis.

6. Ziolkowski makes unclear observations concerning the enlightenment of both Buddha and Vasudeva: "Buddha, who has achieved fulfillment, does not fit into the realm of the spirit any more than does Vasudeva: both show by anticipation the state upon which Siddhartha will enter when he has advanced far enough" (*The Novels of Hermann Hesse* [Princeton, N.J.: Princeton University Press, 1965], 168). He adds later that "the three men [now including Siddhartha] who share this perception [awareness of unity, totality, and simultaneity of all being] also share the same beatific smile, even though each reached his goal by following a completely different path" (172).

7. Compare Hermann Heilner's kissing Hans Giebenrath to Demian's kissing Sinclair. The male-male kiss, as noted, symbolizes the passing on or merging of qualities from one individual to another. Hans understands and joins, or tries to join, Hermann Heilner's world; Sinclair joins Demian's. Here, Siddhartha's kiss is simply a stylistic device enabling Siddhartha to share his vision with Govinda.

8. Ziolkowski calls the river "the natural symbol of synthesis . . . the natural border between the realms of the *spirit* [emphasis provided] and sense" (*Novels* 161). Translation of the word *Geist* as "spirit" in this context is misleading and again underscores the difficulty encountered with Hesse's duality motifs. As mentioned, the real spirit world in Hesse is the world beyond "Geist und Natur." Siddhartha's thoughts clearly indicate this (using Ziolkowski's translation): "The body was surely not the self, nor was the play of the senses . . . this world of thoughts also was not part of the beyond . . . the ultimate meaning lay hidden beyond both of them" (*Novels* 166). Ziolkowski does note at another point that Siddhartha devoted twenty years to the cultivation of the "intellect," or *Geist* (167) in the Vedas, the teachings of his elders, etc.; Narcissus will search for the spirit via the mind in the scriptures. Castalia is intended to search via the mind for wisdom that can be passed on to the world. Masculine/feminine, father/mother, and mind/senses are dualities of this world, but *Geist* and *Natur* must be carefully interpreted according to the immediate context.

9. Rose calls this final vision Christian: "Mystic union in the last instance means a loving embrace of the world. One could justifiably quote Christ's pronouncement that 'God is not the God of the dead, but of the living' (Matt. 22:32)" (*Faith from the Abyss* [New York: New York University Press, 1965], 71). Boulby also finds a Christian context: "Siddhartha's experience leads him away from Buddhistic 'pessimism'; it leads him away from ethical judgments to the total amoralism of chaos; while the universal love points away from Indian teachings altogether toward that of St. Francis" (138). Hesse, himself, calls this love a "return to Christianity, a truly Protestant quality" ("Mein Glaube," *GS VII* 372). Stelzig casts ironic aspersions at such a lofty message, noting that "despite its ironic and light touches, the sermon of the concluding chapter cannot rise above the contradiction inherent in its logic, something that makes Hesse's most popular wisdom book a problematic achievement: it inspires to communicate wisdom even as it maintains that wisdom is not communicable" (*Hermann Hesse's Fictions of the Self* [Princeton, N.J.: Princeton University Press, 1988], 187).

Chapter 9: *Der Steppenwolf*

1. *Der Steppenwolf* is perhaps even more autobiographical than is *Demian*. For an excellent summary of the similarities between Hesse and his Harry Haller counterpart, see Joseph Mileck, *Hermann Hesse: Life and Art* (Berkeley: University of California Press, 1978), especially pages 175–9.

2. *GB II* erroneously lists the year as 1925 in note no. 1, p. 80.

3. Thomas Mann also calls the novel an example of "experimental daring," and Theodore Ziolkowski relates this remark, at least in part, to the novel's confusing external form. In an attempt to show that *Der Steppenwolf* is as tightly constructed in "sonata

form" as Hesse claims, Ziolkowski has written one of the most interesting of the *Steppenwolf* analyses (*The Novels of Hermann Hesse* [Princeton, N.J.: Princeton University Press, 1965], 178–228). Mileck, too, relates the "new" (i.e., the "daring") to the stylistic obfuscations: "The new obviously did not lie in the matter but in the manner, the multimethod of his portraiture" (*Life and Art* 195).

4. Tusken's Jungian interpretation of Hesse's *Der Steppenwolf* was first published in "The Question of Perspective in Hesse's *Steppenwolf,*" *Theorie und Kritik. Festschrift für Gerhard Loose,* ed. Stefan Grunwald (Bern and Munich: Francke, 1974), 159–66. The article was an extension of a previous Jungian interpretation offered by Edward Abood in "Jung's Concept of Individuation in Hesse's *Steppenwolf,*" *Southern Humanities Review* 3 (Summer 1968): 1–12. Although modified, the discussion holds to the same basic Jungian concepts. The adaptation is reprinted with permission of the Francke Verlag.

5. Hesse had friends named Leuthold who often invited him to stay with them when he visited Zurich. In December of 1925, they helped him locate an apartment where he would live for several winters.

6. Edwin Casebeer, *Hermann Hesse,* Writers for the Seventies Series (New York: Warner, 1972), 98–9.

7. Egon Schwarz, "Zur Erklärung von Hesses *Steppenwolf,*" *Monatshefte* 53 (Summer 1961): 191–8.

8. To my knowledge David Horrocks is the first to point out that Nietzsche is an obvious source for the dance as well as the laughter motif in *Der Steppenwolf.* He quotes from *Also sprach Zarathustra* [my translation]: "You superior people, the worst thing about you is: none of you learns to dance as one must dance—above and beyond yourselves [über euch hinweg]" (136). (Zarathustra says the same about learning to laugh.) In "Harry Haller as 'höherer Mensch': Nietzschean Themes in Hermann Hesse's *Der Steppenwolf,*" *German Life and Letters* 46 (April 1993): 134–44.

9. Abood calls Pablo "the perfect man" the "all-powerful, all-knowing Magus archetype" in "Jung's Concept of Individuation in Hesse's *Steppenwolf,*" *Southern Humanities Review* 3 (Summer 1968): 8, but his analysis falls short of finding a way to bring Harry, Hermine, and Pablo together as an integrated personality. At the end of his essay, Abood says, "Harry has not achieved his goal and perhaps never will" (11).

10. In German *Trottel* means fool or imbecile, so Hesse can make a pun with the word *Foxtrottel.*

11. When Dr. Timothy Leary popularized *Der Steppenwolf,* Hesse was interpreted by many as approving the use of drugs, but Hesse was only after a means of artistic expression. When the novel ends, with Harry ridding himself of all his crutches, the reader sees that the theme of the novel is anything but escape.

12. Heidi M. Rockwood's interpretation of Pablo as the more encompassing Mercurial figure of the alchemical process, the "catalyst for all the actions and developments that take place," exemplifies the problem of making Pablo fit into a particular archetypal mold. He does, in fact, fit the all-encompassing catalyst role quite perfectly, as Rockwood suggests, but it is probably more by coincidence than by design, since alchemy does not ever seem to have been the object of any in-depth study on Hesse's

part. In "The Function of Pablo in Hesse's *Steppenwolf*," *South Atlantic Review* 59 (November 1994): 54.

13. In the oft-quoted foreword to the 1942 edition of the novel, Hesse complained that so many saw only the negative side of the message: "the story of Steppenwolf, to be sure, represents a sickness and crisis, but not one that leads to death, not a decline, but the opposite: a healing" (as quoted in *Hermann Hesse: Eine Werkgeschichte* [Frankfurt am Main: Suhrkamp, 1973], 108–10). Hesse seems almost to contradict this claim to faith in a later statement: "It is something else if you call Knecht [Joseph Knecht of *The Glass Bead Game*] a Steppenwolf. He is his opposite. The Steppenwolf flees from a death of desperation by his razor into the naive, sensual life. Knecht, however, the mature one, leaves serenely and bravely a world that offers him no further opportunites for development" (114). At the time he wrote these remarks in a letter; however, Hesse was seventy-eight, and it can easily be seen that he is comparing only the as-yet unenlightened Harry Haller to Knecht.

14. For example, Abood states: "Although [Harry] has not achieved this ideal and never will, he has come a long way since his first reading of the 'Treatise on the Steppenwolf'" (11–2). Seymour L. Flaxman claims that "Hesse gives us no formal solution to the problem in *Steppenwolf*. . . . But Hesse does give us a way out, a *modus vivendi*. . . . It is a tragic story, to be sure. It tells what happens when the intellectual becomes isolated from the society" in "*Der Steppenwolf*: Hesse's Portrait of the Intellectual," *Modern Language Quarterly* 15 (1954): 356. Oscar Seidlin remarks that the "shrill and cacophonous tones . . . remain unresolved in *Steppenwolf*" in "The Exorcism of the Demon," *Symposium* 4 (1950): 332–3. Boulby notes: "The resolution we are offered . . . is spurious" (*Hermann Hesse: His Mind and Art* [New York: Cornell University Press, 1967], 163). Ziolkowski comments that "[Harry], too, may hope to learn magical thinking and to enter the ranks of the immortals . . . but must transcend himself in order to be able to maintain constantly this new view of life" (*Novels* 222).

Chapter 10: *Narcissus and Goldmund*

1. Another book, *Hermann Hesse* by H. R. Schmid, would appear the following year (1928) with the Huber Publishing House in Frauenfeld. A dissertation by Hugo Mauerhofer, "Die Introversion. Mit spezieller Berücksichtigung des Dichters Hermann Hesse," came out in Bern in 1929. Hesse was quite amused with Schmid's work, saying he had created himself a Hesse and a biography and psychology, as well, calling his efforts a "freely invented Hesse-doll." See *GB II* 203, 222.

2. Gisela Kleine, *Ninon und Hermann Hesse* (Sigmarinen: Thorbeck, 1982), 129.

3. This discussion is based on Tusken's "Thematic Unity in Hermann Hesse's *Narziss und Goldmund*: The Tree Symbol as Interpretive Key," *Modern Fiction Studies* 29 (Summer 1983): 245–51. Adaptation of the material has been granted by Purdue University.

4. Ziolkowski finds another reason for the change: "Maulbronn trained boys for . . . the Protestant clergy, while Mariabronn is wholly Catholic. . . . Hesse deserted the

Protestant faith of his family . . . and subsequently never belonged to any church. But the idea of Catholicism, and particularly its ritual and symbolic aspects, appealed to him immensely" (*The Novels of Hermann Hesse* [Princeton, N.J.: Princeton University Press, 1965], 236).

5. Further evidence that this duality is intentional may be found in the fairy tale *Piktors Verwandlungen* (written in 1922, published in Zurich by Gesellschaft der Büchernfreunde, 1925), where the "tree of life" is "both man and woman."

6. In his essay "Trees" ("Bäume") Hesse writes, "Trees are shrines. Those who know how to speak to them, those who know how to listen to them, will learn the truth" (*GS III* 405). Credit should be given to Peter Gontrum for his study on Hesse's tree imagery, "Oracle and Shrine: Hesse's *Lebensbaum,*" *Monatshefte* 56 (April–May, 1964): 183–90. He says, of the chestnut tree in *Narcissus and Goldmund,* that it is "poised over the whole life of the spirit represented in the cloister" (188). Note again the translation of *Geist* as "spirit." Hesse intends the cloister—via its primary representative, Narcissus—to represent the life of the mind, which falls short in its search for the spirit, just as will Castalia, because it excludes the feminine world. Thus, the tree-cloister image—the intercourse of the two worlds—is an ideal that Goldmund, but not Narcissus, will attain. Boulby also notes that the tree is "related in concealed affinity with the slender sandstone twin pillars of the portal and the stone carving of the window" (*Hermann Hesse: His Mind and Art* [New York: Cornell University Press, 1967], 218). Casebeer sees the symbolic connection of tree and cloister but does not capture it completely: "Hesse's tree seems to me to belong to the world of the mother. . . . Yet its 'gold crown' links it to the more general symbolism of the tree" (117–18). A number of other critics either fail to mention the tree or make only brief comments: Hans Jürgen Lüthi, *Hermann Hesse: Natur und Geist* (Stuttgart: Kohlhammer, 1970); Kurt Weibel, *Hermann Hesse und die deutsche Romantik* (Winterthur: Keller, 1954); Ziolkowski, *Novels;* Rose, *Faith from the Abyss* (New York: New York University Press, 1965); and G. W. Field, *Hermann Hesse* (Boston: Twayne, 1970).

7. The reader should be aware of the nuances in the mother/father metaphor, which Hesse uses in sufficient variation to avoid obvious thematic redundancy from work to work. Demian had a mother, but he wore a sign of mourning on his sleeve symbolically to indicate that he was free of any authoritative father figure. Siddhartha found the father's path in life inadequate at every attempted level (i.e., his own father's, the Samanas', and the Buddha's), and his mother was present in name only, meaning that he had had little experience with the "feminine side" of life, which he would explore in the city. In *Der Steppenwolf* Harry Haller has been living at a higher level of a father-world of his own making and goes out to find meaning in the feminine side of life. Narcissus and Goldmund present yet another paradigm. Goldmund's father has been inadequate and gives his son into the hands of the cloister, which, with Narcissus as its representative, becomes a surrogate father. Goldmund has no mother except for his suppressed dream figure and must search her out. In so doing, he will discover the role of the father-world as well. The mother/father and masculine/feminine metaphors appear in still other variations in *Journey to the East* and *The Glass Bead Game.*

8. It is of interest that this Narcissus statement is identical in content to another intellectual's statement on the same theme. Ivan Karamazov, in his conversation with Alyosha at the tavern, says, "It isn't God I don't accept . . . it's the world created by Him." Fyodor Dostoevsky, *The Brothers Karamazov,* trans. David McDuff (London: Penquin Books, 1993), 270. There is, in fact, a good deal of thematic similarity in Hesse and Dostoevsky, especially in the latter's *Brothers Karamazov,* that has not yet been brought to light.

9. This discussion of Goldmund's carvings follows closely the same discussion in Tusken's essay "Thematic Unity in Hermann Hesse's *Narziss und Goldmund:* The Tree Symbol as Interpretive Key," *Modern Fiction Studies* 29 (Summer 1983): 245–51.

10. Russel Neuswanger, "Names as Glass Beads in Hesse's *Narziss und Goldmund,"Monatshefte* 67 (Spring 1975): 48–58; Mileck, *Hermann Hesse: Life and Art* (Berkeley: University of California Press, 1978), 206–9.

11. Hesse adds a personal note as the same quotation continues: "In the same way I, the artist Hesse, need completion through a Hesse who reverences the intellect, thought, discipline, even morality, who has been raised in a pious environment and must continue to discover anew the innocence of his activity, including his art, within the moral entanglements [of life]" (*GB II* 275).

Chapter 11: *Journey to the East*

1. Freedman says of *Journey to the East* that there is a "near absence of *anima*— of female *eros*" (*Hermann Hesse: Pilgrim of Crisis* [New York: Pantheon, 1978], 331) and continues on to say that the novel "had become a counterpoint to Goldmund. It contained only Narcissus" (332). While Freedman's point is well taken as far as the narrative itself is concerned, in comparing H.H.'s bewildered intellectual attempts to write about the League with Goldmund's erotic adventures, it becomes clear that the *anima* role is readily implied by the fact that all journeyers have personal goals—H.H.'s was to find Fatima. Their respective searches, symbolically speaking, include forays into alluring side streets. It is very often what is implied, as one novel takes up where the previous one left off that, makes Hesse's thematic continuum apparent.

2. The reader recognizes "lion" in the name Leo and "andros" (man) in the name Andreas. Also, Leo is a sign of the zodiac. In "Who is Leo? Astrology in Hermann Hesse's *Die Morgenlandfahrt,"* *Monatshefte* 67 (1975): 167–72, John Derrenberger investigates the astrological possibilities of the name Leo, noting that Hesse was a Moon Child, or Cancer, and that Leo is the next ecliptic sign and is ruled by the sun. Thus, the sun is the "dominant primary light" to which the moon "stands in a feminine or passive relation." Leo and H.H., accordingly, "reflect the novel's thematic core of dominance and submission in the question of self." While the analogy fits in principle, and while we are aware that Hesse was at least knowledgable in astrology, chances are that there is a much simpler explanation for the name: the "strong man" is the "perfect servant."

3. The silently working journeyers also reflect Hermine's words in *Steppenwolf,* when she is waxing philosophical with Harry: "We who are filled with longing, we with

a dimension too many, could not live if there were not another air to breathe aside from the air of this world . . . and this is the realm of all that is genuine" (*GS IV* 345). The League headquarters can be symbolically understood as the home of the immortals, the place of refuge to which the living journeyers can flee, where they can commune with their own.

4. A similar theme is found in the poem "Buchstaben" ("Letters"), appended to *The Glass Bead Game* (*GS VI* 546–7).

5. In *Demian* Hesse had commented that everything is written in every soul—that is, if all knowledge were destroyed, it would eventually reappear. It is the inner voice that leads one to meaning. Paradoxically, anyone who has gained access to the archives no longer needs them.

6. Freedman calls *Journey to the East* "one of the most affirmative books [Hesse] had written . . . it celebrates his new life with marvelous enthusiasm." Freedman also adds, without explanation, that "a negative note asserts itself in the end" (330).

Chapter 12: *The Glass Bead Game*

1. Hesse's ideas for his magnum opus had obviously undergone many changes. In a letter to Thomas Mann dated late 1933, he notes that "the idea of my two-year-old plan (the mathematical-musical *Geist*-game) is growing into an idea for a many volume work, into a library." In *Hermann Hesse Briefe,* (Frankfurt am Main: Suhrkamp, 1965), 111. For a detailed chronology of Hesse's progress with the novel, see *Materialien zu Hesses "Das Glasperlenspiel,"* ed. Volker Michels, 2 vols. (Frankfurt am Main: Suhrkamp, 1973, 1974), 1: 33–51.

2. The word *Geist* is left in its original German in two sentences in this paragraph to indicate the difficulty of interpretation and translation.

3. Kurt J. Fickert, "The Mystery of Hesse's *Das Glasperlenspiel," Forms of the Fantastic. Selected Essays from the Third International Conference on the Fantastic in Literature and Film,* eds. Jan Hokenson and Howard Pearce (Westport, Conn.: Greenwood Press, 1986), 221.

4. Dorothy Cox Ward, for instance, comments: "Indeed, as his best known and most admired novels . . . progress, women become less and less important, until in the last two novels, there are few, and these of no significance" ("Two Marys: A Study of the Women in Hermann Hesse's Fiction" [Ph.D. diss., Columbia University, 1976], 11). Stelzig speaks of "the exclusion of eros and the feminine by a masculine hierarchy" (*Hermann Hesse's Fictions of the Self* [Princeton, N.J.: Princeton University Press, 1988], 250), but he says at another point, in seeming contradiction, "Hesse was only able to achieve a precarious identification with the masculine spirit and paternal authority (*Geist*) in his later works" (56). Freedman says that "the figure of Narcissus dominates his last two important books" (*Hermann Hesse: Pilgrim of Crisis* [New York: Pantheon, 1978], 335).

5. As Mileck points out, Carlo Ferremonte is a Latinization of Karl Isenberg, Hesse's musically gifted nephew. In "Names and the Creative Process: A Study of Names in

Hesse's *Lauscher, Demian, Steppenwolf,* and *Glasperlenspiel." Monatshefte* 3 (1961): 175.

6. Siegfried Unseld, "Hermann Hesse's Influence: Ethics or Esthetics?" in *Hermann Hesse: Politische und wirkungsgeschichtliche Aspekte,* eds. Sigrid Bauschinger and Albert M. Reh (Bern: Franke, 1986), 129; first given as a paper at the Amherst Colloquium for German Literature in April 1984. See also Roger Norton, "Variant Endings of Hesse's *Glasperlenspiel," Monatshefte* 60 (1968): 141–6. Norton discusses two brief notes found among Hesse's papers, in which he was considering different endings for his novel. One, "fragment B," shows Knecht in a discussion with the political dictator, who is trying to convince Knecht to place the Bead Game at the service of the state. Knecht refuses, knowing it would mean the end of the province and the death of its leaders. In a last game, however, a contest between the dictatorial powers and pure spirit, the latter wins, showing Hesse's optimistic view of the future.

7. In her address to the Sixth International Hermann Hesse Colloquium in Calw ("Hermann Hesse und die fernöstliche Philosophie" *Hermann Hesse und die Religion,* ed. Martin Pfeifer (Bad Liebenzell: Verlag B. Gengenbach, 1990), Luise Rinser also commented on Hesse's stance during the Hitler era: "He was politically . . . consciously against Hitler, against the new German anti-intellectualism, against the war, against inhumanity. In the countless private letters that secretly made their way to Germany, he immunized many of us against Fascism, myself included" (19). Hesse's stance, however, can be regarded as "black and white" only if one is able to view it in the same way that he regarded Goethe's stance toward the French Revolution in his youth: "For Goethe there was no French Revolution, because he stood higher than the highest of red suns . . . (*GB I* 10). For a detailed account of Hesse's relationship to National Socialism, see Egon Schwarz, "Hesse und der Nationalsozialismus" in *Hermann Hesse: Politische und wirkungsgeschichtliche Aspekte,* 55–71.

8. Mileck says, "Fritz Tegularius, the lonely aristocratic genius, the student of classical philology with a penchant for philosophy and disdain for history, could only be Friedrich Nietzsche" ("Names" 175). This is a generally accepted observation, but nonetheless Tegularius also bears an unmistakable resemblance to a Hesse that could have been.

9. *Hermann Hesse. Briefe, erweiterte Ausgabe* (Frankfurt am Main: Suhrkamp, 1965), 64.

10. Kenneth Negus, "On the Death of Josef Knecht in Hermann Hesse's *Glasperlenspiel," Monatshefte* 53 (1961): 189.

11. It is interesting, in reference to Hesse's concept of the elite, to note that he looked upon Americans as childish and thought that his writing would never be properly understood in that country. Had he lived but one more decade, he would have seen how Dr. Timothy Leary elevated him, virtually overnight, to guru status among thousands of American youth. It may be true that the typical American—provincial, pragmatic, and hard working—would have no interest in, or (like the same kind of people the world over) patience for, Hesse's lofty universal ideals in their primarily materialistic world. But Dr. Leary was able to touch a universal chord in the younger, disillusioned genera-

tion of the Vietnam era. Unfortunately, he understood and preached only half the Hesse message. What appealed to Leary in Hesse, and what became his legacy to the youth, was a misdirected escape into their own private world (in many cases via drugs), precisely the failure for which Hesse had admonished Germany's and Europe's vital thinkers. In other words, the great majority of these potential American Cains, this new generation of seekers, failed, for the most part, and retreated into a self-centered world rather than dealing positively with the problems of the times. Hesse was well aware, throughout his life, that there are few true journeyers who can subordinate their personal lives to a universal vision, and the American Hesse experience underscores this point. Those few, he believed, should be sought out and nurtured in the hope that they can become the Leos and inspire other potential journeyers, even a single one, as is stressed with *The Glass Bead Game*'s conclusion and in the appended "lives." It was obviously Hesse's hope that the insights, the caring, and the visions of the few would keep a universal vision alive. The complexity and interrelationships of current world problems, in a state of change far more rapid than Hesse could have imagined at the time, make it even more difficult for such a small elite to have a significant effect at this point in time.

12. Here is evidence that Hesse's intent with "The Father Confessor," one of the appended biographies, is to stress the early church's retreat from the world—i.e., from its feminine aspect, which is what Father Jakobus continually strives to bring to the church.

13. Note that this situation is a variation of the Goldmund/Narcissus plot. It is Goldmund who is driven to return to the masculine sphere of life, where he can express what his experiences have taught him. Narcissus, on the other hand, does not leave his cloistered existence to risk what Knecht does risk.

14. Hilda Cohn, in "The Symbolic End of Hermann Hesse's *Glasperlenspiel*," *Modern Language Quarterly* 11 (1950): 347–57, sees Knecht's life only as a new beginning: "In his last transformation Knecht enters new, unborn, and mysterious lands. . . . He does not go as a master, but as a beginner in a new, inexperienced role, a 'Knecht'" (355). By placing the emphasis on Knecht's death as a new beginning for *him*, Cohn fails to deal with the meaning of the sacrificial aspect. Sidney Johnson finds that "Knecht is not destined to unite the two poles of life himself, but he does transmit the spark which may enable his pupil to do so" (169–70); in "The Autobiographies in Hermann Hesse's *Glasperlenspiel*," *German Quarterly* 24 (1956): 160–71. Mileck offers basically the same conclusion: "Knecht's death is a symbol both of failure and success—a failure because he himself does not attain his ideal, and a success so far as he is instrumental in the eventual realization of that ideal in another" (258); in "Hermann Hesse's *Glasperlenspiel*," *University of California Publications in Modern Philology* 36 (1952): 243–70. Although Walter Naumann does not see the duality or the sexual metaphor with which my interpretation deals, we agree on the sacrificial aspect: "There is even sacrifice, the sacrifice of the highest, the one who embodies the unity of the mind, for the sake of the continuation of the whole" (41); in "The Individual and Society in the Work of Hermann Hesse," *Monatshefte* 41 (1949): 33–42. Edwin Casebeer, in a rambling analysis, comes close to pulling the mother/father metaphor together in an analysis simi-

lar to Hilda Cohn's: "Castalia is in mountain country, the land of the father. The lake is . . . a mother-element . Although it frequently symbolizes the very opposite of the mountain, especially disaster and death, I believe that the lake here carries in addition one of its other meanings, water being the element between earth and air, life and death—the element of transition. Knecht doesn't simply die, he transcends" (184); in *Hermann Hesse,* Writers for the Seventies (New York: Warner, 1972). Inge Halpert, in "*Vita activa* and *Vita contemplativa,*" *Monatshefte* 53 (1961), says, "Knecht, in the outside world, is not afforded the opportunity to satisfy his newly acquired appetite for life and for activity. . . . Although neither [Hesse] nor his fictional counterpart permanently attains the fusion of the doer and the thinker, Hesse still recommends this fusion as the only hope of man's salvation" (166). Halpert does not see death as the fusion. Ziolkowski's interpretation appears to be contradictory. He first states, "Knecht's death is his only act in the entire novel which has no exemplary significance, but a purely personal and existential meaning for him as an individual" (*Novels* 333), yet two pages later, he notes, "So Knecht plunges to his death. His unhesitating willingness to commit himself summons up a new sense of responsibility in Tito" (335). For more critical reactions to the death of Knecht, see the introductory chapter of Remys's *Hermann Hesse's "Das Glasperlenspiel: A Concealed Defense of the Mother World"* (Bern: Peter Lang, 1983), where he concentrates on the basic interpretations of the novel, most of which deal directly with Knecht's death. (Remys confuses Hugo Ball's name with another, however. He gives Ball's comments on Knecht's death, but Ball died in 1927.)

15. Dr. Harold Round, professor emeritus of the Department of English at the University of Wisconsin–Oshkosh, pointed this out.

16. This interpretation was first published in Tusken, "A Mixing of Metaphors: Masculine-Feminine Interplay in the Novels of Hermann Hesse," *Modern Language Review* 87 (July 1992): 626–35. It is adapted here with permission of the *Modern Language Review.*

17. J. C. Middleton was the first to point out the signficance of the name Belpunt. He also calls the death a "consummation" and a "marriage of heaven and earth" but interprets it in terms of *I Ging [I Ching]* ideograms. He does not comment on the sexual-intercourse connotation. "An Enigma Transfigured in Hermann Hesse's *Glasperlenspiel,*" *German Life and Letters* 10 (1957): 298–302.

18. A brief though solid background study on Hesse's evolving plans for what would be entitled *The Glass Bead Game* and its basic narrative structure is G. W. Field's "On the Genesis of the *Glasperlenspiel,*" *German Quarterly* 41 (November 1968): 673–87. Field points out that Hesse's first thoughts on the autobiographies were written on the back of a letter dated April 30, 1931, which does not mean that this was the date Hesse made the notation, but it did include "five numbered headings," according to Field, with a few notes on each, a "primitive life" listed first (675).

19. Another incarnation was planned—an eighteenth-century Swabian theologian, a pupil of the Pietist theologian Johanne Albrecht Bengel, who was to give up theology for music. Johnson notes: "We can only speculate as to what the motivation for this step would be" (165), but if we recall that Bengel was the object of conversation between

Knecht and Father Jakobus, with Knecht pointing out that Bengel "had wanted to piece together all knowledge symetrically and synoptically" (*GS VI* 249), it is not difficult to understand that such symbolic expression exists in music, in which the Bead Game has its origins. Bengel's move would be a natural transition to the final incarnation.

20. Johnson does not seem to see the harmony that Hesse is attempting to portray, saying that in "all the *Lebensläufe* Knecht advocates the spiritual-intellectual life exclusively" (169). Rose, on the other hand, points to the Rainmaker's life as "one of service in the first stage of man's development, the stage of complete harmony with nature and unquestioned acceptance of its laws" (*Faith from the Abyss* [New York: New York University Press, 1965], 135). Rose makes no attempt to compare the Rainmaker's life to Joseph Knecht's, other than the obvious implication embodied in his description.

21. Johnson shows that he is aware of the ambiguities of the German word *Geist* by noting that the Rainmaker "represents the spiritual-intellectual [both words are used to translate *Geist*] pole of that early age, as opposed to the worldly pole represented by the mother of the tribe" (162).

22. Johnson rightly points out that "the younger seeks out the older" in the three autobigraphies, while, in contrast, Knecht seeks out Tito (166). This appears to be an intentional difference and again relates to Hesse's theme of responsiblity of the intellectuals to serve posterity, to take more initiative in shaping the world.

23. Johnson says of the two deaths that "only indirectly is there any parallelism," noting that the Rainmaker "offers his own life in the interest of the tribe," whereas Knecht loses his "accidentally," a "sacrifice made on the spur of the moment" (168). This view is representative of the misunderstanding of Knecht's death (which Johnson calls "puzzling"). Knecht is ready to sacrifice himself at any time, just as was the Rainmaker. As noted earlier, Negus also failed to see the sacrificial aspect of Knecht's death.

24. "Edel sei der Mensch / Hilfreich und gut / denn das allein unterscheidet ihn von anderen Wesen." ("Let man be noble / helpful and good / for this alone separates him from other creatures.")

25. The finished manuscript of "An Indian Life" was sent to *Die neue Rundschau* in April 1937, and printed in July, prior to its appearance as part of *The Glass Bead Game.* See *Materialien zu Hermann Hesses Das Glasperlenspiel,* 43.

Conclusion

1. For a concise, perceptive, and sensitive view of Hesse's later years see Freedman, *Hermann Hesse: Pilgrim of Crisis* (New York: Pantheon, 1978), 372–91.

2. In a letter to Ernst Morgenthaler in May of 1934, Hesse wrote, "There are two or three dozen people to whom my idea [the *Glasperlenspiel* theme of building a utopia into the future, but also anchoring it in the past] is not just fun and enjoyment, but rather a breath of life, a consolation and a bit of religion, and it is for these few people that it [at this point he was referring specifically to "The Rainmaker" but really meant the entire *Glass Bead Game* work in progress] has been written, and above all for myself." As quoted in *Materiellen zu Hermann Hesses "Das Glasperlenspiel,"* ed. Volker Michels,

2 vols. (Frankfurt am Main: Suhrkamp, 1973, 1974), 1:89.

3. It should be recalled that Hesse expressed this same imagery in 1914 in the fantasy "Dream of the Gods" (*GS III* 927–31), showing, once again, that his vision was intact even at that time. Such evidence supports an important emphasis of this study—that Hesse's major prose works were consciously written as stages of a thematic continuum.

Bibliography

The selected works by Hermann Hesse listed below (with exception of the Boccaccio and Franz von Assisi monographs and collected letters) are all included in *Hermann Hesse: Gesammelte Schriften* (7 vols. Frankfurt am Main: Suhrkamp, 1968), my primary sources for this study. The date and place of first publication is also given. Critical literature is divided into bibliographies, books, related works, and articles and includes most sources cited in this study plus several additional titles.

Selected Works by Hermann Hesse

Novels

> *Peter Camenzind.* Berlin: Fischer, 1904.
> *Unterm Rad (Beneath the Wheel).* Berlin: Fischer, 1906.
> *Gertrud.* Berlin: Fischer, 1910.
> *Roßhalde.* Munich: Langen, 1914.
> *Demian.* Berlin: Fischer, 1919.
> *Siddhartha.* Berlin: Fischer, 1922.
> *Der Steppenwolf.* Berlin: Fischer, 1927.
> *Narziß und Goldmund.* Berlin: Fischer, 1930.
> *Morgenlandfahrt (Journey to the East).* Berlin: Fischer, 1932.
> *Das Glasperlenspiel (The Glass Bead Game).* Zurich: Fretz & Wasmuth, 1943.

English Translations of the Novels

Demian. Trans. N. Priday. New York: Boni/Liveright, 1923. New York: Holt, 1948. Trans. W. Strachan. London: Vision Press, 1958. London: Panther, 1969. Trans. M. Roloff and M. Lebeck. New York: Harper & Row, 1965. New York: Bantam, 1966.
Steppenwolf. Trans. B. Creighton. London: Secker, 1929. New York: Holt, 1929. Toronto: Oxford University Press, 1947. New York: Ungar, 1957. New York: Holt, Rinehart & Winston, 1970. Rev. J. Mileck and H. Frenz. New York: Holt, Rinehart & Winston, 1963. New York: Bantam, 1969. Rev. W. Sorrell. London: Modern Library, 1963. London: Penguin, 1964.
Death and the Lover (Narziß und Goldmund). Trans. Geoffrey Dunlop. London: Jarrold, 1932. New York: Ungar, 1959. *Goldmund.* London: Vision Press, 1959. *Narziß and Goldmund.* London: Penguin, 1971. *Narcissus and Goldmund.* Trans. U. Molinaro. New York: Farrar, Straus & Giroux, 1968. New York: Bantam, 1971.

233

Magister Ludi (*Glasperlenspiel*). Trans. M. Savill. London: Aldus, 1949. New York: Holt, 1949. New York: Ungar, 1957. *The Glass Bead Game.* Trans. Richard and Clara Winston. New York: Holt, Rinehart & Winston, 1969. New York: Bantam, 1970. London: Cape, 1970. London: Penguin, 1972.

Siddhartha. Trans. H. Rosner. New York: New Directions, 1951. London: Vision Press, 1954. New York: Ungar, 1957. New York: Bantam, 1971. London: Pan, 1974.

The Journey to the East (*Morgenlandfahrt*). Trans. H. Rosner. London: Vision Press, 1956. New York: Noonday Press, 1957. New York: Farrar, Straus & Giroux, 1968. New York: Bantam, 1972. St. Albans: Panther Press, 1973. London: Pan Books, 1974.

Peter Camenzind. Trans. W. Strachan. London: Vision Press, 1961. London: Penguin, 1973. Trans. M. Roloff. New York: Farrar, Straus & Giroux, 1968. New York: Bantam, 1969.

Beneath the Wheel (*Unterm Rad*). Trans. M. Roloff. New York: Farrar, Straus & Giroux, 1968. New York: Bantam, 1970. As *The Prodigy.* Trans. W. Strachan. London: Vision Press, 1957. London: Penguin, 1973.

Roßhalde. Trans. R. Mannheim. New York: Farrar, Straus & Giroux, 1969. New York: Bantam, 1972. London: Cape, 1971. London: Pan, 1972.

Shorter Prose Works and Short-Story Collections

Eine Stunde hinter Mitternacht (*An Hour beyond Midnight*). Leipzig: Diederichs, 1899. Nine short prose studies. Written "beyond midnight" during sleepless hours, an "escape into the night" from the storms of daily life.

Hinterlassene Schriften und Gedichte von Hermann Lauscher (*Posthumous Writings and Poems by Hermann Lauscher*). Basel: Reich, 1901. Poems and prose vignettes from Hesse's early life.

Diesseits (*This Side*). Berlin: Fischer, 1907. Five short stories written in Gaienhofen during early years of Hesse's marriage.

Knulp. Berlin: Fischer, 1915. A three-story novella portraying Hesse's favorite "vagabond" hero—intelligent and independent, who does not let life around him dictate his own life.

Märchen (*Fairy Tales*). Berlin: Fischer, 1919. Sentimental remnants of Hesse's romantic dreams. Eight tales, all of which reach into Hesse's "other reality."

Klingsors letzter Sommer (*Klingsor's Last Summer*). Berlin: Fischer, 1920. Three novellas written in a brief period following Hesse's separation from his wife and his move to Ticino (Tessin). The medieval magician Klingsor becomes the painter Klingsor-Hesse who must now somehow recognize the "magic" of his inner life and live accordingly.

Kurgast (*Guest at the Spa*). Berlin: Fischer, 1925. A satirical and psychological study of himself and fellow guests at a spa.

Die Nürnberger Reise (*Trip to Nürnberg*). Berlin: Fischer, 1927. An account of a "pilgrimage" through southern Germany, a conscious counterpoint to his isolated existence in Montagnola.

Gedenkblätter (Memories). Berlin: Fischer, 1937. Memories from the years 1902–36.
Traumfährte (Dream Journeys). Zurich, 1945. Stories and fairy tales, written 1910–32.
Späte Prosa (Late Prose). Berlin, 1951. Stories and memories, 1944–50.

Collected Poems

Romantische Lieder (Romantic Songs). Dresden: Pierson, 1899.
Gedichte (Poems). Berlin: Grote, 1902.
Unterwegs (Underway). Munich: Müller, 1911.
Musik des Einsamen (Music of a Lonely Person). Heilbronn: Salzer, 1915.
Ausgewählte Gedichte (Selected Poems). Berlin: Fischer, 1921.
Krisis (Crisis). Berlin: Fischer, 1928. Forty-five poems related thematically to *Der Steppenwolf.*
Trost der Nacht (Consolation of the Night). Berlin: Fischer, 1929.
Neue Gedichte (New Poems). Berlin: Fischer, 1937.
Die Gedichte (The Poems). Zurich: Fretz & Wasmuth, 1942.
Der Blütenzweig (The Blossoming Branch). Zurich: Fretz & Wasmuth, 1945.
Gedichte, Neudruck (Poems, Reprint). Berlin: Suhrkamp, 1953.
Die späten Gedichte (The Late Poems). Frankfurt: Insel, 1963.

Selected Essays

"O Freunde, nicht diese Töne" ("Oh, Friends, Not these Tones"), 1914. An appeal for peace. The title derives from Schiller's "Ode to Joy," used as the text for the last movement of Beethoven's Ninth Symphony. (*GS VII* 44–49).

"Brief an einen Philister" ("Letter to a Philistine"), 1915. An open letter to a businessman who had insulted artists. Hesse chastizes himself for not speaking out at the time. (*GS VII* 50–56).

"Die Zuflucht" ("The Refuge"), 1917. The Bible verse "nor will people say, 'Here it is,' or 'There it is,' because the kingdom of God is within you" (Luke 17:21) reveals the message that was to remain so important to Hesse: God speaks from within everyone. (*GS VII* 62–68).

"Krieg und Frieden" ("War and Peace"), 1918. Hesse points out that peace is an ideal, but because humans are capable of understanding the words "Thou shalt not kill," they are above the animals, not as a finished product, but as an expression of nature's longing for new forms and possibilities. This is what we must live up to. (*GS VII* 117–20).

"Künstler und Psychoanalyse" ("Artists and Psychoanalysis"), 1918. Hesse had recently been introduced to Jung's theories and methods and elaborates on the close relationship between psychoanalysis and art. (*GS VII* 137–43).

"Die Brüder Karamasoff oder der Untergang Europas" ("The Brothers Karamasov, or the Decline of Europe"), 1919. Hesse relates the fate of the Karamazov family to the collapse of Europe in World War I. (*GS VII* 161–78).

"Gedanken über Dostojewskijs Idiot" ("Thoughts on Dostoevsky's Idiot"), 1919. Both Christ and Dostoevsky's Prince Muishkin were alone. Both had to "accept the chaos" if they were to move on to a higher life. (*GS VII* 178–86).

"Eigensinn" ("Selfwill"), 1919. In praise of self-will, our inner spirit and driving force, which everyone should heed. This becomes an abiding theme in Hesse's works. Just as every stone and flower develop according to inner law, so should humanity. (*GS VII* 194–200).

"Zarathustras Wiederkehr" ("Zarathustra's Return"), 1919. The prophet returns to chastise defeated Germans who seek to place blame on others and look to others for directions. Direction comes from within. (*GS VII* 200–230).

"Über Dostoevskij" ("On Dostoevsky"), 1925. Reveals many of the Dostoevsky themes and ideas that influenced Hesse. (*GS VII* 292–94).

"Mein Glaube" ("My Belief"), 1931. This and the following essay reveal and detail the history and formulation of Hesse's religious thoughts and beliefs and the stages of religious enlightenment toward which most major religions appear to strive. (*GS VII* 370–74).

"Ein Stückchen Theologie" ("A Bit of Theology"), 1932. (*GS VII* 388–402).

"Weltkrise und Bücher" ("World Crisis and Books"), 1937. (*GS VII* 408–9).

"Nachwort zum *Steppenwolf*" ("Epilogue to *Steppenwolf*"), 1942. Written 15 years after the initial publication, stressing the fact that Hesse had intended *Steppenwolf* to express a positive message. (*GS VII* 412–13).

Monographs

Boccaccio. Berlin: Fischer, 1904.

Franz von Assisi (Francis of Assisi). Berlin: Fischer [1904]. Portrays the "real" Christianity of St. Francis, whose life remained a discernible influence in Hesse's writings.

Collected Letters

Hermann Hesse. Briefe. Frankfurt am Main: Suhrkamp, 1951. Erweiterte Ausgabe, 1959, 1964, 1965.

Hermann Hesse–Peter Suhrkamp. Briefwechsel 1945–59 (Hermann Hesse–Peter Suhrkamp. Correspondence 1945–59). Ed. Siegfried Unseld. Frankfurt am Main: Suhrkamp, 1950.

Hermann Hesse–Romain Rolland. Briefe (Hermann Hesse–Romain Rolland. Letters). Frankfurt am Main: Suhrkamp, 1954.

Hermann Hesse: Kindheit und Jugend vor 1900. Ed. Ninon Hesse. Vol. 1, 1877–95. Frankfurt am Main: Suhrkamp, 1966.

Hermann Hesse–Thomas Mann. Briefwechsel (Hermann Hesse–Thomas Mann. Correspondence). Ed. Anni Carlsson. Frankfurt am Main: Suhrkamp, 1968. Expanded edition 1975.

Hermann Hesse–Helene Voight-Diederichs. Zwei Autoren Porträts in Briefen, 1897–1900 (*Hermann Hesse–Helene Voight-Diederichs. Portraits of Two Authors in Letters, 1897–1900*). Leipzig: Diederichs, 1971.

Hermann Hesse: Gesammelte Briefe. Ed. Ursula and Volker Michels with Heiner Hesse. 4 vols. Frankfurt am Main: Suhrkamp, 1973, 1979, 1982, 1986.

Hermann Hesse: Kindheit und Jugend vor 1900. Vol. 2, 1895–1900. Ed. Ninon Hesse, Gerhard Kirchhoff. Frankfurt am Main: Suhrkamp, 1978.

Selected Critical Works

Bibliographies

Barreiss, Otto. *Eine Bibliographie der Werke über Hermann Hesse.* 2 vols. Basel: Karl Maier-Buder, 1962, 1964.

Mileck, Joseph. *Hermann Hesse and His Critics: The Criticism and Bibliography of Half a Century.* University of North Carolina Studies in Germanic Languages and Literatures, 21. Chapel Hill: University of North Carolina Press, 1958. Reprinted New York: AMS Press, 1966.

———. *Hermann Hesse. Biography and Bibliography.* 2 vols. Berkeley: University of California Press, 1977.

Pfeifer, Martin. *Hermann Hesse Bibliographie. Primär-u. Sekundärschriftum in Auswahl.* Berlin: Schmidt, 1973.

Waibler, Helmut. *Hermann Hesse: Eine Bibliographie.* Bern: Francke, 1962.

Books, Monographs, and Dissertations

Ball, Hugo. *Hermann Hesse: Sein Leben und sein Werk.* Berlin: Fischer, 1927. Reprinted Frankfurt am Main: Suhrkamp, 1977. The first Hesse biography, in honor of his fiftieth birthday. Ball was a close personal friend.

Böttger, Fritz. *Hermann Hesse.* Berlin: Verlag der Nationen, 1974. A GDR publication which must make the attempt to place Hesse, the individualist, in the ranks of the socialists.

Boulby, Mark. *Hermann Hesse: His Mind and Art.* New York: Cornell University Press, 1967. A well-written, insightful study of Hesse and his works. Like Ziolkowski's and Milek's studies, one of the seminal works on Hesse in English.

Bran, Friedrich. *Hermann Hesses Gedanken über Heimat.* Bad Liebenzell/Calw: Gengenbach, 1982. Captures Hesse's love for Calw and its environs during his early years.

Casebeer, Edwin F. *Hermann Hesse.* Writers for the Seventies Series. New York: Warner, 1972. A study written at the height of the Hesse craze in the United States. Style often rambles, but some analyses are perceptive.

Field, George W. *Hermann Hesse.* Twayne's World Author Series. Boston: Twayne, 1970. A good, basic introduction to Hesse.

Freedman, Ralph. *Hermann Hesse: Pilgrim of Crisis.* New York: Pantheon, 1978. Perhaps the most readable study of Hesse. A thorough, perceptive treatment of his life and detailed study of all significant works.

Kleine, Gisela. *Ninon und Hermann Hesse.* Sigmarinen: Thorbeck, 1982. A personalized look at Hesse through the eyes of his third wife.

Lüthi, Hans Jürgen. *Hermann Hesse: Natur und Geist.* Stuttgart, Berlin, Cologne, and Mainz: Kohlhammer, 1970. Traces the duality theme through Hesse's works. Conclusion gives a brief but very informative historical overview of duality theme in literature.

Michels, Volker, and Hans Mayer. *Hermann Hesse. Sein Leben in Bildern und Texten.* Frankfurt am Main: Suhrkamp (1979).

Michels, Volker, ed. *Materialien zu Hesses "Das Glasperlenspiel."* 2 vols. Frankfurt am Main: Suhrkamp, 1973, 1974. *Materialien* are comprehensive studies of the conception, content, and critical perceptions of the individual novels. They are most helpful for any critical research.

———. *Materialien zu Hesses "Siddhartha."* 2 vols. Frankfurt am Main: Suhrkamp, 1975, 1976.

———. *Materialien zu Hesses "Steppenwolf."* Frankfurt am Main: Suhrkamp, 1972.

———. *Über Hermann Hesse I: 1904–62.* Frankfurt am Main: Suhrkamp, 1976.

Mileck, Joseph. *Hermann Hesse: Life and Art.* Berkeley: University of California Press, 1978. Mileck is a most prolific Hesse scholar. This work is a solid and thorough treatment of Hesse's life and works. Emphasizes the confessional nature of his writing and convincingly proves that Hesse is best understood via this approach.

Otten, Anna. *Hesse Companion.* Albuquerque: University of New Mexico Press, 1977.

Pfeifer, Martin, ed. *Hermann Hesse und die Religion.* Proc. of Sixth International Hermann-Hesse Colloquim. Bad Liebenzell: Verlag B. Gengenbach, 1990. (Individual contributors are listed separately in "Articles" section.) Eleven essays by leading Hesse scholars. A timely and significant collection.

Quispel, Gilles. *Gnostic Studies.* Netherlands Historisch-Archaelogisch Institut te Istanbul, 1975. A study that helps to explain how Hesse's "good and evil" world can, in fact, be one of harmony. Of specific interest for *Demian* interpretation.

Remys, Edmund. *Hermann Hesse's "Das Glasperlenspiel: A Concealed Defense of the Mother World.* European University Studies, Series I: German Language and Literature 668. Bern, Frankfurt, and New York: Peter Lang, 1983. An especially informative first chapter, where Remys summarizes various interpretations of Joseph Knecht's death in *The Glass Bead Game.*

Rose, Ernst. *Faith from the Abyss: Hermann Hesse's Way from Romanticism to Modernity.* New York: New York University Press, 1965. A "spiritual biography" that follows the gradual evolution of Hesse's romantic world view into his problematic religious faith.

Stelzig, Eugene. *Hermann Hesse's Fictions of the Self.* New Jersey: Princeton University Press, 1988. An examination of what it means to be an "autobiographical writer." Stelzig builds his discussions around Hesse's self-will (*Eigensinn*). A solid, scholarly work with heavy comparative-literature content.

238

Unseld, Siegfried, ed. *Hermann Hesse: Eine Werkgeschichte*. Frankfurt am Main: Suhrkamp, 1973. As the title indicates, the book contains information relating to the conception, the writing, and the content of Hesse's works. Includes numerous quotations from Hesse relating to individual novels as well as critical comments. A most helpful guide.

Ward, Dorothy Cox. "Two Marys: A Study of the Women in Hermann Hesse's Fiction." Diss. Columbia University, 1976. A seminal English-language study of the role of feminine characters and characterization. Has shortcomings but very helpful.

Weibel, Kurt. *Hermann Hesse und die deutsche Romantik*. Winterthur: Keller, 1954. Weibel praises Hesse as a visionary who could see where "modern life" was leading, namely to war and destruction. Weibel labels Hesse's "inward path" his "magic way out."

Wolf, Uwe. *Hermann Hesse: Demian—Die Botschaft vom Selbst*. Bonn: Bouvier, 1979. Deals primarily with the gnostic influence apparent in *Demian*.

Ziolkowski, Theodore. *Fictional Transfigurations of Jesus*. Princeton: Princeton University Press, 1972, 151–61. Hesse's Demian is included among fictional characters discussed as Christ-transfigurations.

———. *The Novels of Hermann Hesse: A Study in Theme and Structure*. Princeton, N.J.: Princeton University Press, 1965. Along with Joseph Milek, Ziolokowski is recognized as a leading American Hesse scholar. This work remains one of the most in-depth studies of Hesse's major prose works, especially in terms of structure-content relationship.

Related Works

Campbell, Joseph. "Joseph Campbell: Myths to Live By." *Bill Moyers' Journal* (PBS, April 17 and 24, 1981; transcript: Educational Broadcasting Corp., 1981; produced by Journal Graphics, Inc., New York).

———. *The Power of Myth*. New York: Doubleday, 1988.

Chesterton, G. K. *St. Francis of Assisi*. N.p.: Doubleday, Doran, 1924. New York: Image, 1957.

Cunningham, Lawrence. *St. Francis of Assisi*. Twayne World Author Series. Boston: Twayne, 1976.

Jung, Carl Gustav. *The Integration of Personality*. Trans. Stanley Dell. London: K. Paul, Trench, Trubner, and Co., 1940.

Reese, William. *Dictionary of Philosphy and Religion*. New Jersey: Humanities, 1980.

Articles

Abood, Edward. "Jung's Concept of Individuation in Hesse's *Steppenwolf*." *Southern Humanities Review* 3 (Summer 1968): 1–12.

Breugelmann, René. "Hermann Hesse and Depth Psychology." *Canadian Review of Comparative Literature* (Winter 1981): 10–47.

Cohn, Hilda. "The Symbolic End of Hesse's *Glasperlenspiel." Modern Language Quarterly* 11 (September 1950): 347–57. Interprets Joseph Knecht's death as personal transcendance, a new beginning for *him*.

Dahrendorf, Malte. "Hermann Hesse's *Demian* und C. G. Jung." *Germanische-Romanische Zeitschrift* 39 (1958): 81–97.

Derrenberger, John. "Who is Leo? Astrology in Hermann Hesse's *Die Morgenlandfahrt." Monatshefte* 67 (Summer 1975): 167–72. Relates Hesse's personal "signs" to "Leo" to determine meaning of H.H.-Leo relationship.

Fickert, Kurt J. "The Mystery of Hesse's *Das Glasperlenspiel. Forms of the Fantastic." Selected Essays from the Third International Conference on the Fantastic in Literature and Film.* Contributions to the Study of Science Fiction and Fantasy 20, ed. Jan Hokenson and Howard Pearce. Westport, Conn.: Greenwood Press, 1986. 219–25.

Field, George W. "Hermann Hesse: Polarities and Symbols of Synthesis." *Queens Quarterly* 81 (1974): 87–101.

———. "On the Genesis of the *Glasperlenspiel." German Quarterly* 41 (November 1968): 673–88.

Flaxman, Seymour L. "*Der Steppenwolf:* Hesse's Portrait of the Intellectual." *Modern Language Quarterly* 15 (December 1954): 349–58.

Gignac, Patrick J. "Homosexual Identity (Mis)information in Hesse's *Demian." The German Mosaic: Cultural and Linguistic Diversity in Society.* Contributions in Ethnic Studies, 33, ed. Carol Aisha Blackshire-Belay. Westport, Conn.: Greenwood Press, 1994, 295–300.

Gontrum, Peter. "Oracle and Shrine: Hesse's *Lebensbaum." Monatshefte* 56 (April–May 1964): 183–90. A very helpful study dealing with tree symbolism in Hesse's works.

Halpert, Inge. "*Vita activa* and *Vita contemplativa." Monatshefte* 53 (Spring 1961): 159–66. Concludes that Hesse sees the fusion of the active life and the contemplative life as "the only hope of man's salvation."

Horrocks, David. "Harry Haller as "höherer Mensch': Nietzchean Themes in Hermann Hesse's *Der Steppenwolf." German Life and Letters* 46 (April 1993): 134–44.

Johnson, Sydney. "The Autobiographies in Hermann Hesse's *Das Glasperlenspiel." German Quarterly* 29 (May 1956): 160–71.

Küng, Hans. "Hermann Hesse als ökumenische Herausforderung." *Hermann Hesse und die Religion.* Proc. of Sixth International Hermann-Hesse Colloquim. Ed. Martin Pfeifer, Bad Liebenzell: Verlag B. Gengenbach, 1990, 57–86. Draws attention to the ecumenical challenge that Hesse's religious themes present.

Mann, Thomas. "Introduction to Hermann Hesse's *Demian." Demian.* Trans. Michael Roloff and Michael Lebeck. New York: Harper and Row, 1965.

Michels, Volker. "Gegen den Nationalismus der Konfessionen." *Hermann Hesse und die Religion.* Proc. of Sixth International Hermann-Hesse Colloquim. Ed. Martin Pfeifer, Bad Liebenzell: Verlag B. Gengenbach, 1990, 147–66. Adds emphasis to Hans Küng's essay (above). Notes similarities of religious nationalism to political nationalism.

Middleton, J. C. "An Enigma Transfigured in Hermann Hesse's *Glasperlenspiel.*" *German Life and Letters* 10 (1957): 298–302.

Mileck, Joseph. "Hermann Hesse's *Glasperlenspiel.*" *University of California Publications in Modern Philology* 36 (1952): 243–70.

———. "Hermann Hesse und der Osten: Ziel oder Zweck? Bekehrung oder Aesthetik?" *Hermann Hesse und die Religion.* Proc. of Sixth International Hermann-Hesse Colloquim. Ed. Martin Pfeifer, Bad Liebenzell: Verlag B. Gengenbach, 1990, 87–103.

———. "*Das Glasperlenspiel:* Genesis, Manuscripts, and History of Publication." *German Quarterly* 43 (January 1970): 55–83.

———. "Names and the Creative Process: A Study of Names in Hesse's *Lauscher, Demian, Steppenwolf,* and *Glasperlenspiel.*" *Monatshefte* 53 (Summer 1961): 167–80. A helpful study that points out various real-life figures who served as models or inspiration for Hesse characters.

Naumann, Walter. "The Individual and Society in the Work of Hermann Hesse." *Monatshefte* 41 (Spring 1949): 33–42.

Negus, Kenneth. "On the Death of Josef Knecht in Hermann Hesse's *Glasperlenspiel.*" *Monatshefte* 53 (Summer 1961): 181–9.

Neuer, Johanna. "Jungian Archetypes in Hermann Hesse's *Demian.*" *Germanic Review* 57 (Winter 1982): 9–15. The most recent and detailed study of Jungian concepts found in *Demian.* Parallels are carefully drawn and convincing, but Neuer does not deal with the "mysterious events" which are also helpful in explaining Jungian relationships.

Neuswanger, Russel. "Names as Glass Beads in Hesse's *Narziss und Goldmund.*" *Monatshefte* 67 (Spring 1975): 48–58. Adds to Milek's study of names.

Norton, Roger. "Variant Endings of Hesse's *Glasperlenspiel.*" *Monatshefte* 60 (1968): 141–6.

Rinser, Luise. "Hermann Hesse und die fernöstliche Philosophie." *Hermann Hesse und die Religion.* Proc. of Sixth International Hermann-Hesse Colloquim. Ed. Martin Pfeifer, Bad Liebenzell: Verlag B. Gengenbach, 1990, 17–32.

Rockwood, Heidi M. "The Function of Pablo in Hesse's *Steppenwolf.*" *South Atlantic Review* 59 (November 1994): 47–61. Interprets Pablo as the mercurial figure of the alchemical process, the "catalyst for all the actions and developments that take place." Pablo fits the mold in which Rockwood casts him, but she does not convince the reader that Hesse was consciously using the alchemical model as a Pablo pattern.

Schwarz, Egon. "Hermann Hesse und der Nationalsozialismus." *Hermann Hesse: Politische und wirkungsgeschichtliche Aspekte.* Bern: Francke, 1986, 55–71. Helps to point out political relevance in Hesse's works which is not always apparent.

———. "Zur Erklärung von Hesses *Steppenwolf.*" *Monatshefte* 53 (Summer 1961): 192–8.

Seidlin, Oskar. "Hermann Hesse: The Exorcism of the Demon." *Symposium* 4 (1950): 325–48.

Sokel, Walther. "The Problem of Dualism in Hesse's *Demian* and Musil's *Törless.*" *Modern Austrian Literature* 9, 3/4 (1976): 35–42.

Tusken, Lewis W. "Hermann Hesse's *Roßhalde:* The Story in the Paintings." *Monatsheft* 77 (Spring 1981): 60–6.

―――. "A Mixing of Metaphors: Masculine-Feminine Interplay in the Novels of Hermann Hesse." *Modern Language Review* 87 (July 1992): 626–35.

―――. "The Question of Perspective in Hermann Hesse's *Steppenwolf.*" *Theorie und Kritik. Festschrift für Gerhard Loose.* Ed. Stefan Grunwald. Bern and Munich: Francke, 1974, 159–66. An expansion of Abood's study of Jungian individuation in *Steppenwolf.*

―――. "Thematic Unity in Hermann Hesse's *Narziss und Goldmund:* The Tree Symbol as Interpretive Key." *Modern Fiction Studies* 29 (Summer 1983): 245–51.

Unseld, Siegfried. "Hermann Hesse's Influence: Ethics or Esthetics?" *Hermann Hesse: Politische und wirkungsgeschichtliche Aspekte.* Eds. Sigrid Bauschinger and Albert M. Reh. Bern: Francke, 1986, 117–33.

Zeller, Bernhard. "Hermann Hesse und die Welt der Väter." *Hermann Hesse und die Religion.* Proc. of Sixth International Hermann-Hesse Colloquim. Ed. Martin Pfeifer, Bad Liebenzell: Verlag B. Gengenbach, 1990, 33–55.

Index

Michels, Volker, 6–7, 97
Middleton, J. C., 230n. 17
Mileck, Joseph, 1, 2, 60, 74, 86, 98, 114, 154, 218n. 1, 219nn. 2, 5, 220n. 8, 222–23nn. 1, 3, 227–28nn. 5, 8. 229n. 14
miracles, 203, 204, 213
Montagnola, 99, 108
Morbio Inferiore, 145, 150, 166
Morgenthaler, Ernst, 231n. 2
Moses, 75, 120
mother of God. *See* Eve
Moyers, Bill, 220–21n. 10
Mozart, Amadeus, 148, 120, 198. *See also* characters in Hesse's novels—*Steppenwolf*
music, 46, 93, 113, 118, 120, 127, 154, 156, 157–58, 160, 161, 179, 185, 194, 199, 230n. 19. *See also* duality themes: music-mathematics
"My Belief" (Hesse: "Mein Glaube"), 222n. 9. *See also* "A Bit of Theology"; religion
mysterious events, 88, 90, 92, 94, 106, 113, 143, 144, 148–50. *See also* magic theater
myth/mythology, 3, 48, 84, 85, 93, 202, 203, 213. *See also* new mythology; "On a Tocatta by Bach"; Snow Princess

Narcissus and Goldmund (Hesse), 60, 69, 80, 128–41, 144, 145, 225n. 6, 226n. 9. *See also* characters in Hesse's novels—*Narcissus and Goldmund*
National Socialism, 153, 161–62, 166, 198, 228n. 7. *See also* Fascism; Hitler; Second World War
Naumann, Walter, 229n. 14
Natur. See Duality themes: *Natur-Geist*
nature, theme of, 47, 48–49, 50, 68, 69,

70, 78, 97, 129, 139, 165, 188. *See also* duality themes: *Natur-Geist;* "The Rainmaker"
Negus, Kenneth, 167
Neuer, Johanna, 90, 95
Neuswanger, Russel, 139
new mythology, 3, 192, 200, 212–13. *See also* myth/mythology
Nietzsche, Friedrich, 50, 85, 91, 111–12, 223n. 8, 228n. 8
Nirvana, 100, 101, 106, 108
Nobel Prize, 1, 7, 38, 211
Norton, Roger, 228n. 6
Novalis, 212

"Oh Friends, Not these Tones" (Hesse: "O Freunde, nicht diese Töne"), 73
"On a Toccata by Bach" (Hesse: "Zu einer Toccata von Bach"), 190–92, 212. *See also* myth/mythology; new mythology
outsider, 14, 57, 63, 96, 111, 175, 217n. 2

pantheism, 31
Perrot, Heinrich, 33, 35
Peter Camenzind (Hesse), 36, 45, 46–53, 59–60, 62, 70, 106, 151, 216n. 5, 217n. 1. *See also* characters in Hesse's novels—*Peter Camenzind*
Petit cénacle, 38, 40, 43, 163
Pfisterer, Pastor Jakob, 26–27
Pietists/Pietism, 3, 6, 7, 8, 9–10, 11, 12, 13, 16, 18, 19, 21–22, 24–25, 27, 28, 30, 42, 48, 56, 89, 96, 98, 99, 100, 167, 200. *See also* Christian/Christianity; Protestantism; religion
polarities. *See* duality themes
politics, theme of, 43, 81, 84, 164, 166, 169, 183, 184, 188, 210
Protestantism, 9, 99, 165. *See also* Catholic/Catholicism; Pietists/Pietism; religion